# INDIA AND ASEAN:

## ECONOMIC PARTNERSHIP IN THE 1990s AND FUTURE PROSPECTS

# INDIA AND ASEAN :

## ECONOMIC PARTNERSHIP IN THE 1990s AND FUTURE PROSPECTS

*Editors*

PROF. SHRI PRAKASH

DR. VANITA RAY

DR. SANJAY AMBATKAR

GYAN

GYAN PUBLISHING HOUSE

NEW DELHI-110 002

The responsibility for the facts stated, and the views, if any, expressed or conclusions drawn in any article of this book is entirely that of the author(s). The editors are in no way responsible for the same.

INDIA AND ASEAN :
ECONOMIC PARTNERSHIP IN THE
1990S AND FUTURE PROSPECTS
*(Current Affairs, Economics, International Relations, Political Science)*

ISBN : 81-212-0522-0



Published in 1996 in India by
Gyan Publishing House
5, Ansari Road
New Delhi 110 002



Printed at Mehra Offset Press, New Delhi

# Contents

# List of Contributors

| | |
|---|---|
| PROF. V.V. BHANOJI RAO | National University of Singapore, Singapore. |
| PROF. CHARAN D. WADHVA | Research Professor, Centre for Policy Research, New Delhi. |
| DR. SANJAY AMBATKAR | Research Associate, Academy of Third World Studies. |
| PROF. B. BHATTACHARYYA | Dean (Research), Indian Institute of Foreign Trade, New Delhi. |
| MR. T.K. BHAUMIK | Senior Advisor (Policy), Confederation of Indian Industry, New Delhi. |
| MR. K.K. TRIVEDI | Senior Advisor (Economic), Indian Investment Centre, New Delhi. |
| PROF. K.V. KESAVAN | Chairperson, Centre for East Asian Studies, JNU, New Delhi. |
| PROF. I.N. MUKHERJI | Centre for South Asian Studies, JNU, New Delhi. |
| MR. M.C. VERMA | Senior Fellow, ICRIER, New Delhi. |

| | |
|---|---|
| DR. V.L. RAO | Senior Fellow,<br>Research and Information Systems for the Non-Aligned Countries (RIS),<br>New Delhi. |
| PROF. SHRI PRAKASH | Offg. Hon'y Director,<br>Academy of Third World Studies,<br>Jamia Millia Islamia. |
| DR. NITISH SENGUPTA | Director General,<br>International Management Institute,<br>New Delhi. |

# Preface

The spectacular economic performance of the ASEAN countries in the recent past has aroused much interest around the world and particularly, in many developing nations of Asia. For such developing economies this achievement is like an "economic miracle" which inspires them to develop economic ties with the ASEAN countries. India, being a neighbouring state, is keen to intensify its age-old economic relationship with the ASEAN, especially with the launching of the economic reform programme since July 1991 and adopting a "Look East" policy in international economic relations.

India's recent keenness emanates from the principle of "mutual cooperation". Over the years, India too has achieved technological excellence in the manufacture of engineering goods, agro-based products, automobile spare parts; skill in erecting small and medium scale industries, etc. Similarly, India's human resource base is widely recognised the world over, particularly in medical and engineering sciences, science and technology, financial and managerial administration, etc. More interestingly, India's consumer market is also growing speedily and presently estimated to have the strength of about 250-300 million middle-income consumers.

To discuss the commonalities and complementarities existing between India and ASEAN (and exploring new) a two-day seminar was organized at the Academy of Third World Studies in March 1995 and a cross-section of subject experts presented their research papers highlighting various aspects of the issue. This volume is the direct outcome of the seminar papers. The seminar was financially supported by the Ministry of External Affairs and the Planning Commission and we are grateful for their generous consideration. We also thank Dr. Sanjay Ambatkar for convening and successfully handling the seminar.

We are confident that this volume would be useful to the researchers as well as policy-makers who are involved in the studies and decision making in the field of international economic relations.

Prof. SHRI PRAKASH
Offg. Hon'y Director
Academy of Third World Studies.

# I

# INTRODUCTION

The central question this volume proposes to address is: "What kind of economic partnership would emerge between India and Southeast Asia in the coming decades? And whether such a partnership would lead to a new pattern of economic cooperation leading India to become an integral part of the Asia-Pacific region"? More specifically, we are interested in searching the diversified sphere of economic cooperation based on "mutual benefit" a theme which would sustain for a longer period and in the process spread to other areas like culture, security, human resource, etc., to create a healthy environment wherein India would gain an indispensable position in the region.

The Southeast Asian and more particularly, ASEAN countries in the recent period have attracted the attention of the world and India being the next door neighbour is watchful of their economic development. India, too, is surging ahead, economically, since the process of economic reforms initiated in 1991. Would this bring India nearer to the "most vibrant" area of the world?

In the field of international relations nowadays, economics assumes precedence over political factors. Nevertheless, while analysing the situation, if essential, we would touch upon political factors. Dr. Bhanoji Rao strongly maintains in the first chapter that till late 1980s politics played an important role in keeping India away from Southeast Asia. India had been considered the satellite country of the former Soviet Union till its disintegration and the USA had a louder say in most part of the SEA. However, the situation had changed since 1980s because of two reasons: first, the breakdown of Soviet Union ended the Cold War enabling India to come out from the "Soviet Umbrella" and second, India opened its economy with the launching of a far reaching reform programme.

India's economic interest in SEA increased since 1991 mainly owing to the rise of the combined share of the latter in world exports. The economic strength of SEA has tremendously increased due to the rise in its intra-regional trade and therefore India needs to take measures to boost up its trade with this region. However, even to deepen the economic relations, India would have to widen the overall understanding of SEA through increasing cultural ties. The exchange of academics, businessmen and government officials between India and SEA may help to fill the existing communication gap.

Among the Southeast Asian countries the ASEAN is the leading success story with the implementation of "inward looking" trade and investment policies. The experience of the last four decades according to Dr. N.K. Sengupta reveals that the countries with "outward looking" policies lagged behind in accelerating the rate of economic development and this makes India's case stronger to fall back on "inward cobweb" of the Asia-Pacific region. It would much depend upon India's initiative to forge economic relations with this area and the adoption of realistic domestic economic policies, as well.

However, is it always for India to initiate the process of economic interaction with Southeast Asia? Is it not equally significant and of benefit to Southeast Asia to look upon India as a worthy business partner? Prof. Wadhwa and Dr. Ambatkar raised these questions after analysing the existing economic relations and came out with the conclusion that economic interdependence of India and SEA is essential for the mutual benefit of both regions. India, with large and sound human resource base could provide ample opportunities to ASEAN's surplus capital to reap advantages by investing in India. More essentially, India's skill and entrepreneurship in establishing small and medium scale industries could open more employment opportunities in Southeast Asia, particularly in the Indo-China region. Indian technical expertise, particularly, in textile and agro-based industries is still relevant in Vietnam, Cambodia, Myanmar, etc.

The authors strongly argue India's prospects as an investment destination in coming years vis-a-vis Southeast Asia following the appreciation in real effective exchange rates of some of the ASEAN economies. The "flying geese" pattern of foreign investment may find a favourable environment in India being a low-wage economy with added advantage of "regenerated enthusiasm" (due to economic reforms) in the private sector. There need to be special efforts on the part of India and SEA to establish trade generating joint-ventures for promoting intra-India-ASEAN trade relations. And equally important is to boost-up trilateral or quadrilateral growth centres for enhancing investment in the relatively less developed Indochina region.

What determines the quantum of trade in the changed international economic scenario? The goods produced with comparative advantage and marketed at competitive prices, may sound the right answer. But in a recent period a new paradigm has emerged, mostly led by Japan, which demonstrates that a large investment in manufacturing activities in the overseas countries decides the trade volume. The developing Asian countries are often advised to follow this "Japanese Model" to expand trade. Mr. T.K. Bhaumik also underlines the significance of Indian investment in ASEAN countries to boost up India's trade in this region. Trade follows investment and ASEAN economies provide ample opportunities for Indian investment because of technological upgradation of these economies. Similarly, India, too provides a favourable investment environment to ASEAN investors with the opening of the Indian economy.

To attract ASEAN's investments mere macro level economic reforms are not adequate. What is essential is widespread improvement at the micro level in the basic infrastructure. Prof. Bhattacharya emphasises that unless India improves the basic facilities such as arterial roads and ports, water resources, power and software, etc., no large scale foreign investment could be expected.

Similarly, Mr. Trivedi airs his views more clearly while comparing India and China as an investment destination. China being the forerunner in economic reforms (beginning in late seventies) had the distinct advantage of attracting large foreign investment during the 1980s. However, with the 1991 economic reforms India certainly has scored over some of its Asian competitors in attracting investment. India with a democratic form of government (with economic and political stability) coupled with the availability of cheap labour and ample scientific and technical manpower as well, looked upon by many Southeast Asian countries as a better place for investment, although this has to materialize.

Japan has a different policy for investment in South and

Southeast Asia. Japanese investment follows its ODA (Official Development Assistance) and this is evident from the bulk volume of investment it made over the years in Southeast Asia. Prof. Kesavan says that Japanese FDI has proportionately increased in the ASEAN countries since the 1980s following its large-scale flow of ODA in 1970s and 1980s—creating a wide-range of infrastructure for its private investors to pour their funds. India, too has attracted Japanese attention since economic reforms and has been the recipient of sizable (Japanese) ODA following which one can expect a flow of investments in the coming years.

On the trade front, India, since 1989 has impressively improved its position with the ASEAN countries. Not only the volume but its composition of trade has substantially moved in India's favour turning the balance of trade positive as well as enhancing the proportion of high-tech products exports to the ASEAN countries (except Singapore). Nevertheless, India should not be complacent over these achievements as Prof. Mukherjee points out and suggests rather it must strive to penetrate the ASEAN markets by diversifying the export basket instead of concentrating on few products.

Apart from investment and trade, the service sector is also another significant area where India and Southeast Asia could interact in the coming years. Many of the Southeast Asian countries have already excelled in providing varied kind of services to the world. India, too has achieved a remarkable excellence in building a strong base of high-skilled human resource in the field of construction, technology, banking and financial services, etc., and thus is a right partner to do business with the Southeast Asian countries. Mr. Verma feels that with the knowledge of English, computer literacy and mastery of mathematics, etc. India is poised to become a natural choice for Southeast Asian countries to widen the scope of cooperation in the service sector.

Similarly, the financial sector is also an important area where the possibility of interaction between India and ASEAN countries could be tapped following widespread reforms in various fields. Dr. Rao finds that with the doing away of various controls and barriers from the financial sector, particularly in India, the possibility of cooperation with the ASEAN countries has been intensified especially, in the field of commercial banking. India needs to heighten efficiency and range of financial instruments and institutions. More specifically, India has to bring a pragmatic approach involving trade policy so that hasty and sweeping liberalization, if any, may not adversely affect its chances to tie with the ASEAN countries.

Among Asian nations, India and China stand at equidistance when it comes to the ASEAN countries to promote mutual business cooperation. China with the presence of its large ethnic population in the whole ASEAN region obviously has better opportunities and easier ways to transact business. Moreover, most of the Chinese ethnic community in the ASEAN countries are engaged in business distribution channels which usually handle China's trade. Despite all these advantages ASEAN's trade and investment deals with China has slowed down with the emergence of India as a strong competitor because of economic liberalization since 1991. Prof. Shri Prakash through his extensive analysis of international trade data shows how till 1989 China and ASEAN had a growing and a substantial interest in each other's trade but after the end of the Cold War this has been markedly reduced, owing to the greater diversification and internationalization of ASEAN's exports and imports, which has become possible because of trade and investment liberalization in many countries.

Whatever it may be, since the end of the Cold War India's chances to tie up (economically) with the ASEAN nations have increased. Even the ODA of Japan and Taiwan which earlier used to go to China are being diverted towards India and ASEAN (and may eventually lead to a rise in their FDI flow). The improved image of India in the outside world with a successful implementation of the reform programme and withering away of China's economic significance for the ASEAN countries may usher in a strong economic interaction between India and ASEAN.

Finally, the book turns to the Asia-Pacific Economic Cooperation (APEC), a wider and crucial area in the current discussion. The APEC know as the "enlarged shadow" of ASEAN, certainly is significant for India's trade and investment, as 42 per cent of the world's total trade is concentrated in this group (and is predicted to cross the 50 per cent mark with the turn of the 20th century). From the investment view point, APEC accounts for 50 per cent of total approved FDI in India during 1991-94. In the backdrop of its commendable position in the global economic affairs, India cannot afford not to knock on the doors of APEC to acquire its membership. Dr. Bhanoji Rao feels, for India, it is indispensable to establish strong linkages with APEC so that it could become a prospective springboard to jump into the global markets.

Already, with good economic relations with almost all the prominent members of APEC, India can claim to have prepared the ground to be "considered" as a part of this group. To foster India's prospects to tie economically with APEC, as a group, calls for special efforts such as continuing the process of liberalization and spreading it to areas like insurance; trying to establish links with AFTA in order to garner benefits of free trade; upgrading key bilateral relations especially with Japan and Australia (being influential players in APEC); and finally bringing in sophistication in economic and commercial diplomacy while dealing with the countries of this group.

*By way of a conclusion:* To policy makers and to those responsible for making effective decisions about international economic relations this book may sound inevitable considering the earnestness of the subject matter. India is standing on the threshold of becoming an "economic tiger" in the very near future and its integration with the already established ASEAN tigers would be the first step in the right direction. Of course, India has initiated this process by demanding its present status of a sectoral dialogue partner to be raised to full dialogue partnership with ASEAN. Once this aim is achieved India could become an integral part of ASEAN economic activities enhancing its chances of getting APEC membership in the future.

More importantly, India has to improve its image (in the light of economic reforms) in the outside world so that the reforms get properly projected. Here comes the role of the Indian government which has to effectively interact with the various governments of Southeast Asia. Further, the government has to nurture the Indian community (settled in this region) to establish business distribution channels so that such channels may help in promoting the growth of India's commerce.

India's balanced and long term approach towards building a strong interaction with Southeast Asia would not only bring economic rewards but also peace and prosperity in the Asia-Pacific region.

# II

# INDIA AND SOUTHEAST ASIA

# 1

# India and Southeast Asia: New Partnership

V.V. BHANOJI RAO

## A Temporary Break in Historical Ties

The contacts between India and Southeast Asia (SEA) have been historical. There are many words in Bahasa Melayu and Bahasa Indonesia which have relatively pure Sanskrit roots. A million people on the island of Bali and Indonesia are Hindus. Not too long ago, a Balinese tourist guide impressed me with his Sanskrit hymns in praise of the sun. 'Rama' is a common name of Thai kings. Temples of Cambodia recall the historical ties with India. Islam, too, travelled via India to SEA while Buddhism moved from India earlier on. At Bandung, four decades ago, Nehru provided leadership to the Non-Aligned Movement. The momentum in the historical links, however, did not go very far in the economic realm, largely because of diverse politico-economic strategies followed by India on one side and most SEA nations on the other.

Amidst the international politics of the Cold War, the two sides' foreign policies became aligned to the former USSR and the USA respectively. Instead of a naturally flourishing multidimensional relationship between India and SEA, almost until recently, India could not find enough time for SEA, and SEA had no inclination to build bridges to India, since India did not emerge as the economic powerhouse, it was supposed to become.

Added to the lack of warmth in political relationships and negligible economic linkages, India's stance in regard to Vietnam and Cambodia also irked many Southeast Asian leaders (Sridharan, 1995). I should also add that Indian democracy, with its factions and divisions inclusive, combined with closed-door economic policies, never really could mesh with the relatively authoritarian regimes and open economies in some of the key SEA nations. Some time in the future, economic historians might opine that thanks to India's closed-door policy of some four decades, the now prosperous parts of SEA could attract foreign investments and develop niches in export markets.

**Recent Attempts at Building Bridges**

Successive Indian governments, even before the disintegration of the USSR and the end of Cold War, recognized the need to *Look East* for geo-political and economic reasons. The attempts to forge a closer relationship, however, received a tremendous boost since 1991, when India launched a relatively more significant economic liberalisation programme which involves a conscious attempt to link India with the global productive forces (Asher, 1994). Attracting foreign direct investments and promoting two-way trade have been the two-key pillars of the new relationship, leaving behind the baggage of the Cold War, Vietnam and Cambodia. What I am going to do is to make a case for strong economic linkages and draw some policy conclusions for India and SEA. The scope for a strong India-SEA partnership is there. Much depends on nurturing it.

The Association of South East Asian Nations (ASEAN is a regional organization comprising of Brunei, Indonesia, Malaysia, Philippines, Singapore, Thailand and Vietnam) have accorded a sectoral dialogue partner status to India for mutually beneficial interaction in trade, investment, tourism and science and technology. It is widely believed that India will soon become a full dialogue partner as well as a member of the ASEAN Regional Forum (ARF) where Asian security concerns are addressed. India has also expressed interest to join the Asia-Pacific Economic Cooperation (APEC) forum with 18 members including the ASEAN nations, the USA, Japan and Australia among others.

Among the Indian attempts since 1991 to forge strong bilateral ties with SEA, the India-Singapore link has been particularly successful. Prime Minister Goh Chok Tong was the chief guest at the 1994 Republic Day of India. He visited India again in December to be the chief guest at the CII celebrations at Calcutta. In the meantime, Prime Minister Narasimha Rao visited Singapore in September 1994 and delivered the prestigious Singapore Lecture.

The following excerpts from Prime Minister Rao's Singapore

Lecture on September 8, 1994 are useful to set the tone and provide the background for the on-going Indian efforts at cultivating the SEA nations:

> What we see in the Asia-Pacific region cannot be called a clash of civilizations but a mesh, interwoven with religious, ethnic, racial, linguistic and professional strands.
>
> And it is this diversity which gives the resilience that enables this mesh to sustain the almost unbelievable growth rates that Asia has seen in the past decade and will continue to see well into the next century.
>
> I am consciously including India in this reality and this vision of the Asia-Pacific that I propound.
>
> India has already taken steps to liberalise its currency regime, open the economy to move imports and investment, and educate its people on the benefits of exposure to the outside world. The Asia-Pacific could be the springboard for our leap into the global market place....
>
> I am happy to have had this opportunity to enunciate my belief in this vision of a new relationship between India and the Asia-Pacific from Singapore, which I consider the geographic and symbolic centre of the Asia Pacific.
>
> I trust this vision will be realized... and that the next century will be a century of partnership for us all.

## RATIONALE FOR PARTNERSHIP

### Growth of Regional Markets

The share of Asian NIEs in the world exports rose from 3.8 per cent in 1980 to 10.2 per cent in 1993. ASEAN-4 share rose from 2.3 per cent to 3.6 per cent. In contrast, India's share rose from 0.4 per cent to just 0.6 per cent. With about 15 per cent of the world labour force located in India, its share in the world exports is minuscule. Also, trade to GDP ratio for India at 16 per cent in 1992, for instance, was the way below the 50-150 range of ASEAN-4. Consistent with its efforts to boost exports, the country naturally looks to the fast growing Asia-Pacific region in general and SEA in particular.

A recent study by ESCAP (1994) points out that intra-regional trade has been a significant factor in the growth of SEA trade and it will gain further momentum in the coming years due to various factors. First, the developing economies of the region are expected to grow rapidly and thus provide markets for a wide variety of products. Second, developing economies of the region will become increasingly outward oriented. Third, intra-regional investment and relocation of production facilities from Japan and NIEs to other countries in the region will increase, and will give further impetus to intra-regional trade.

The ESCAP region as a whole exported the US $ 140 billion to the world in 1975 and $ 962 billion in 1992. Two trends are an integral part of this growth. First, the share of manufactures in total exports rose from less than 40 per cent in 1975 to 73 per cent in 1992. Second, the share of exports to ESCAP region (that is, intra-regional exports) increased from 33 per cent in 1975 to 45 per cent in 1992. Intra-regional trade is much more heavily concentrated in agricultural (60%) and mineral products (82%) and somewhat less in manufactures (39%).

In 1992, some of the key ESCAP regions had the following intra-regional trade to total trade ratios: 56.5 per cent in ASEAN-4, 40 per cent in Australia, New Zealand and Japan and 44 per cent in the four NIEs of Asia. In contrast, India's intra-regional trade to total trade ratio was 27.5 per cent. This can increase substantially, especially in agricultural and mineral products.

**Investment Flows**

Within the rapidly growing Asia-Pacific countries, the investment flows also have a regional bias. During 1981-91, each of the Asian NIEs received an FDI inflow of about US $ 2 billion per annum on the average. During 1988-90, most of them received roughly half the investment from the ESCAP region and the latter half from outside the region. ASEAN-4 also follow a similar pattern. South Asia is characterized by minuscule inflows and 90 per cent of it came from outside the region.

During 1981-86, FDI into India was an annual average of the US $ 69 million. During 1986-91, the annual average rose to the

US $ 173 million. During these years, the FDI quantum from outside the ESCAP region was 90 per cent of the total. Thus, during the decade of the 1980s, even when FDI was permitted into India, it was not from its Eastern neighbours.

The *Look East* policy, however, began to bring about a change. As can be seen from the accompanying table on FDI flows into India, Australia and Singapore shares, for instance, have increased in recent years. A number of investment missions went to Singapore especially and their impact is being felt to some extent. It is notable that the West Bengal government and the newly installed Karnataka government have recently had investment missions soliciting FDI in Singapore. This is a trend that has prompted outside investors to appreciate the present Indian political climate. Many outside India are understanding India's political stability in a proper perspective even Indian political actors keep changing.

**Approved foreign investment, 1991-94**

| | *1991* | *1992* | *1993* | *1994* |
|---|---|---|---|---|
| *Total Investment* | | | | |
| Rs. Billion | 5.3 | 38.9 | 88.6 | 89.6** |
| US $ Million* | 169 | 1243 | 2831 | 2863 |
| *Shares (%) of Top 12 (1994) Economies* | | | | |
| USA | 34.8 | 31.7 | 39.1 | 38.9 |
| UK | 6.0 | 3.0 | 7.0 | 14.5 |
| Germany | 7.8 | 2.2 | 2.0 | 6.4 |
| Mauritius*** | 0.0 | 0.0 | 1.4 | 6.0 |
| Japan | 9.9 | 15.7 | 2.9 | 4.5 |
| Italy | 3.3 | 2.3 | 1.3 | 4.4 |
| Australia | 0.5 | 2.0 | 0.3 | 4.3 |
| Singapore | 0.3 | 1.5 | 0.8 | 3.0 |
| Netherlands | 10.5 | 2.5 | 3.6 | 2.3 |
| Hong Kong | 3.9 | 1.5 | 1.0 | 1.8 |
| Korea | 1.2 | 1.0 | 0.3 | 1.2 |
| Russia | 1.6 | 0.3 | + | 1.2 |

* at Rs. 31.3 per dollar
** Excluding Rs. 52 billion of GDRs
*** not necessarily investments of Mauritius origin
\+ negligible

Source of basic data : *SIA Newsletter, January 1995.*

To a large extent, FDI flows into India can be expected to grow substantially due to its human resource base, and low wage costs. In 1990, with Japan = 100, the average wage cost index was 76 in Australia and 34-40 in NIEs. The index for ASEAN-4, China and South Asia are as follows (ESCAP, 1994a).

**Average wage cost, 1990, Japan = 100**

| | | | |
|---|---|---|---|
| Indonesia | 3.5 | Bangladesh | 3.9 |
| Malaysia | 12.0 | Pakistan | 6.3 |
| Philippines | 7.1 | | |
| Thailand | 9.7 | Sri Lanka | 2.4 |
| China | 1.9 | India | 5.5 |

One may not read too much into the numbers, yet their message is clear. Indonesia, China and South Asia can absorb large quantums of FDI into labour intensive industries, provided they create the necessary investment climate. It is not out of place here to mention that India must constantly be aware of the economic trends in China, which has seen a jump in exports from US $ 18 billion in 1980 to close to US $ 100 billion in 1993.

## COOPERATION AND LINKAGES

### Greater Understanding

Relations between Singapore and India have been placed on a strong footing as a result of the high level commitment to cooperate for mutual benefit. The recent cooperative initiatives between the two countries have gone beyond the economic sectors and embraced cultural relations also (Yong and Rao, 1995). But, the root is in economic relations and this receives emphasis in SEA in all bilateral and multilateral relations. Like Singapore, other ASEAN nations too should respond favourably in due course to collaborate with India. In the meantime, at all levels, attempts must be made to move towards the goal of harmonious relations between academics, businessmen and governments.

### Reforms with Strategic Planning

Why is it that outsiders are taking note of India? They know that it is an emerging mega economy, that economic liberalization alone is consistent and compatible with its liberal democracy and secularism, and that once its productive forces are released, they are unstoppable. Every conceivable product can be made in India simply by adding value through its powerful human resources, especially with due skill development. SEA will follow the USA, Germany, United Kingdom and Australia — and recognize India's market power, skill power and entrepreneurial power.

As the indicative projections in my study on APEC-India linkages show, the Indian economy can easily achieve a 6.5 per cent growth during 1995-2000. What this means is really awesome. GDP will grow from US $ 319 billion in 1995-96 to US $ 504 billion in 2000-2001. Per capita GDP will reach the US $ 500 level by the turn of the century. Foreign capital requirements will be in the US$10-20 billion range annually. Exports could reach US$60 billion and imports a staggering US$70 billion by 2000-2001. The next century, people will acknowledge as time goes on, is an Indian century — not exclusively and in isolation, but as part of the Asia-Pacific.

Today, Indonesia, Malaysia, Philippines, Thailand, Brunei, Myanmar, Laos, etc., may not appear to see the emerging India. All that is needed is to let India grow, let its reserves grow, let its international competitiveness be based on human resource skills and at the same time let it build strong and enviable democratic institutions not for export, but, for home consumption for the bliss that emanates from the fragrance of freedom. The challenge is now for India to take actions not only on the economic front, but also on other fronts. Among the latter are industrial relations and attitudes and values of the people. (Rao, 1993).

Continuation of economic reform, targeted reliefs for the poor, a visionary housing development plan to transform the looks of India by arresting visible inequities, improving the educational and economic status of women and an overall sensitivity to the way outsiders react to what Indians say and do at home — these will prompt SEA to adopt a "Look to India" policy in course of time.

India has to strengthen its strategic planning. An example at the micro level is worthy of note. The Indian made Sumit mixer is not only strong and rugged, it has a very important mechanism which is appreciated by most users. It is the facility to stir manually the stuff being blended without opening the top cover, or in some cases, without switching off. Presently, for the Sumit, Indians abroad are the main customers. In my view, Sumit has the potential to invade the world market! But, how does one go about it? What will the government do to help without violating WTO obligations? Can the employers, employees and government sit together with cool heads to formulate a market penetration plan for Sumit? I say the same about Titan watches. They are beautiful and elegant, but are not available outside the country. For Rs. 2000, that is, S $ 100 or US $ 60, one can have that little beauty on one's wrist. How can Titan penetrate the world markets?

Strategic and indicative planning are much more important now than the planning that India used for the past four decades. There is no Japanese, German or Swiss management school that can teach the real art of market penetration. Often, successful managers write books, and succeed in book sales, but no experience or strategy can be replicated at the market place! National level strategic planning in unconventional and inimitable ways may be the only way out, if India has to be a major player in the global market place.

**SAARC Level Initiatives**

It is unfortunate that SAARC was unable to freeze all the bilateral concerns for the sake of multilateralism. One hopes that investment, trade, educational and cultural exchanges and similar interactions can take place without waiting for political preconditions. Any positive movement in greater intra SAARC understanding will attract attention from others, notably, members of ASEAN, APEC and similar forum.

**Trade Promotion**

To a large extent, trade promotion has to complement the tariff reforms in India, ASEAN and other Southeast Asian countries. The duty rates in the ASEAN Free Trade Area (AFTA) will be 5 per cent or less by 2003. Indian government, academics and the businessmen should examine the case for a special trade relationship between India and the ASEAN. It may be possible for India and the ASEAN to agree on preferential duty rates for specific products and sectors, as a prelude to eventual free trade between them. The specially cordial relations that have existed between India and Vietnam should be turned around for mutual economic advantage. Educational, health and credit rating services are examples of sectors that can be nurtured as important Indian export sectors.

**Investment Promotion**

Several of the ASEAN nations have the financial capability to invest in Indian infrastructure. The latest Indian budget provides a five-year tax holiday for such ventures. In regard to foreign direct investments, Indian missions in ASEAN countries must have a soliciting and facilitating role. Indian investments in SEA have been growing and these too should be encouraged. Especially important are trade promoting investments. Indian investments should be stepped up in Myanmar and the Indo-China states.

**Information and Research**

Latest information on SEA is vital for trade and investments. Government, industry and the academia together should set up viable institutional mechanisms to collect and quickly disseminate up-to-date quantitative and qualitative information on SEA. Research issues identification and efforts to address them should also be carried out on a tri-partite basis. Strategic and confidential research should have priority over routine, descriptive, and superficial accounts.

**Ideas on India-Indonesia Linkages**

The route to take in regard to India-SEA partnership is by building strong bilateral linkages with key countries. The following is an illustrative account of the possible, and hopefully feasible, in regard to India-Indonesia linkages.

Physically and demographically, Indonesia is a large country. Rich in natural resources, especially coal, oil, timber and various other minerals and agricultural products, the country has the largest population (close to 200 million) among all the SEA nations. India and Indonesia can collaborate for mutual benefit in coal mining, meat processing, nuclear power, pulp and paper (Indonesian multinational Sinarmas is launching production operations at Poona) and oil, gas and petrochemicals. There are opportunities for joint investments in tourism. Australians and pacific islanders can come to India from Indonesia as an extended tour package. Europeans can go to Indonesia from India in similar package tours. India can set up in Indonesia a series of excellent joint venture educational establishments in science, technology, medicine and computer software. Both countries have considerable expertise on small and medium industries, and exchanges in this area will be mutually beneficial.

Institutional support is also needed for India-Indonesia collaboration. The private sectors in the two countries should establish formal exchange mechanisms. The commerce ministries of both countries could set out a trade promotion agenda.

## IN SUM

For now at least, it would appear that India-SEA economic linkages depend relatively more on Indian initiatives. This is not totally unacceptable. However, as Indian economic reforms proceed and as the economy's potentials are realized, SEA will take greater interest in India, as a matter of pragmatic economic calculus.

## REFERENCES

Asher, Mukul G. 1994. The 1994-95 Budget: Implications for India's "Look East" Policy. *Doing Business with India,* Singapore: Singapore Indian Chamber of Commerce and Industry, 51-62.

ESCAP, 1994. Review and Analysis of Intra-regional Trade Flows in Asia and Pacific. Secretariat note for the Fifth Meeting of the Steering Group of the Committee for Regional Economic Cooperation. Bangkok: ESCAP.

Rao, V.V. Bhanoji. 1993. *India's Economic Future: Government, People and Attitudes,* Delhi, Tata McGraw Hill.

Sridharan, Kripa. 1995. The Evolution and Growth of India-Singapore Relations, In Yong and Rao (1995).

Yong Mun Cheong and Rao, V.V. Bhanoji. 1995. *Singapore-India Relations: A Primer,* Singapore: University of Singapore Press, (in press).

# 2

# India's Sectoral Dialogue Partnership with ASEAN

CHARAN D. WADHVA

*and*

SANJAY AMBATKAR

It is by now commonly acclaimed that the coming century would belong to the Asia-Pacific region as the principal source of dynamism in the global economy. ASEAN sub-region constitutes an integral part of the dynamic Asia-Pacific region. In India's efforts for closer economic integration with the global economy in general and the Asian-Pacific Economy in particular, ASEAN region provides the first natural economic region for targeting such integration.

ASEAN presently comprises Brunei, Indonesia, Malaysia, Singapore, Thailand, Vietnam and Philippines, Singapore is an Asian tiger while Malaysia, Thailand are on their way to become Asian tigers by 2020 A.D. India too is poised to emerge as an Asian tiger in the not too distant a future. India, therefore, provides an ever expanding size of the market for foreign goods and for foreign investors due to the country's growing affluent middle class currently estimated conservatively at 250 million people. Indian skills and ASEAN's surplus capital provide the solid foundations for new economic complementarities for mutually profitable business cooperation in the twenty-first century. Recognising the economic potential of India in the post Cold War era after the break up of the former Soviet Union, ASEAN accorded India the status of its dialogue partner in January 1992 at the meeting of its foreign ministers held in Singapore.[1]

India's recently acquired status of ASEAN's sectoral dialogue partner has opened up new opportunities for mutually beneficial cooperation in the four designated areas of sectoral dialogue. These areas are : trade; investment; tourism; and science and technology. The trend towards rising wage rates and appreciating currencies (against the US dollar) in countries like Singapore, Malaysia and Thailand together with growing resources for foreign investment in all ASEAN countries are likely to shift the "flying geese" pattern of investment away from ASEAN countries towards neighbouring country like India. This is already happening at present. Foreign direct investment (FDI) in the manufacturing sector from major sources (including Japan) has of late been either following or continuing at decelerated growth rate in all ASEAN countries including the currently hottest favourite Malaysia.[2] This is because Malaysia, Singapore and Thailand are no longer as attractive destinations as low wage countries compared to China, Vietnam and even India. Moreover real effective exchange rates of some of the ASEAN countries like Malaysia, Singapore and Thailand have been appreciating since 1985 as revealed by the Asian Development Bank in its annual Asian Development Outlook. Even the investors from these ASEAN countries (especially the land constrained and the capital surplus Singapore) are relocating the overseas investment in other countries especially in the Growth Triangle (like the one of the Indonesian Batham Island) and in Vietnam.

The evolution of the proposed ASEAN Free Trade Area (AFTA) in the next ten years would provide new business opportunities for India for locating its investments in the expanded ASEAN region (including Vietnam and other countries of the Indochina region in the very near future).[3]

Indian technologies still appropriate in many areas for being transferred to the countries of Southeast Asia especially in the Indochina region (comprising Myanmar, Cambodia, Laos and Vietnam). The new world order being shaped by the World Trade Organisation (as a successor of GATT from 1995) also provide new vistas for mutual economic cooperation. These include among others joint R&D projects for developing "Asian Patents" cooperative ventures in exporting agro-based and textile related products and skill-intensive services like consultancy services and software. Joint ventures in textiles between India and some of the ASEAN partners for meeting the demand in the markets of the developed countries are likely to prove to be more useful towards the year 2005 A.D. This in view of the time limit of the year 2005 A.D. setup by the WTO for fully returning to the MFA-Regime in the "Textiles and Clothing" sectors. By that time, the competitive advantage in this sector is likely to slip away from some of the ASEAN countries and to be substantially diluted for India in favour of other low-wage developing countries.

Besides these favourable economic developments, political climate for commercial cooperation between India and the ASEAN countries has further improved in the post-Cold War era and especially since 1992 when India became the sectoral dialogue partner country of the ASEAN. Gone are also the imagined fears of possible dominance of the Indian ocean by the Indian naval forces. In some of the ASEAN and the neighbouring countries of the Indochina region which are all intending to become full members of the ASEAN beginning with Vietnam's expected entry into the ASEAN in July 1995, India is implicitly perceived as an additional and useful "balancing factor" (to China's feared supremacy) for promoting peace and security in the Southeast Asian region.

The continued high prosperity of most ASEAN countries (termed as Newly Industrialising Economies) and their structural transformation to successful export-oriented manufacturing activities and as exporters of capital have brought out new complementarities in the economies of ASEAN countries and India. The ASEAN capital and its newly acquired technologies from the Multi National Companies (of the West as well as Japan and South Korea from the East) combined with Indian technical and managerial skills provide a powerful combination for providing further source of dynamism in the entire region.

The far-reaching economic reforms launched by India since July 1991 oriented towards a more open and competitive market economy have dramatically improved the business and economic environment for expanding mutually beneficial cooperation with the ASEAN countries.[4]

These economic relations will get strengthened through the sizeable and influential Non-Resident Indian community residing permanently in the ASEAN countries.

The areas of potential cooperation include two-way expansion of trade in goods and services; investment through joint ventures in manufacturing and trading (bilaterally and through third countries); and associated flows of technology; expansion of two-way tourism; and mutual cooperation in science and technology including medical, engineering, management and other forms of scientific education where India has recognisable comparative advantage. All these areas of cooperation have been explicitly identified for sectoral dialogue between India and ASEAN.

Briefly but, the potential for mutually beneficial economic cooperation between India and ASEAN countries at bilateral, regional and global levels is enormous and is waiting to be tapped. In future, in all probability, investments will lead trade flows in this combined region.

## BUILDING ON THE EXISTING BASE

The economic relations and especially trade relations between India and ASEAN countries (though relatively small compared to their share in the world trade) have been growing rapidly in recent years especially in the period since 1991 and more so since India has become sectoral dialogue partner of the ASEAN in 1992. These provide building blocks for further expanding economic relations in line with the principle of dynamic comparative advantage.

### Trade Expansion

The recent dynamism noticed in the two-way trade expansion between India and ASEAN countries is reflected through data provided in Table 1. As can be seen from this Table India's export to the ASEAN grouping increased more than five times from a low base of US $ 301 million in 1980 to US $ 1534 million in 1993. Within the same period, the share of the ASEAN grouping in India's global exports more than doubled from 3.6 per cent in 1980 to 7.7 per cent in 1993. The rate of growth of India's export to the ASEAN grouping has accelerated in the period since India launched its economic reforms in 1991 and more so in the period since India became the sectoral dialogue partner of the ASEAN in Jan. 1992. Thus as Table 1 reveals, India's exports to the ASEAN grouping increased dynamically from little over US $ 1.5 billion in 1993. Singapore alone account for nearly 46 per cent of India's exports to the ASEAN grouping in 1993. The annual rates of growth of India's exports to the ASEAN work out to 28.5 per cent in 1992 and 19.7 per cent in 1993. The member country-wise picture of India's export to the ASEAN grouping for the same period is also provided in Table 1. The simple annual average growth rates of India's exports during the four year period 1990-93 works out to 30 per cent for Indonesia; 22.6 per cent for Malaysia; 38.1 per cent for the Philippines (because of extremely low base value in 1990); 32 per cent for Singapore; and 17 per cent for Thailand. Indian companies like the I.T.C.-Global based in Singapore have been actively promoting India's export to Singapore and through Singapore to Vietnam and other Southeast Asian countries.

India's imports from the ASEAN countries have also grown during the 1991-93 period (after registering sharp fall in 1991 over 1990 level). Thus India's imports from the ASEAN grouping had registered an increase from US $ 849 million in 1991 to US $ 950 million and to U.S. $ 991 million in 1993. This works out to annual growth rate of 11.8 per cent in 1992 and 4.3 per cent in 1993. The share of ASEAN grouping in India's total import had gone down during the 1990-93 period from 6.1 per cent level in 1990 to 4 per cent level in 1992 but had recovered to 4.4 per cent level in 1993. As in the case of export, Singapore is the largest source of India's imports from the ASEAN grouping accounting for a dominant 62 per cent share in 1993 (see Table 1). Malaysia came next in this respect accounting for 23 per cent share of India's export from the ASEAN grouping. India's imports from Indonesia, the Philippines and Thailand have been of marginal nature either depicting relative stagnation or even decline in recent years.

As a result of the much faster growth of India's export to the ASEAN grouping in the 1990s compared to import, India had dramatically converted its typical trade deficit with the ASEAN grouping of the 1980s to rising trade surplus in 1991-93 period. However, a trade surplus of mere US $ 543 million in India's favour in 1993 is too small to be noticeable in the ASEAN strongly export oriented economies.

Of the two most important trading partners in the ASEAN countries, namely, Malaysia and Singapore, the commodity composition of India's trade with these two countries has been gradually moving in favour of higher value added manufactured goods. In case of Malaysia, exports of buffalo meat has significantly

## TABLE I (A)
## India's trade with ASEAN

(Value in Million US$)

| Country | Exports to (value) | | | | | Imports from (value) | | | | | Balance of trade (value) | | | | |
|---|---|---|---|---|---|---|---|---|---|---|---|---|---|---|---|
| | 1980 | 1990 | 1991 | 1992 | 1993 | 1980 | 1990 | 1991 | 1992 | 1993 | 1980 | 1990 | 1991 | 1992 | 1993 |
| Indonesia | 50 | 92 | 145 | 167 | 203 | 25 | 173 | 67 | 67 | 90 | 25 | -81 | 78 | 100 | 113 |
| Malaysia | 68 | 126 | 203 | 246 | 240 | 342 | 546 | 391 | 440 | 228 | -274 | -420 | -188 | -194 | 12 |
| Philippines | 9 | 21 | 64 | 77 | 53 | 12 | 4 | 31 | 11 | 7 | -3 | 17 | 33 | 66 | 46 |
| Singapore | 127 | 308 | 386 | 535 | 700 | 475 | 689 | 311 | 367 | 612 | -348 | -381 | 75 | 168 | 88 |
| Thailand | 47 | 201 | 199 | 257 | 338 | 24 | 62 | 49 | 65 | 54 | 23 | 139 | 150 | 192 | 146 |
| ASEAN | 301 | 748 | 997 | 1282 | 1534 | 878 | 1474 | 849 | 950 | 991 | -577 | -726 | 148 | 332 | 543 |
| World | 8441 | 17813 | 17872 | 18528 | 19964 | 14822 | 23990 | 19509 | 24206 | 22493 | -6381 | -5177 | -1637 | 5678 | -2529 |

*Source* : Direction of Trade Statistics Year Book, 1994.

## TABLE I (B)
## India's trade with ASEAN

*(Value in Million US $ and Percentage of Trade with World)*

| *Country* | *Exports to* | | | | *Imports from* | | | | *India's Balance of Trade with* | |
|---|---|---|---|---|---|---|---|---|---|---|
| | 1980 | | 1992 | | 1980 | | 1992 | | 1980 | 1992 |
| | *Value* | *%* | *Value* | *%* | *Value* | *%* | *Value* | *%* | *Value* | *Value* |
| Indonesia | 50 | 0.59 | 160 | 0.77 | 25 | 0.17 | 54 | 0.23 | 25 | 106 |
| Malaysia | 68 | 0.80 | 322 | 1.55 | 342 | 2.30 | 473 | 2.00 | -274 | -151 |
| Philippines | 9 | 0.10 | 71 | 0.34 | 12 | 0.08 | 36 | 0.15 | -9 | 35 |
| Singapore | 127 | 1.50 | 425 | 2.05 | 475 | 3.20 | 342 | 1.44 | -348 | 83 |
| Thailand | 47 | 0.55 | 304 | 1.47 | 24 | 0.16 | 72 | 0.30 | 23 | 232 |
| ASEAN | 301 | 3.56 | 1284 | 6.20 | 878 | 5.92 | 977 | 4.13 | -577 | 301 |
| World | 8441 | | 20683 | | 14822 | | 23638 | | -6381 | -2955 |

*Source* : International Monetary Fund, *Direction of Trade Yearback*, 1986 and 1993 Issues.

grown in the post-1990 period. But other items of India's export to Malaysia have not shown buoyancy in this period as India's total export to Malaysia has actually declined from US $ 246 million in 1992 to 240 million in 1993. Malaysia is the most important exporters of palm oil to India in the world. And this position has continued for more than two decades. India's major export to Singapore included textile manufactures, gems and jewellery, leather products and marine products. The main products imported by India from Singapore include petroleum products (refined); electronic valves; electric machinery and chemical products.

**Investment Expansion**

Two-way Investment Cooperation between India and ASEAN through joint ventures has witnessed a second big wave of expansion in the post-1991 era of reforms in India. It is well known that even in the era of pre-1991 economic reform in India. Indian entrepreneurs had set up the largest numbers of joint manufacturing ventures in the ASEAN compared to any other region in the world. As of early 1992, India's operational joint ventures numbered 19 in Malaysia; 15 in Thailand; 13 in Singapore; 11 in Indonesia and only one in Philippines.[5] It is important to note that most of the operational Indian joint ventures in Singapore are in high-tech areas.

Singapore had emerged as the largest single investor from ASEAN countries in India in the post-1991 era of reforms. A "mild India fever" had gripped Singapore on the eve of Singapore Prime Minister Goh Chok Tong's visit to India in January, 1994. This fever has somewhat subsided in the latter part of 1993 and in the first half of 1994. However, it is most likely that India would continue to be an attractive destination for Singaporean investment. The Bangalore Technology Park and the Madras-Singapore Corridor (being revived as the Madras Industrial Park) would prove to be landmarks of Singapore-India business cooperation. Singapore Airlines proposal to set up a joint venture company in India with the Tata group for domestic air services is currently under the active consideration of the Government of India.

During the visit of the Indian Prime Minister to Singapore in September 1994, the visiting Indian Business Delegation signed as many as 13 new proposed joint ventures in India involving investment worth US $ 534 million. These include among others projects involving shipbuilding aquaculture; telecom equipments; the construction of mini township near Delhi named after Singapore's Sentosa Island and a new banking company jointly by Singapore's indigenous Keppel Bank and India's 20th Centenary Finance Corporation Ltd. Singapore and Indian businessmen also agreed on trilateral investment cooperation ('trioka' approach) in third countries like Vietnam where Singaporeans have substantial business interests. The Prime Minister of Singapore assured the Indian Prime Minister of Singapore's support to India's seeking membership of the 17 nations Asia Pacific Economic (APEC) forum including the ASEAN-6; Australia; New Zealand; Canada; Chile; Papua New Guinea; South Korea; Japan and the three other China's (People Republic of China, Hong Kong and Taiwan). Goh Chok Tong's repeated visit to India in January, 1995 reconfirmed Singapore's continued interest for supporting two-way expansion of India-Singapore economic relations particularly for expanding Singapore's investment in India. India and Singapore are currently (March, 1995) negotiating signing of an MOU on cooperation in the field of Marine environment.

Of late, Malaysia has shown strong interest in promoting its economic and defence ties with India. Malaysian companies are actively exploring investing in toll road and highway construction in India. India and Malaysia had signed an MOU on micro satellites using technology developed by India.

Thai investors especially second generation NRIs have recently shown keen interest in acquiring private sector Indian's banks.

The visit by Prime Minister P.V. Narasimha Rao to Vietnam and Singapore in Sept. 1994 had also clearly brought out the possibilities of strengthening defence cooperation with India playing a supportive role in the security and stability of the ASEAN region in which India had a stake. India is already assisting some ASEAN countries like Malaysia in conducting joint naval exercises and assisting Malaysia in supply of parts for MiG planes bought by Malaysia from Russia. The Indian Prime Minister had reiterated India's desire to explore the possibilities of a meaningful role for India in the recently floated ASEAN Regional Forum

(ARF) under the APEC-umbrella for discussing emerging security environment and possible options for cooperation in the Asia Pacific Region.[6]

**New Specific Opportunities and Constraints**

The first official level sectoral dialogue between India and the ASEAN held at Bali in January 1994 had reviewed the potential business opportunities for mutual expansion of business in the four selected areas. These are: (1) Trade; (2) Tourism; (3) Investment; and (4) Science and Technology. The institutional mechanism for making progress on this and future sector dialogues between ASEAN and India was set in place at the first meeting of the standing ASEAN-India Joint Sectoral Committee (AIJSCC) held at Bali. In addition to the AIJSCC, an ASEAN-New Delhi Committee (ANDC) and an ASEAN-India Business Council (AIBC) had also been set up as regular bodies. Throughout the deliberations of the first sectoral dialogue, the primacy of private sector led business to business initiative for strengthening ASEAN-India economic cooperation in four selected areas was recognised and recorded.

The second government-to-government level sectoral dialogue between India and the ASEAN was held at New Delhi during February 13-17, 1995. This dialogue reviewed the progress of India-ASEAN economic cooperation and considered areas which required greater attentions in future.[7] Considerable attention was focussed on the need to promote two-way tourism and tourism related investments (like hotels and airlines) between India and the countries of the ASEAN regions as well as in third countries. The Indian tour operators observations regarding the need to relax visa restrictions for the Indian tourists was noted for being conveyed to the Malaysian authorities. The difficulties being experienced by some of the ASEAN investors due to somewhat restrictive Indian civil aviation policy were conveyed to the Indian authorities. The issue of opening bank branches on reciprocal basis for facilitating expansion of trade and investment between India and the ASEAN countries was also sympathetically considered. The two sides agreed on the need to work together to fight the proposed introduction of social clause in exports from the developing countries to the markets of the European Union and of other developed countries under the new rules being debated under the auspices of the World Trade Organisation. A positive outcome of this second sectoral dialogue was the assurance given by India's Prime Minister P.V. Narasimha Rao to Ajit Singh, Secretary General of the ASEAN that India would favourably consider raising the cash ceiling on investment by the Indian companies in the ASEAN region to enable them to take advantage of emerging mutually beneficial business opportunities due to the progress being made towards the establishment of an ASEAN Free Trade Area by 2008 A.D. Both sides are reported to have expressed satisfaction over the successful completion of the second round of the sectoral dialogue as well as the cumulative progress made towards strengthening India-ASEAN economic partnership in the future. The business-to-business contacts through visits at individual level and at the level of exchange of visits by several delegations sponsored through national and ASEAN-level Chambers of Commerce and apex industry associations of India and the ASEAN countries have been intensified since India became a sectoral dialogue partner of the ASEAN in January 1992. Besides Singapore, Thailand has significantly increased its investments in the Indian joint ventures in 1993. Malaysian investors are also actively exploring the possibilities of investing in India's toll paying highways. The Malaysian government has expressed the desire to finance setting up new captive medical colleges in India to produce Malaysian doctors through Indian medical education. Similar training for Malaysian defence personnel is also likely to be favoured by some of the governments in the ASEAN countries.

Besides above-mentioned business opportunities, several specific areas of business opportunities between India and ASEAN countries have been indicated in a study by V. L. Rao and R. Upendra Das.[8] In our view, investment in services will provide several mutually profitable opportunities for strengthening economic partnership between India and the countries of the ASEAN region. Joint ventures in hostels, construction, tourism, higher education (through Fellowship exchange), software and consultancy services of various types (medical, architectural, finance and accounting, and other management services) provide good examples of possibilities of investment in services for two-way expansion of business in the combined region.

Based on an earlier research study on the specific areas of mutual trade expansion between the member countries of the South Asian Association for Regional Cooperation (SAARC-7, namely, Bangladesh, Bhutan, India, Maldives, Nepal, Pakistan and Sri Lanka of South Asia) on the one side and ASEAN on the other (which is still largely relevant), reproduced below is the following list of 16 products with good potential for mutual expansion of trade between India and the ASEAN countries :[9]

1. Oils of Vegetable origin; 2. Newsprint; 3. Dyestuffs, synthetic; 4. Nitrogenous fertilisers; 5. Phosphatic fertilisers; 6. Potassic fertilisers; 7. Rubber and products; 8. Cement; 9. Pig Iron; 10. Tinplates; 11. Steel Castings; 12. Copper Refined; 13. Aluminium and products; 14. Lead Refined; 15. Zinc; and 16. Tin.

Long term contracts for the procurement of palm oil from Malaysia and Indonesia by India need to be institutionalised.

The intra-industry India-ASEAN trade needs to be expanded. Detailed market research is required for scientifically examining the feasibility of proposals in this regard. We provide two illustrative examples in this connection.[10] The first example relates to export of auto-parts from India to the Proton Car of Malaysia and of some parts of Proton Car for Indian cars. Another example of intra-industry trade potential relates to the subdivision of publications business in terms of design and printing in Singapore and work processing-copy editing as well as proof reading in India.

**Trilateral or Quadrilateral Growth Centres**

There is tremendous scope for extending the concept of the growth triangles like the one functioning at Batam Island. Calcutta-Bangkok-Jakarta air and land based industrial park and a quadrilateral Madras-Colombo-Kuala Lumpur-Singapore sea-route and land-based (involving Sri Lanka) industrial park provide illustrative ideas which can be further examined.[11]

**Trade Generating Joint Ventures**

A new special breed of "Trade Generating Joint Ventures" (TGJVs) involving investment and regional technology can be examined for creating new complementarities for specifically promoting intra-India-ASEAN trade in the first phase.[12] Later this conception can be extended to third country ventures and global marketing of products and services of such TGJVs between the leading firms of India and the ASEAN countries (and in course of time also involving selected firms from the countries of the Indo-China sub-region of the expanded ASEAN region).

**Major Constraints in Economic Partnership**

Despite no political problems between India and the ASEAN countries and the growing contacts between India and the ASEAN countries both at official and business-to-business delegation levels in the past 1991 period, there are yet no signs of reaching the full crescendo of "ASEAN fever" in India and "India fever" in the ASEAN countries. As the Japanese experience (as investor of FDI) and the Chinese experiences (as recipient of FDI) amply demonstrate, given a sufficient level of understanding and encouragement at the political level between or among the countries concerned, intending business investors (not just delegations) have to frequently visit the target destination countries for appraising their planned investments. The foreign businessmen (investors) have to make their personal presence felt through active interaction with the local government officials and the local potential business partners. Surjit Man Singh has observed from her recent trips to the Asia-Pacific (East and Southeast Asia) region that as far as Indian business travellers are concerned, "India has practically no visibility in the Asia-Pacific region which is easily the most creative, dynamic and vibrant part of the world today.[13] The same is more or less true of the frequency and regularity of exploratory business trips by ASEAN entrepreneurs to India.

The major constraints to the process of strengthening economic partnership between India on the one side and the ASEAN countries on the other side include. Lack of adequate market information; inadequate infrastructure for servicing the needs of two-way expansion of trade and investments; low level of business-to-business contacts on regular basis as business partners in joint ventures; and (till 1991) relatively lukewarm diplomatic efforts; combined with the basic problem of lack of export-competitiveness of Indian products (price, quality, delivery schedules, etc.)[14]

To these factors, we must add the image problem of India at the official bureaucratic level and at the level of the Indian business community. The investor entrepreneurs from the ASEAN countries (as from any other developed country) recent experiencing inordinate delays in India for the implementation of the decisions already taken. There is a widespread perception that Indian (and India-origin) business community generally keeps to itself and does not very freely mix and interact with the multi-ethnic local business communities in most ASEAN countries (especially of the Chinese origin). Right or wrong, these perceptions often stand in the way of forging active strategic alliances (including the joint ventures in marketing and distribution channels) between the firms in India and in the ASEAN countries.[15] It should now be possible to reduce the impact of these problems with the recent setting up of the ASEAN-India Joint Business Council and of the India-ASEAN Economic Coordination Committees at apex level of Chamber of Commerce and Industry to deal with their counterpart in the ASEAN countries.

Singapore in September 1994 has highlighted the yet untapped vast potential for economic cooperation between India and the countries of ASEAN region for these mutual benefit. Surely but steadily, investing private companies from the ASEAN region have discovered the potential of the Indian market as natural extension of their overseas business plans. Detailed market research studies need to be conducted to further identified specific areas of profitable business opportunities. Increasing two-way interaction at both business and political levels between India and several ASEAN countries since 1991 has brought out the need for evolving a coordinated strategic action plan between the government and the business for converting potential opportunities for business cooperation into concrete business operations.

## MAJOR ELEMENTS OF ACTION PLAN

The strategic action plan for concretising opportunities for business cooperation between India and ASEAN countries will have to be evolved primarily by the business entrepreneurs and their organisations like the Joint Business Councils. The forging of strategic business alliances between the business entities in the concerned countries would serve as the principal tool for realising the above objective. The Indian business entities with promotional support of their government should identify and woo large foreign investing companies of ASEAN origin interested in investing in infrastructural project in India on Build-Own-Operate-and Transfer basis assuring fare rates of return on such FDI. The governments of the concerned countries will have to play a well carved out supportive role in smoothening this cooperative process and speedily actualising the relevant proposals for business-to-business cooperation across the concerned countries (including the "third country" ventures as well). Effective follow-up action will have to be taken on continuous basis to strengthen this cooperation.

We list below the specific supplementary role for the governments, especially the Government of India, for strengthening the process of business-to-business cooperation between India and the countries of ASEAN region :[16]

(i) The concerned governments should upgrade political relations with the other governments to a level which would give added priority and credibility to the process of strengthening of mutually beneficial economic and business partnership in this combined region. In this connection, the Government of India needs to pay special attention to Indonesia, Philippines and Brunei for propagating and seeking support of their governments for strengthening integration of India with the ASEAN economies;

(ii) The governments should evolve joint negotiating positions on regional and international economic policies and problems in the post-Uruguay Round World especially as they affect the businessmen of the combined region (e.g. on the delinking of social clauses on labour conditionalities and phasing of environmental requirements from trade);

(iii) The Government of India in consultation with the ASEAN secretariat and keeping in mind the steps progressively taken by the present full dialogue partners from their status as sectoral dialogue partnership (e.g., South Korea) should evolve an appropriate three yearly plan of action to achieve full dialogue status soon;

(iv) The Government of India should seek the help of the governments of the ASEAN countries while seeking membership of the APEC;

(v) The concerned governments should do their best to support infrastructural development (especially infrastructure for exports). The Government of India should seek the help of the governments of the ASEAN countries to bring to India reputed investor companies of ASEAN origin interested in projects in India and put them in touch with the concerned business entities and authorities;

(vi) The concerned governments could enter into feasible defence cooperation agreements especially for training and joint exercises for strengthening collective security;

(vii) The most important new role of the government (especially in India) is to create a favourable macro and micro environment which will facilitate independent decision making by the private business within the framework of more open competitive economy as pursued in most ASEAN countries. Sustained high growth of GDP and expanding foreign trade in an open economy will automatically make India a more acceptable and more keenly sought after economic partner in the ASEAN region;

(viii) Foreign policy of India should be heavily oriented towards serving India's economic interests;

(ix) The institutional and administrative capacity for efficient, transparent and speedy decision making and implementation of the government policies should be vastly improved in India. This will enhance India's credibility in the area of market-oriented economic reforms in the ASEAN region; and

(x) The concerned governments and the ASEAN Secretariat should take greater interest in activating and following up on the 'Action Taken Reports' of the institutional mechanisms at business apex level organisations already in place (such as the ASEAN — India Business Council and the ASEAN — New Delhi Committee) by sending governmental observers (and not official representatives) and publicising the efforts being made both at the government-to-government and business-to-business levels and progress achieved as well as action plans agreed for strengthening India-ASEAN economic partnership at bilateral as well as multilateral levels.

**Conclusions**

With concerted efforts, India can rapidly increase its trade, investment, tourism and other linkages with the ASEAN countries in the next five years and emerge as ASEAN's significant economic partner. The same would be true for India as far as ASEAN's importance to India is concerned. India will then not only be able to graduate to a full dialogue partner of the ASEAN but also become strong contender for membership of the expanded ASEAN and expanded APEC.

## NOTES

1. ASEAN had invited India earlier in the 1970s to become its sectoral dialogue partner. But India had missed out on this opportunity due to India's recognition of the regime in Kampuchea (Cambodia) following the Soviet lead. Much valuable time has been lost in this process.
2. Total approved investment in Malaysian manufacturing sector fell from M$ 27.7 billion 1992 to M$ 13.3 billion. Within this overall proposed investment, foreign investment fell by 66 per cent to M$ 6 billion. For further details of noticeable reduction in FDI inflows to the ASEAN countries in 1993 compared to 1992 sourcewise (such as from Japan, Taiwan, South Korea), see the news item in this effect in the *Financial Times,* (London) Jan. 7, 1994 (p. 10). Even if it is a temporary setback, it is likely to reappear in the near future for reasons explained above in the text.
3. The original ASEAN-5 at the launching of this grouping in 1967 comprised of Indonesia, Malaysia, Philippines, Singapore and Thailand. Brunei became its sixth member in 1984. The ASEAN-6 became ASEAN-7 in 1995 with the inclusion of Vietnam as its seventh member. Cambodia is very soon likely to be accorded the status of "Observer" following its active application for seeking the membership of the ASEAN. Laos and Myanmar are also likely to be admitted as members of the ASEAN thereby covering the entire "Southeast Asia" in the next few years. Thus ASEAN-7 looks like expanding to the ASEAN-10 in the next five years or so (by 2000 A.D.).
4. For a comprehensive account and appraisal of the economic reforms launched by India since June 1991, see Charan Wadhva, "Economic

Reforms in India and the Market Economy", Allied Publishers, New Delhi, 1994.

5. For more up-to-date data on this subject, the reader is referred to the latest publications by the Indian Investment Centre, New Delhi.

6. India appears to be facing difficulties in securing even an observer's (or special invitee) status in the ARF. Some of the ASEAN countries (notably Indonesia) and some other ASEAN countries have reservations for extending membership of the APEC. APEC has decided to consolidated itself and not to admit any new country into its fold for a period of three years ending in 1997. Based on the recommendations of the Eminent Persons Group, APEC countries have recently agreed to move towards "Open regionalism" and establishing the world's largest free-trade area by 2020 A.D. Some countries of ASEAN are similarly opposed to India's membership of the ASEAN at least at present.

7. The following account of the progress made at the second India ASEAN sectoral dialogue on the news report publish in the *Indian Express*, New Delhi, Feb. 18, 1995 and on the editorial comments in the *Indian Express*, dated Feb. 22, 1995.

8. V. L. Rao and R. Upendra Das, India and ASEAN; Issues in Sectoral Dialogue Partnership, New Delhi; Published by Research and Information System for the Non-Aligned and Other Developing Countries, 1993 (RIS Occasional Paper No. 41). This publication also presents data on the Commodity Composition of trade between India and the ASEAN countries.

9. From Charan D. Wadhva, "Economic Cooperation between Countries of ASEAN and SAARC in Prem Vashishtha (ed.), Commonalities, Complementarities and Cooperation: Asian Pacific Region, New Delhi, Association of Development Research and Training Institute of Asia and the Pacific and the National Council of Applied Economic Research (Ch. IV), 1989.

10. Ibid.

11. These ideas are contained in Charan Wadhva, "India-Southeast Asia Economic Partnership in 1990s: role of governmental policies in B. D. Ghoshal (ed.), Southeast-Asia: Indian Perspectives", New Delhi, Konark Publishers, 1995, Ch. 4 (Forthcoming).

12. For the conceptual clarity and an illustrative list of possible "Trade Generating Joint Ventures" between SAARC (of which India is a leading member) and the ASEAN, see Charan D. Wadhva, "Possibilities of Trade Generating Joint Ventures among SAARC-ASEAN" in Bhabani Sengupta (ed.). SAARC-ASEAN: Problems of Inter-regional Cooperation, New Delhi: South Asian Publishers, 1988.

13. Surjit Man Singh, "Hope in the East": It is high time India explored the Asia-Pacific, the *Indian Express*, October 29, 1993.

14. Cf. Charan D. Wadhva, "Regional Economic Cooperation between SAARC and ASEAN and other countries of the Asia-Pacific Region" in K.K. Bhargava, et al 'South Asia: Towards Dynamism and Cooperation', Popular Prakashan, 1994.

15. Cf. Charan D. Wadhva "India-Southeast Asia Economic Partnership in the 1990s" role of governmental policies.

16. This last section heavily draws upon Charan D. Wadhva's "India-Southeast Asia Economic Partnership in the 1990s: Role of Governmental Policies" in B. D. Ghoshal (ed.) "Southeast Asia: Indian Perspectives", New Delhi, Konark Publishers, Ch. 4 (Forthcoming).

# III
# INVESTMENT

# 3

# Indo-ASEAN Investment Relations

B. BHATTACHARYYA

The trade and economic relations between India and countries of the ASEAN region though quite old were not quantitatively significant. There is possibility of substantial expansion of trade and investment between them, provided there are focussed programmes and projects covering trade liberalisation, facilitation and promotion.

The trends in trade flows in various countries show that it is investment flows that drive trade flows, particularly when the largest increases in trade flows take place in the form of inter-industry or intra-firm trade. The key to greater economic relationships with ASEAN thus lies in increasing mutual flows of investment. This includes both Indian investments in ASEAN countries and ASEAN investments in India.

There is evidence to show that India has managed to improve its image among foreign investors after the liberalisation process which started in 1991. The spate of newspapers articles and features in prominent newspapers demonstrate that India has been able to attract media attention.

Details of country-wise approvals for foreign direct investment and foreign technology agreement from August 1991 to December 1994 are given in the table below:

**Country-wise approvals for foreign direct investment and foreign technology agreement from Aug.'91 to Dec.'94**

*(Value: Rs. Crore)*

| S. No. | Country | Approvals Total | Tech | Fin | Amount of Foreign Investment |
|---|---|---|---|---|---|
| 1. | USA | 1093 | 568 | 525 | 8382.79 |
| 2. | UK | 652 | 371 | 281 | 2063.19 |
| 3. | NRI | 352 | 3 | 349 | 1756.01 |
| 4. | Japan | 371 | 251 | 120 | 1258.26 |
| 5. | Switzerland | 234 | 125 | 109 | 1189.10 |
| 6. | Germany | 694 | 416 | 278 | 899.89 |
| 7. | Netherlands | 242 | 117 | 125 | 663.34 |
| 8. | Mauritius | 16 | 0 | 16 | 658.98 |
| 9. | Italy | 251 | 145 | 106 | 620.60 |
| 10. | Oman | 6 | 1 | 5 | 560.36 |
| 11. | Australia | 114 | 55 | 59 | 531.90 |
| 12. | UAE | 20 | 2 | 18 | 462.37 |
| 13. | Hong Kong | 61 | 13 | 48 | 460.56 |
| 14. | Singapore | 148 | 49 | 99 | 392.59 |
| 15. | Thailand | 35 | 17 | 18 | 380.92 |
| 16. | France | 187 | 109 | 78 | 261.30 |
| 17. | Mexico | 8 | 2 | 6 | 244.26 |
| 18. | South Korea | 136 | 58 | 78 | 181.75 |
| 19. | Ireland | 13 | 3 | 10 | 172.05 |
| 20. | Russia | 63 | 15 | 48 | 124.84 |
| 21. | Denmark | 56 | 27 | 29 | 112.88 |
| 22. | Malaysia | 23 | 7 | 16 | 108.31 |
| 23. | Belgium | 38 | 19 | 19 | 91.30 |
| 24. | China | 31 | 18 | 13 | 88.90 |
| 25. | Canada | 66 | 38 | 28 | 74.85 |
| 26. | Sweden | 83 | 57 | 26 | 67.65 |
| 27. | Austria | 96 | 70 | 26 | 47.21 |
| 28. | Taiwan | 60 | 30 | 30 | 38.67 |
| 29. | Kuwait | 6 | 0 | 6 | 34.73 |
| 30. | Bermuda | 3 | 1 | 2 | 29.35 |
| 31. | Finland | 39 | 24 | 15 | 25.29 |
| 32. | Philippines | 17 | 8 | 9 | 22.34 |
| 33. | Portugal | 9 | 6 | 3 | 15.36 |
| 34. | Spain | 29 | 19 | 10 | 14.07 |
| 35. | Israel | 25 | 16 | 9 | 11.24 |
| 36. | Saudi Arabia | 9 | 0 | 9 | 11.17 |

*(Contd.)*

| *S. No.* | *Country* | *Approvals* *Total* | *Tech* | *Fin* | *Amount of Foreign Investment* |
|---|---|---|---|---|---|
| 37. | Bahamas | 3 | 0 | 3 | 8.87 |
| 38. | British Virginia | 8 | 4 | 4 | 8.78 |
| 39. | Estonia | 1 | 0 | 1 | 7.00 |
| 40. | Cayman Islands | 2 | 0 | 2 | 6.50 |
| 41. | Czech Republic | 14 | 11 | 3 | 5.70 |
| 42. | Bahrain | 6 | 0 | 6 | 5.65 |
| 43. | Qatar | 1 | 0 | 1 | 4.53 |
| 44. | Norway | 18 | 9 | 9 | 4.29 |
| 45. | Sri Lanka | 5 | 0 | 5 | 3.94 |
| 46. | Luxembourg | 2 | 0 | 2 | 2.90 |
| 47. | Panama | 3 | 1 | 2 | 2.55 |
| 48. | Hungary | 14 | 6 | 8 | 2,43 |
| 49. | Indonesia | 6 | 2 | 4 | 2.28 |
| 50. | Ukraine | 8 | 2 | 6 | 1.57 |
| 51. | Nigeria | 2 | 0 | 2 | 1.54 |
| 52. | Kazakhstan | 1 | 0 | 1 | 1.50 |
| 53. | Channel Islands | 3 | 0 | 3 | 1.25 |
| | Total (incl. others) | 5462 | 2740 | 2722 | 22141 |

**Inward Investment Flows from the ASEAN**

As will be observed from the table, total number of foreign investment proposals approved in the country from the world for the period August 1991 to December 1994 was 5462 which included 2740 technical proposals and 2722 financial proposals. As a result of these proposals, the total inflow of FDI during the above mentioned period stood at Rs. 22,141 crore. As compared to these figures, the number of foreign investment proposals approved from ASEAN region stood at 229 which included 83 technical proposals and 146 financial proposals involving a sum of Rs. 906.44 crore. Thus out of the total FDI of Rs. 21,141 crore only 4.09 per cent came from the ASEAN region during the period August 1991 to December 1994. This is a very meagre amount as compared to the potential that exists.

Further out of total FDI flows of Rs. 906 crore from ASEAN region during the period August 1991 to December 1994, more than 85 per cent came from two countries of the region, viz., Singapore and Thailand. FDI flows from the Philippines, Indonesia and Brunei have been negligible while Malaysia accounted for

Rs. 108 crore during the above period. Details of country-wise approvals from the ASEAN nations from August 1991 to December 1994 are given in the table below :

**Country-wise foreign direct investment**

*(Value: Rs. crore)*

| *S. No.* | *Country* | *Approvals* Total | *Approvals* Tech | *Approvals* Fin | *Amount of Foreign Investment* |
|---|---|---|---|---|---|
| 1. | Singapore | 148 | 49 | 99 | 392.59 |
| 2. | Thailand | 35 | 17 | 18 | 380.92 |
| 3. | Malaysia | 23 | 7 | 16 | 108.31 |
| 4. | Philippines | 17 | 8 | 9 | 22.34 |
| 5. | Indonesia | 6 | 2 | 4 | 2.28 |
| | Total | 229 | 83 | 146 | 906.44 |

India can invite ASEAN expertise in areas such as the following:

- Oil and gas based industries,
- Packaging and quality upgradation for export products,
- Port management,
- Pineapple and palm fibre extraction,
- Energy efficiency in multi-stored buildings and
- Renewable energy (based on paddy husk and other agro-residues).

**Outward Investment Flows from India**

Apart from inviting foreign investors from the ASEAN region to our country, Indian joint ventures and wholly owned subsidiaries in these countries have played an important role in promoting exports, trade expansion and economic cooperation. These projects have served as an outlet for Indian entrepreneurs to internationalise and in the process, expose themselves to the latest technological developments, management practices, etc.

As on December 31, 1993, there were 430 joint ventures in different parts of the world. Out of these joint ventures, 167 were in operation and 263 were at different stages of implementation. The total quantum of Indian equity in the 167 joint ventures in operation was about Rs. 141.79 crore, while approved Indian equity of the joint ventures under implementation amounts to Rs. 1035.24 crore.

Indian joint ventures are dispersed over 62 countries. More than 70 per cent of the approved joint ventures are concentrated in 13 countries. Details are given in the table below :

**Country-wise Indian joint ventures as on 31st December, 1993**

| *Sl. No.* | *Country* | *No. of Joint Ventures* |
|---|---|---|
| 1. | Malaysia | 36 |
| 2. | Singapore | 29 |
| 3. | Thailand | 20 |
| 4. | Indonesia | 13 |
| 5. | United Kingdom | 38 |
| 6. | Sri Lanka | 28 |
| 7. | UAE | 29 |
| 8. | Nigeria | 16 |
| 9. | Nepal | 21 |
| 10. | USA | 29 |
| 11. | Kenya | 10 |
| 12. | Uzbekistan | 10 |
| | Total (incl. others) | 430 |

Out of the total 430 approved joint ventures mentioned above, 98 are located in the four countries of ASEAN, viz., Malaysia, Singapore, Thailand and Indonesia. The size and scale of operations of the Indian joint ventures in the ASEAN region has generally been small. In most of the operating joint ventures, India's share holding is less than 50 per cent and value of investments less than Rs. 50 lakh in each case.

As on December 31, 1993 there were 172 wholly subsidiaries abroad, located in 30 countries out of which 52 are in operation and the remaining 120 are under various stages of implementation. Out of the 120 subsidiaries which are in operation, seven are located in Singapore, three in Malaysia and one each in Thailand and Indonesia. Out of the subsidiaries which are under implementation, 15 are located in Singapore.

Some of the fields where India is offering its expertise and could expand its role in ASEAN countries include :

- Small and medium industries development,
- Tool room and training centres,
- Vocational-cum training centres,
- Setting up of natural-resource based rural industries,
- Information technology and computer software,
- Oil-drilling,
- Chemicals and pesticides,
- Drugs and pharmaceuticals and
- Cement.

Apart from certain other economic areas, ASEAN and India agreed to begin active cooperation in the area of investment through the establishment of ASEAN-India Joint Sectoral Cooperation Committee (AIJSCC). The first meeting of AIJSCC was held in Bali during January 7-8, 1994. This meeting, co-chaired by the ASEAN Secretary-General and Indian Foreign Secretary, was a follow-up to the meeting to establish ASEAN-Indian Sectoral Dialogue Relations which was held in March 1993 in New Delhi. India's transition from a sectoral dialogue partner to a full dialogue partner is expected to be a long affair. The progress in achieving the limited goals has been extremely slow and the private sector is not fully involved, even though at the sectoral dialogue held in Bali, it was agreed to extend cooperation to the areas of trade, investment, tourism, agriculture, science and technology. Consequently, the ASEAN-New Delhi Committee consisting of the heads of diplomatic missions of ASEAN member countries in New Delhi has been formed to facilitate the sectoral dialogue relations.

Some of the countries of South East Asia are looking for basic infrastructures such as development and upgradation of arterial roads and ports, water resources development, generation of power and development of software from India. Since these countries face a severe resource crunch a number of projects can be financed by private sector which can draw Indian investments. Different Indian firms operating in the same field can come together to form consortia to tap the ASEAN markets.

With the opening of sectors in India like housing, real estate and infrastructure including hotel and tourism-related industries, mutual funds, etc. to foreign and, in particular, NRI investments, and encouragement by the ASEAN Governments to its citizens and especially those of Indian-origin, a significant rise in investment and trade flows is expected to take place between India and ASEAN.

A number of NRI groups like Thakral Brothers, Scotts Holdings, Chandaria Group and Dadi Balsara from Singapore are already investing in India on individual basis. With the encouragement of Singapore's Government, Singapore Indian Chamber of Commerce and Industry has set up a holding company called "Parameswara Holdings" specifically for the purpose of investing in India.

On the other hand, Indian liberalisation has made it possible for Indian companies, both in the government and private sectors, to go to ASEAN countries for doing business. Already the list of Indian companies setting up branch offices in ASEAN is growing rapidly. The State Trading Corporation, MMTC and Shipping Corporation of India are located in Singapore. In the private sector, companies like ITC, Peerless Group, Kirloskars, Greaves, Ispat Alloys, Vedika Investment Services, Mastek, Sumeet, Ranbaxy Laboratories Ltd., Tata Engineering and Locomotive Company, Godrej of India, JG Glass Industries Ltd., the Birla Group and Hindustan Safety Glass, etc., have all gone to ASEAN countries and have succeeded in their ventures in these countries.

The exchange of economic delegation between India and ASEAN countries have sharply increased in 1993 and 1994 as compared to the earlier period. Such visits have led to a number of projects being identified for investment. While the projects are mainly in the infrastructure and core industry sectors, the delegations have concentrated on business opportunities in services where they have qualitative advantage like airport management, port management, logistic services and the like.

A record number of Indian delegations visited ASEAN countries during the past three years. In 1994, high-level delegations from ASSOCHAM, CII, Maharashtra Government, Haryana Government, Federation of Karnataka Chambers and West Bengal Government have visited ASEAN countries.

The increased level of economic interaction has been responsible to a great extent in ASEAN's growing interest in investing in India, of course, with the opening up of the Indian economy. A number of small, medium and large projects are under negotiations. The interested investors are not merely from among the NRI community but also from other companies.

In the establishment of joint ventures, India has a comparative advantage in terms of qualified but cheap labour, natural resources like marine products, horticultural products, leather, minerals (granite, sandstone and marble), etc. Some of the countries of ASEAN region have a sound infrastructure for international trading. The Governments of ASEAN countries have been business-friendly and are providing various incentives for doing business in their countries.

# 4

# Indo-ASEAN Cooperation in Investment

T.K. Bhaumik

The investment relationship between India and the ASEAN countries is not a new one. It started over 30 years ago when both India and the ASEAN countries had made a beginning of their planning for development and conditions were not so favourable. During the 1960s some of the Indian entrepreneurs ventured into some of the ASEAN countries and put up industrial units in collaboration with their counterparts in those countries.

While some of them did not survive, others have been very successful and have made a reputation as successful Indian ventures. The failures have been due to under-capitalisation, lack of adequate management support from the Indian headquarters, using the foreign ventures primarily for the purpose of exporting Indian capital goods, etc.

One of the leading industrial houses of India, who had put up their first manufacturing unit in Thailand 25 years back, and have since expanded their operations manifold, has recently celebrated silver-jubilee function. There are several others as well with successful experience of operation in the ASEAN region for a list of some of the Indian ventures in ASEAN.

However, the overall impact of such ventures on the economies of the host countries has not been significant; nor has the growth of Indian ventures kept pace with the growth of industrialisation in these countries. Since the early 1980s, overall Indian investment in the ASEAN region has been insignificant.

Investment from ASEAN countries to India, on the other hand, has been even less. Until recently, practically none of the ASEAN countries made any significant investments in India (some data to be given). Various factors have contributed to such low two-way investment flows. An important one is that a conducive economic environment and availability of surplus capital are two pre-requisites for fostering the flow of investment. These necessary pre-conditions were not existing until recently on either side.

The decade of the 1980s, and the subsequent years, have been significant for ASEAN countries and India. The ASEAN countries witnessed major changes in economic policies, leading to significant improvement in the overall economic environment. This is evident from the trend in the GDP growth of respective countries and flow of foreign direct investment. These economies are now, to a large extent, full-fledged market economies, free from historical controls and regulations and the governments now play the role of facilitator. Trade and investment policies are now very conducive to competition and free interplay of market forces.

In India, the process of liberalisation started during the 1980s, but major policy reform began in 1991. Since then it has culminated into substantial liberalisation of trade and investment policies coupled with lowering and restructuring of tax rates, reducing the tight controls on banking and finance, restructuring of the capital market, limiting the role of the public sector and a liberal policy towards foreign investment.

The new economic policies have evoked considerable interest in India as a profitable ground for investment. This is reflected in the fact that between August 1991 and August 1994, foreign equity investment worth Rs. 200.5 billion (US $ 6.4 billion) has been approved; the total number of cases approved is 4809, of which 2363 cases involved financial collaboration.

On conservative assumption of debt to equity ratio of one and foreign equity being 50 per cent of the total equity, the above equity investment implies project cost of US $ 25.56 billion. There has been a significant improvement in the net capital inflows on account of investment in the capital market by the foreign institutional investors. Apart from the new policy environment that has attracted the attention of the international investors, faster growth of India's domestic market has been a major source of attraction for the foreign investors. The potential of the domestic market ensures profitability of investment in India.

The important point that needs to be taken note of is that there is a growing convergence of trade and investment policies between India and the ASEAN countries. Similarly, both have high growth potential and provide large opportunities for expansion of the internal markets. All these should pave the way for smooth investment flows between India and the ASEAN countries. The time is, therefore, favourable for strengthening existing investment links and also exploring new areas for investment.

## METHODOLOGY

The study is based purely on the feedbacks received from the industry and the policy-makers in India and ASEAN countries and reflects their perceptions and viewpoints. No attempt has been made to tamper with the views expressed.

To begin with a detailed questionnaire was sent to a large cross-section of Indian entrepreneurs. The mailing list included not only those who have business interests in the ASEAN, but also those who do not have any interest at present. The target group for the questionnaire was primarily small and medium enterprises.

The large enterprises, particularly those having substantial business interest in the ASEAN region and those who can be key players, have been covered through personal interviews.

## OBSERVATIONS

The responses to the questionnaire and feedbacks from personal meetings reflect keen interest, particularly among the Indian entrepreneurs. From the responses to the questionnaires issued to a cross-section of enterprises (a total of 70 responses), it is observed that while nine companies have joint ventures either in India or in ASEAN countries, 47 companies have expressed their willingness to have joint ventures in the ASEAN region and six are willing to have joint ventures in India.

Practically all the Indian companies whom the expert group met considered ASEAN as the most promising region in Asia and felt it could provide platform for globalised operation of Indian companies.

There is a general perception that the ASEAN countries can be natural business partners for Indian companies in view of cultural affinity, geographical proximity as also presence of large

Indian community. There may be a language problem however it is not a serious barrier.

Large Indian companies are aware of the developments in the ASEAN region and particularly establishment of ASEAN Free Trade Area (AFTA) and its impact on the growth process in the entire region. Besides, considerable concern, coupled with sense of business opportunities, was also observed about formation of APEC and regional economic grouping or growth areas such as East Asian Growth Area (EAGA). The feeling is that Indian companies must establish their presence to take advantage of the developments.

All the Indian companies that the expert group had met are of the opinion that investment climate in the ASEAN region is very conducive. There are no obvious policy and procedural problems and the governments are very pragmatic, though there may be invisible cultural and attitudinal barriers.

The Indian entrepreneurs are appreciative of the competitive environment in these countries, opportunities for growth and expansion, disciplined workforce and high productivity in the region.

India has strong managerial and technical capabilities that get best opportunities for flourishing in the competitive environment of the region. In fact, Indian managers are a source of great strength for Indian companies. Their adaptability to the local conditions of ASEAN is excellent.

However, can India be a large investor? In other words, do Indian companies have sufficiently large amounts to invest overseas at a time when domestic demand on that investible fund is rising? Opinions were divided on this. We shall deal with this question in the next section.

On the ASEAN side, the fact that India offers vast market potential is very well appreciated. It is widely accepted that market is no constraint. Apart from her own large and growing domestic market, India can be a potential base for South Asian and West Asian markets. However, the expert group could not find equally overwhelming response from the ASEAN side. As compared to their Indian counterparts, the entrepreneurs in some of the ASEAN countries betrayed lack of information about the changes in India, resulting in considerable perception gap. It appeared that developments within their own economics and within the regional economy were sufficient to make them look inward. What was appalling, however, was the misconception that resulted from lack of knowledge.

At the same time, there seems to be considerable psychological barriers that prevent the entrepreneurs from taking interest in promoting commercial relationships with their Indian counterparts. The respective governments of the ASEAN will have to take interest in promotion of trade and investment links with India as this will give clear signals to the business community in the region.

The on-going economic reforms are well known and appreciated. There are, however, certain areas of concern which are widely shared. Without going into the details, which will be referred to in subsequent paragraphs, the broad areas of concern are:

- Lack of changes at the state-level economic policies,
- Unhelpful bureaucracy at the state-level,
- Labour laws and low level of labour productivity,
- Infrastructural deficiencies,
- Overall investment climate not comparable to that in the ASEAN countries. One primary concern in this connection is delay in conceptualisation as well as implementation of project. Nobody would like to have avoidable cost-overruns and
- Investors do not get welcome treatment at the immigration and customs counters.

## INDIAN INVESTMENT IN ASEAN

From the responses received through questionnaires and personal interviews, a large number of areas have been identified as having potential for investment in the ASEAN region by the Indian entrepreneurs. In the process of identification of items, we have looked at the region as a whole and not the individual countries, since the whole of ASEAN is looked at as a single market block.

**Constraint of Capital**

India, it may be mentioned, is not a capital surplus country, though the foreign exchange reserves are currently over $ 19 billion. Also, investible surplus available with most of the Indian companies may not be large enough for investment abroad after meeting the requirements of the domestic market. In this context, the expert group wanted to examine the question of the ability of the Indian entrepreneurs to invest abroad.

The general feeling is that the Indian industry in general will need to invest significantly for modernisation of the existing units, besides investing in new ventures within the country. Liberal economic policy has opened up vast opportunities for investment within the country. Accordingly, total quantum of surplus for investment abroad may not be enough for large projects.

**Is Substantial Investment Possible?**

One has to also take into account the control exercised by the Government of India. The policy with regard to joint ventures abroad by the Indian entrepreneurs is far from liberal, in spite of some relaxation in the policy. Indian entrepreneurs cannot invest more than $5 million in any venture outside the country. This severely restricts the ability of the entrepreneurs to acquire substantial equity in joint ventures abroad. They have to still ensure higher equity participation through plants and equipments. This is not the case with other foreign investors.

In other words, large Indian companies, with ability to invest, are restricted from having substantial financial stake in the joint venture company. According to the large industrial houses, no worthwhile projects can be undertaken, since with such limitation it is not even possible to assess a project adequately.

**Scope for Medium Scale Ventures**

A section within the Indian industry, however, feels that relaxation in the policy would enable them to set up medium scale projects abroad. While Indian industry cannot invest in value added hi-tech industries, they can certainly invest in areas that require intermediate technologies. For instance, Indian industry can now think of investment in areas such as castings and forgings, secondary manufacturing including machining and finishing and export related service industries such as warehousing and distribution.

Another area where the Indian industry can make profitable investment within the limits fixed by the Government of India is software, the market for which is growing at a fast rate in Japan, Singapore, China, Hong Kong and also ASEAN countries. The current policy is also conducive for sub-assembly operations and thus establish presence in the market.

**Role of Existing Ventures**

Problem of substantial investment, however, does not arise in the case of such Indian companies who have achieved success in this region and expanded their operations. Such companies can easily overcome the limitation imposed by the policy. Since one successful venture can finance another venture, besides facilitating recourse to capital markets in the host countries. Such enterprises can make a real breakthrough in Indian investments.

For an Indian company venturing into the region for the first time, it may be wise to start on a somewhat low key and make a small but successful beginning and then expand. Five factors are important in this context.

(i) identification of right partner,

(ii) proper homework,

(iii) need to avoid over-ambition,

(iv) selection of best technology, and

(v) commitment of the top management.

It may be mentioned that in the past several projects could not succeed because of such factors.

**Closer Look Needed**

However, the Indian industry will do well to take a much closer look at the developments taking place within the region and find opportunities. In this context, mention can be made of formation of growth triangles or sub-regional cooperation zones or growth areas, where there may be ample scope for setting up resource-based processing units and small scale assembly or manufacturing units. For instance, the Northern Sub-regional Cooperation Zone, consisting of South Thailand, North Sumatra and the Malaysian states of Pelang, Kedah and Perlis is likely to develop as a major growth area. South Philippines, Sabat and North Sulaweshi, the Sarawak, Bourice and Kalimanthan and Johor-Singapore-Riau are other sub-regions. Brunei is also in the process of diversifying the economy and offers opportunities for small scale units such as garments, leather goods, etc.

**Joint Investment in Vietnam and Myanmar**

During discussion with the large Indian entrepreneurs it was also revealed that many of them were exploring the possibility of joint investment into the neighbouring countries of Vietnam and Myanmar. These countries are in need of foreign investment not only for infrastructure building but also for development of resource-based industries, namely, agro-based industries, mineral products, etc. Since growth of entrepreneurship is at the nascent stage, these countries need appropriate technologies, training in entrepreneurship and management, vocational training facilities, etc. In all these respects, the entrepreneurs from Indian and the ASEAN countries can join hands and make useful contributions to the development process of these countries. In fact, many Indian entrepreneurs are viewing such possibilities very seriously and some have already identified some projects in sectors such as agriculture, pulp and paper, pharmaceuticals, road construction, housing, etc. Other areas to be explored in this connection are oil exploration (where India's ONGC and OIL can play important role), petroleum refining, fertiliser, etc. Indian and ASEAN entrepreneurs can set up joint venture projects with India as a major market.

In addition to joint investment in these sectors, the expert group also feel the need for joint Indian and ASEAN effort in the following areas:

- Entrepreneurship development through setting up of training and management institutions, whereby Indian and ASEAN institutions can join together;
- Vocational training institutes and
- Development of small and medium enterprises.

**Small and Medium Enterprises (SMEs)**

On the question of cooperation at the level of the SMEs considerable enthusiasm was observed among the successful

Indian SMEs. General feeling is that India has the unique advantage of experience and expertise.

Over the years, the Indian policy for development of SMEs has helped to create a nucleus of entrepreneurial skills and facilitated growth of entrepreneurship. Also , India has a well-spread network of institutions for training of small and medium entrepreneurs, development of appropriate technology, etc.

The scope for cooperation has, thus, two aspects, namely,

(i) Investment by the Indian SMEs in the ASEAN region and

(ii) Technical and managerial training for potential ASEAN SMEs.

With regard to the first, while there is significant potential in view of inadequate development of SMEs in some parts of the ASEAN region, the hurdles pertain to (i) lack of information leading to problem of identification of areas and suitable partners and (ii) inability to take risks. The latter is a serious problem in view of very limited financial strengths of the SMEs. Further, in the absence of adequate information and limited finances, it is well-nigh impossible to assess feasibility of investments.

It is generally felt that a regular programme of exchange of SMEs, a programme that can be sponsored by the governments, will go a long way in building contacts and knowledge about investment prospects. Also, India should offer training facilities to prospective entrepreneurs from the ASEAN region.

It is suggested that specialised institutions in India such as National Small Industries Corporation (NSIC), Small Industries Service Institutions etc. and industrial organisations with considerable experience of operation of industries such as Confederation of Indian Industry who have substantial membership from small scale sector should work out viable schemes and coordinate with the governments in the ASEAN.

**Action Plan**

The suggested action plan for promotion of Indian investment in the ASEAN countries is as follows:

(i) Any foreign exchange constraint in India should not be allowed to come in the way of viable projects. Since

ASEAN countries provide opportunities for global operation of many of the large Indian companies, limit for automatic investment approval may be substantially raised.

(ii) Automatic approval still requires the Indian companies to obtain permission from the Reserve Bank of India (RBI) and it takes time, and thus RBI control on investment abroad continues. It suggested that within any prescribed ceiling, the intending investor should be given the same facility as is given to the domestic investors in the case of de-licensed industries. He should be allowed to invest in joint ventures abroad merely by submitting the investment details for the purpose of records.

(iii) The current practice of insisting on equity participation through plant and machinery has to be given up. It should be left to the entrepreneurs to decide in what way they should have higher equity.

(iv) Unlike in India, there is no network of development banks in the ASEAN countries, taking part in equity shares or providing term loans. This makes it difficult to raise term loans. Term loans are provided by the commercial banks, who insist on company guarantees. However, Indian companies are not allowed to give company guarantees. They should be allowed to do so. At least, the large established companies should be allowed to issue guarantees.

(v) Indian companies should be freely allowed to raise loans abroad for purchase of plants and equipments, even if these are procured from within the country.

(vi) Profits earned by the joint venture companies should be allowed for free re-deployment for expansion, modernisation and diversification.

(vii) EXIM Bank has considerable role to play in promotion of Indian joint ventures in the ASEAN region. It should play an active role in identification of projects and assist the prospective entrepreneurs in project appraisal.

Such role is particularly important for those who have no previous exposure to the region and particularly the small and medium enterprises. The expert group would also recommend that EXIM Bank should earmark special fund for equity financing in the case of viable investment projects.

(viii) Multilateral aided projects also offer vast scope for collaboration between the Indian and the ASEAN entrepreneurs. EXIM Bank and suitable financing institutions (to be identified) in the ASEAN countries should join hands to help consortium of Indian and ASEAN entrepreneurs by extending necessary financial support. EXIM Bank of India is favourable to the ideas and would like to work out some viable financing scheme along with one or more banks in the ASEAN region. In view of the vast potential for joint collaboration in multilaterally aided projects, it is suggested that EXIM Bank should take the initiative and find a suitable partner.

**ASEAN Investment in India**

In India, it is accepted without reservation that there is considerable scope for ASEAN investment in India. This is the surest way to getting integrated with the ASEAN economic block and become an integral economic partner or rather extension of what will be AFTA.

The scope for ASEAN investment in India is enormous and the onus lies with the Indian industry and the government, who should facilitate such investment.

Areas having potential for investment are many, but broadly ASEAN strength lies in the area of infrastructure development and service-oriented industries, namely, the following :

(i) Roads and highways including mass rapid transit system,

(ii) Development of seaports,

(iii) Development of airports and airport-related services,

(iv) Power,

(v) Telecommunication,

(vi) Petroleum,

(vii) Tourism and tourist-related services (namely, establishment of air bridges) and

(viii) Development of industrial estates, technology and parks.

**Roads and Highways**

The Government of India has opened roads and highways to private sector investment. Some sections of highways and some toll roads have been identified for immediate investment by the private sector. Further, the Mass Rapid Transit System (MRTS) for the National Capital Regions offer vast scope for foreign investment. A project for Tramways for Delhi has been already formulated with detailed project report and the city government is in the process of awarding the contract.

While these are specific examples, the point that has to be taken note of is that there is vast potential for foreign investment in the roads sector in India that needs drastic improvement not only in terms of construction of new roads, bridges, expressways, etc., but also in terms of maintenance and widening of existing roads on quality upgradation etc. So far as policy is concerned, the Government will welcome foreign investment and has assured a return of 16 per cent on investment.

Considering the expertise available with the ASEAN entrepreneurs in this sector (particularly Singapore and Malaysia), they stand a good chance of acquiring contracts jointly with the Indian entrepreneurs. The ASEAN entrepreneurs will be required to keep track of the developments in India and identify suitable Indian partners.

The Government of India will have to ensure that the projects are cleared without delay. This is important since such projects are capital-intensive and delay in clearance will result in cost overruns, making the projects unviable. Once the proposal is cleared, all other clearances required at the local levels should be automatic. Among other things, environmental clearance and acquisition of lands pose significant hurdles. Such issues should be tackled at the stage of identification of the projects, so that the entrepreneurs do not have to grapple with.

Next, although the Government of India is encouraging private sector investment and particularly foreign investment, there is need for transparency of the policy and a clearly laid-down guidelines, which will help the prospective entrepreneurs in making appropriate assessment of the project.

**Seaports**

Under the liberal economic environment, with emphasis on faster development of external trade, development of major seaports (there are 11 major ports) has received serious attention. Currently, the major ports handle around 170 million tonnes of cargo and this is expected to go up to nearly 250 million tonnes by the end of the decade.

In order to handle the growing volume of cargo in a cost effective manner, there is need for substantial modernisation of the existing ports. Here again, the government expects the private sector to play a major role.

The Ministry of Surface Transport have already taken steps to liberalise rules and procedures relating to maritime transport. Relaxation of the cabotage law, enactment of an ordinance relating to multi-modal transportation of goods, berth reservation facilities, leasing of berths, leasing of land and water fronts for setting up ship repair facilities, privatisation of drydocks, liberalisation of licensing procedure to enable more entrepreneurs to participate in stevedoring activities are some of the changes that have been already introduced to encourage private sector participation.

Many ports have plans to instal and develop complete terminals equipped with fully integrated cargo-handling and transport systems. Investment areas where foreign investors can look for investment include:

- setting up of container terminals,
- setting up of warehousing and storage facilities,
- operation and maintenance of various cargo handling facilities,
- dredging operations,
- dry-docking,

- provision of pilotage and orange services and
- leasing of equipment.

Portwise investment opportunities, as identified, are as below :

| | |
|---|---|
| Haldia Dock Complex | : Container handling facilities, construction of berths and jetties. |
| Paradip Port | : Construction of berths and jetties, handling equipment, supporting infrastructure. |
| Visakhapatnam Port | : Construction of berths, jetties and handling equipment. |
| Madras Port | : Handling equipment, operation and maintenance of port craft and equipment and leasing of equipment. |
| Tuticorin Port | : Container handling facilities, construction of berths, handling equipment, supporting infrastructure, construction and operation of drydocking. |
| Cochin Port | : Container handling facilities, supporting infrastructure. |
| Marmugao Port | : Warehousing and storage, operation and maintenance of port, craft and equipment. |
| New Mangalore Port | : Operation and maintenance of port craft and equipment, dredging. |
| Bombay Port | : Supporting infrastructure, operation and maintenance of port, craft and equipment, storage facilities, leasing of berths and equipment. |
| Jawaharlal Nehru Port | : Container handling facilities and operation and maintenance of port craft and equipment. |

Kamla Port : Container handling facilities, construction of berths and jetties, handling equipment and supporting infrastructure.

The above-mentioned areas of private sector investment highlight the considerable scope for investment which the entrepreneurs in the ASEAN countries may like to look at. The added advantage is that the different ports are under the management of their respective port authorities and, accordingly, there are minimum procedural hurdles. However, the major Port Trust Act, 1963 requires that the schedule of charges to be recovered for services should have prior sanction of the government and the charges to be levied on the user for the services, that are to be provided by the private operators, should be within the limits determined with the approval of the government.

It appears that in order to attract foreign as well as domestic private investment, the Act needs to be amended to enable the investors to earn sufficient rate of return. Besides, the labour laws will also have to be suitably amended to improve productivity and efficient utilisation of equipments.

**Airports**

India has currently five international airports, 88 domestic airports and 28 civil enclaves at defence airports. In addition, there are air cargo complexes for exclusive handling of export cargo at the hinterlands. However, the quality of the existing airports (domestic as well as international) leaves much scope for improvement. Whether looked at from the point of view of domestic and international tourists or trade, there is need for substantial improvement of facilities in most of the airports. Following table gives an idea of the pressure that is likely to be generated on the major airports on account of growth of traffic.

This kind of growth in traffic cannot be satisfactorily managed without substantial improvement of existing facilities and substantial capacity addition. According to a projection, by the year 2001, top 20 airports of India expected to handle 37 million passengers against 15.2 million in 1991-92, i.e.; number of passengers is expected to increase at the rate of 10.4 per cent per annum. While all the airports are in need of upgradation, to begin with one can look at the investment opportunities in these top 20 airports. Twelve of these have been earmarked for development as model airports. The following is an outline of investment opportunities in two of the airports.

**Projected aircraft departures at top six airports**

| *Airport* | *Average Aircraft Departures Per Day* | | |
|---|---|---|---|
| | *May 1993* | *1995* | *2000* |
| Bombay | 33 | 56 | 84 |
| Delhi | 28 | 41 | 65 |
| Calcutta | 19 | 25 | 39 |
| Madras | 15 | 20 | 33 |
| Bangalore | 16 | 19 | 33 |
| Hyderabad | 9 | 12 | 21 |

*Source :* Exposition on Civil Aviation—Indian Aviation Industry—At the Threshold : Background Paper, Confederation of Indian Industry.

**Lucknow Airport**

Lucknow is a prominent tourist destination and an important commercial centre. It is proposed to develop the existing airports as a model airport "fit in every respect for accepting modern wide bodied high speed jet aircraft". The features that are proposed to be added include:

- standard terminal building,
- excellent passenger facilities,
- technical and operational infrastructure for efficient air traffic control services,
- adequate navigational and visual aids for all weather flight operations,
- efficient and reliable aeronautical communication services,
- standard runway for modern wide-bodied jet aircraft,
- spacious apron and
- efficient ground safety services.

**Hyderabad Airport**

Similarly, the National Airport Authority has taken up the modernisation of Hyderabad Airport on a priority basis and the plan includes:

- expansion and remodelling of the present terminal building,
- construction of a new integrated terminal complex,
- construction of a new integrated cargo complex,
- strengthening of the runway and resurfacing of the link taxi track,
- installation of a modern airport surveillance radar and a secondary surveillance radar and
- provision of a round-the-clock automatic information service.

The other airports which are also proposed to be developed as model airports are Nagpur, Vadodara, Bhubaneswar, Patna, Jaipur, Indore, Coimbatore, Calicut, Guwahati and Imphal.

**Tourism**

Tourism offers vast potential for Indo-ASEAN collaboration. More or less all the ASEAN countries are attracting large number of tourists of various types. India also attracts around 1.7 million tourists annually, but the number is small, when considered against the backdrop of the country's potential. India has places of tourist interest that cater to all segments of international tourists, age-groups as well as interest-groups. All the major tourist spots are connected by the domestic air-routes.

However, there are several problems and issues that need to be tackled before India can attract large number of tourists either from ASEAN or elsewhere. Some of the problems can be resolved through large scale investment and those are the areas where ASEAN entrepreneurs can think of investment.

First, while India has a large number of tourist spots spread all over the country, the facilities like hotels, transport, etc., are far from developed. Wherever facilities have been created, these cater to the requirements of luxury tourists. Very little attention has been paid to attract the budgeted tourists, belonging to the middle income class, or other low-budget tourists with their interests in sports, adventure, etc. There is need for development of proper infrastructure such as connecting roads, communication facility, hospitals, low-cost hotels, guest houses, etc.

Second, although many of the major tourist centres are connected by air-routes, the availability of connecting flights and availability of seats (particularly during peak seasons) are uncertain. The hotels and the tour operators hardly play any useful role in this respect. There is total lack of coordination among the key operators, namely, the airlines, the hotel industry, the travel agents and the tour operators.

Third, in most of the tourist places, the authorities are not so much concerned about appropriate hygienic and sanitary conditions.

Fourth, India needs to provide favourable conditions for foreign tourists, who should be made to feel welcome on their arrival. There is a general feeling that visa formalities discourage the intending tourists. Further, the immigration formalities are time taking and cause inconvenience.

It is thus clear that there are several things that need to be taken care of at the Indian end. The basic requirements are:

- development of infrastructure at the tourist centres,
- development of approach roads from the major cities to the tourist centres,
- provision of low cost hotels, rest houses, motels, etc.,
- development of communication facility in the tourist centres,
- appropriate hygienic and sanitary conditions and proper maintenance of the tourist centres and
- development of health care facilities, etc.

As an encouragement to the business tourists as also other tourists from the ASEAN region, the government may like to consider the possibility of visa-free entry for short duration visits. Drastic improvement in the immigration clearance will also have to be considered.

Keeping in view the vast potential for cooperation in the field of tourism between India and the ASEAN countries, some ideas, as suggested by the concerned interests in India, are outlined below:

- the Government of India should work out a Master Plan for development of tourism integrating India with ASEAN countries. The thrust of the Master Plan can be to create certain Tourist Zones covering important tourist centres in India and the ASEAN countries. More particularly, tourist centres along with the eastern and southern parts of India can be very well connected with the tourist centres in Thailand, Singapore, Indonesia and Malaysia.
- In the eastern sector, a suggestion was made that around 10 islands in the Andaman Island can be identified (the whole of Andaman is not considered in view of defence sensitivity). Sunderban in West Bengal, Puri in Orissa, Madras in the south, etc., are some of the tourist areas that can be very well connected.
- However, for this purpose, it is necessary to target the concerned airports for development and ensure integration with the airports in the South East Asian countries and an integrated tourism development plan needs to be formulated. The task of developing such Tourist Zones can be entrusted to the joint initiative of the private sector in India and the ASEAN countries.
- India and ASEAN countries can develop air-bridges which would be joint ventures between the airlines in India and the airlines in the ASEAN countries on a 50:50 basis. In case 50:50 partnership is not feasible, higher equity participation can be permitted to ASEAN airlines with a provision of 60 per cent repatriation.

**Housing and Real Estate**

India also offers vast scope for ASEAN investment in real estates. Development of real estates, including residential houses and commercial complexes, has been given considerable priority in India's development strategy. The government also expects the private sector to play a major role in this area.

The private sector in India, it may be mentioned, has already shown great interest in this area, as is reflected in recent diversification into real estates by several large Indian corporate entities. There is large demand for:

- development of residential complexes,
- development of self-contained townships,
- luxury apartments, and
- commercial complexes so as to de-congest the existing office complexes.

While discussing about to the Indian construction and real estate companies, it was gathered that the companies in ASEAN countries such as Singapore, Malaysia, Thailand, etc., are better equipped in terms of construction material, equipment and technology, and general feeling was that they can play useful role in India. However, currently the Government of India permits investments by the Non-Resident Indians only and the policy needs to be relaxed to permit foreign investment in the real estates.

**Power Generation**

India requires considerable investment for overall improvement of the power scenario. The Eighth Five Year Plan (1992-97) has provided for additional generating capacity of 30538 MW. Even if this target is fulfilled, there would be estimated energy shortage of 37648 million KW and picking shortage of 15253 MW by the terminal year of the plan, i.e., 1996-97. In percentage terms, the energy shortage is estimated to be 9 per cent and the picking shortage would be 20 per cent.

Keeping in view of the importance of improving the power scenario, the government has been encouraging the private sector, and particularly the foreign investor, to invest in the power sector. A detailed scheme of incentives has been announced for the purpose, some element of which are outlined as below:

- Amendment of the Indian Electricity Act 1910 and the Electricity (Supply) Act 1948 to bring about a new legal administrative and financial environment conducive to private enterprises.

- Private sector can set up coal or gas-based thermal power projects, hydel projects and wind, solar energy project of any size.
- Projects worth less than Rs. 250 million need no clearance from the Central Electricity Authority.
- All private companies are allowed a debt equity ratio up to 4:1.
- Promoters have to bring in atleast 11 per cent of total cost of the project.
- Up to 100 per cent foreign equity participation permitted.
- Five Year Tax Holiday beginning from the year of generation of power.
- Lower import tariff for import of power equipment and highly concessional excise duty on indigenously procured capital goods.
- 16 per cent return on foreign equity.
- Generating companies operating coal-based, gas-based and hydro projects can sell power on the basis of a suitably structured two-part tariff.

The policy has already evoked considerable interest among the domestic entrepreneurs as well as foreign investors, which is evident from the table given on the next page.

**Crude Oil and Natural Gas**

India is import-dependent as far as crude oil and petroleum products are concerned. However, there are substantial reserves of both crude oil and natural gas. As on 1 January 1992, estimated reserve of crude oil was 779 million tonnes of oil equivalent, while estimated reserve of natural gas was 615 million tonnes of oil equivalent. Production to reserve ratios were, however, 29 per cent in the case of crude oil and about 40 per cent in the case of natural gas.

In view of the growing import-dependence hand and declining trend in production from the existing oil wells, the emphasis is on rapid exploration of new oil wells and the government would welcome large scale private sector investment in this sector.

**Power projects evinced interest by private sector**

| States | No. of Projects | Capacity (MW) | | | | | Estimated Cost | | Foreign Projects | | |
|---|---|---|---|---|---|---|---|---|---|---|---|
| | | Thermal Gas | Thermal Coal | Hydel | Total | % | Rs. crore | % | No. of Proj. | Capacity (MW) | Cost (Rs. Cr.) |
| Andhra Pradesh | 5 | 443 | 2500 | | 2943 | 9.0 | 9825 | 9.4 | 3 | 1443 | 4575 |
| Arunachal Pradesh | 2 | 48 | | 600 | 648 | 2.0 | 1968 | 1.9 | 2 | 648 | 1968 |
| Assam | 4 | 398 | | 100 | 498 | 1.5 | 1711 | 1.6 | 1 | 360 | 1200 |
| Bihar | 1 | | 500 | | 500 | 1.5 | 1637 | 1.6 | | | |
| Delhi | 1 | 800 | | | 800 | 2.4 | 2000 | 1.9 | | | |
| Gujarat | 2 | 655 | 250 | | 905 | 2.8 | 3053 | 2.9 | 2 | 905 | 3053 |
| Haryana | 2 | 1500 | | | 1500 | 4.6 | 4500 | 4.3 | 2 | 1500 | 4500 |
| Himachal Pradesh | 9 | | | 1884 | 1884 | 5.8 | 5882 | 5.6 | 2 | 301 | 954 |
| Karnataka | 5 | | 2300 | 600 | 2900 | 8.9 | 10319 | 9.7 | 5 | 2900 | 10139 |
| Kerala | 12 | | 420 | 103 | 523 | 1.6 | 1665 | 1.6 | 1 | 420 | 1400 |
| Madhya Pradesh | 5 | | 1340 | 412 | 1752 | 5.4 | 4543 | 4.4 | | | |
| Maharashtra | 7 | 2425 | 2110 | 90 | 4625 | 14.2 | 17353 | 16.7 | 3 | 3515 | 13683 |
| Orissa | 7 | | 6420 | | 6420 | 19.7 | 22324 | 21.4 | 6 | 5420 | 18824 |
| Rajasthan | 2 | | 740 | | 740 | 2.3 | 1622 | 1.6 | 1 | 240 | 586 |
| Tamil Nadu | 5 | 300 | 2960 | | 3260 | 10.0 | 8479 | 8.1 | 4 | 3010 | 7679 |
| Uttar Pradesh | 2 | | 750 | 360 | 1110 | 3.4 | 3238 | 3.1 | 1 | 750 | 2625 |
| West Bengal | 4 | 20 | 1635 | | 1655 | 5.1 | 4211 | 4.0 | 2 | 1020 | 2040 |
| Total | 75 | 6588 | 21925 | 4148 | 32661 | 100.0 | 104151 | 100.0 | 35 | 22432 | 73386 |

*Source :* Current Energy Scene in India, June 1994—Centre for Monitoring Indian Economy Pvt. Ltd.

In the 7th round of bidding that was initiated in January 1994, 45 blocks were offered to private sector, of which 27 were on onshore, 17 offshore and one onshore block extending to offshore. In addition, several blocks were also offered to private parties for geophysical survey with a view to upgrade information on hydrocarbon potential.

Prior to this, in August 1992, the government had offered 31 small-sized and 12 medium-sized oil and gas fields for development by private companies. Following Table gives an idea about the extent of interest shown by domestic entrepreneurs as well as foreign investors in this sector.

**Oil fields contracts awarded to private sector in India**

| *Name of the field* | *Area Sq.Km.* | *Location* | *Contract Awarded to* |
|---|---|---|---|
| Bakrol | 36 | Gujarat | Salen Exploration Tech. Ltd., New Delhi |
| Lohar | 5 | Gujarat | Salen Exploration Tech. Ltd., New Delhi |
| Indrora | 134 | Gujarat | Salen Exploration Tech. Ltd., New Delhi |
| Bhandut | 6 | Gujarat | Gujarat State Petrochemicals Corporation, Ahmedabad |
| Cambay | 161 | Gujarat | Gujarat State Petrochemicals Corporation, Ahmedabad |
| Matar | 6 | Gujarat | Gujarat State Petrochemicals Corporation, Ahmedabad |
| Sabarmati | 6 | Gujarat | Gujarat State Petrochemicals Corporation, Ahmedabad |
| Hazira | 50 | Gujarat | Gujarat State Petrochemicals Corporation, Ahmedabad |
| Wavel | 9 | Gujarat | Gujarat State Petrochemicals Corporation, Ahmedabad. |
| Dholka | 48 | Gujarat | Consortium of Joshi Technologies USA and Larsen & Toubro, Bombay |
| Baola | 4 | Gujarat | Interlink Petroleum, Baroda |
| Asjol | 15 | Gujarat | Consortium of Petrodyne USA, Hindustan Oil Exploration Co., Baroda and Gujarat State Petrochemicals Corporation, Ahmedabad. |
| PY-I | 75 | Cauvery Offshore | Consortium of Mosbacher Energy Co. of USA, Petrodyne, USA, and Hindustan Oil Exploration Co., Baroda |

*Source :* Current Energy Scene in India, June 1994—Centre for Monitoring Indian Economy Pvt. Ltd.

In addition to exploration, there is considerable scope for investment in the refineries. Until recently, this sector was closed to the private sector, but ever since the government announced its intention to allow private sector investment, several private sector companies including foreign companies, have shown considerable interest.

Some of the private sector refineries that are already under implementation are Mangalore Refinery and Petrochemicals (Aditya Birla Group of Companies), Black Gold Refinery (an NRI project), Reliance Petrochemicals (Ambani Group), Eastern India Refinery (Hinduja Group), Essar Refineries (Ruia Group and an NRI Group), and Parmar Refinery (Switzerland-based Parmar Group).

**Telecommunication**

Telecommunication is another area that offers vast scope for joint collaboration between Indian and the ASEAN entrepreneurs, particularly the entrepreneurs from Singapore. The Government of India has the following targets:

- Availability of telephone on demand by 1997,
- All villages to be covered by 1997,
- A PCO for every 500 persons in the urban areas by 1997,
- All value added services available internationally to be introduced in India by 1996-97.

The production of telecom equipments has been delicensed to meet the telecom needs of the country and substantial capacity has been already created for the manufacture of necessary hardware within the country. The following sub-sectors of value added services have been opened up to private sector including foreign investors:

- Electronic mail,
- Voice mail,
- Data services,
- Audio text services,
- Video text services,

- Video conferencing,
- Radio paging, and
- Cellular mobile telephone.

**Aquaculture**

Aquaculture is a highly prospective area of ASEAN investment in India. India has a large coastal area encompassing several states and vast stretch of brackish water, suitable for shrimp culture. Current problems relate to lack of supporting infrastructure and low yield in the absence of adequate attention and extension services.

There is considerable scope for development of hatcheries and processing. Most of the states have also port facilities for exports. What is necessary is for the concerned state governments to take initiatives and come out with clear policy framework for development of this sector. The state governments are conscious of the potential, but have done very little towards attracting the entrepreneurs. As a result, current activities are mostly unorganised and on a small scale.

To give an example, West Bengal has 405,000 hectares of brackish water, out of 1,190,000 hectares in the country as a whole. But there are only 10-15 Aqua units of 200-500 acres each. Present yield is just 0.48 tonne per hectare, which is due to traditional technique of farming.

Given their vast experience and technological advantage, the ASEAN investors can play tremendous role in development of aquaculture in India and create dependable sources of supply for exports.

**Orchids**

Development of orchids in India has great potential and is in conformity with the current thrust on development of fruit processing industry in India. India, it may be mentioned, is the second largest producer of fruits, but currently there is considerable wastage in view of lack of adequate processing facility. Also, fruits grown in India needs induction of appropriate technology so as to conform to international demands.

Thailand has achieved significant progress in the area of fruit growing and processing. Pineapple, watermelon, mango, lichi, etc., are some of the fruits in the growing of which the country is fairly advanced. For instance, it can produce mango throughout the year. The country also specialises in the growing of guava of very high quality. There is considerable scope for collaboration between India and Thailand. Thailand and India can collaborate in production and processing of export-variety pineapple (in north-eastern states), guava (in Uttar Pradesh) and mango (in the eastern state of West Bengal, Uttar Pradesh and the southern states).

A study team of agricultural scientists may be constituted to look into the possibility of collaborative R&D in the production of fruits. The study team should identify specific areas for R&D collaboration. The state governments will have to take the lead by facilitating foreign investment in the development of orchids.

**Competitive Investment Climate Needed**

The above review of some of the sectors clearly highlight the vast scope that exists for ASEAN investment in India. In spite of this, the response of the ASEAN entrepreneurs has been lukewarm so far. The reasons are many, but some can be briefly mentioned.

The ASEAN countries are currently undergoing a phase of development, where their entrepreneurs have lot of opportunities in their own home grounds. They will look outside for investment only if the climate is extremely conducive and returns on investment are sufficiently attractive.

This underlines the need for India offering best investment climate and rates of return that outweighs, or at least match, the ones in the region. In other words, the opportunity cost must be in India's favour.

'Investment is no charity' was pointed out by the Ambassadors or High Commissioners of ASEAN countries in India in a meeting with the Expert Group. This is important. In the competitive environment of the world economy, where the direction of money is influenced by returns and capital flows freely within profitable zones, neither Indian nor ASEAN entrepreneurs can expect charitable investment. Hence, both India and ASEAN countries must offer competitive conditions for investment.

However, as it appears, onus is more on the Indian side. India needs large scale foreign investment in practically all the sectors and has only begun to attract it. It must tap all sources and ASEAN countries are important neighbours. Flow of FDI in the ASEAN region is much larger compared to the FDI flow to India. And now ASEAN entrepreneurs themselves are investing abroad, though primarily for creating and expanding export bases. Need for creating export bases elsewhere and particularly in the large and growing markets will necessitate diversion of investible resources.

Another important factor that must be taken note of is that areas surrounding the ASEAN are now opening up for development, namely, Vietnam and Myanmar. Both are likely to be ASEAN members in the near future, and both require massive investment. One has to also take note of the impact of ASEAN Free Trade Area, progress towards which is rapid, on intra-ASEAN investments.

On the whole, ASEAN entrepreneurs have several preoccupations to keep them busy. India will have to attract them, in terms of policy and overall investment climate and communicate them effectively. Improvement in areas wherein the past, India was known to have disadvantages namely, productivity, work culture, time and cost-overruns, inefficiency of local administration, socio-political environment, etc., should also be effectively communicated.

# 5

# India: An Investment Destination

K.K. TRIVEDI

There is now growing recognition of the importance of foreign investment in the development process. The reasons being that FDI can help to close the investment, saving gap, finance, net imports and generate employment. At the same time, FDI is considered to be an important source of obtaining technology, scarce management skills and improved marketing know-how. That is why it is not surprising that FDI flows world over have been rising much faster than almost all other indicators of economic activity. For example, FDI has grown at around 25 per cent per annum in the latter 1980s, while trade has grown at under 10 per cent and national income at around 2-3 per cent.

Since 1991, India has also joined those developing countries who are making serious efforts to attract foreign investment. In its endeavour to attract non-debt creating foreign capital, the Indian government announced a series of policy changes relating to foreign investment and collaborations, import controls, foreign exchange, industrial licensing, etc. All these changes have been a part of the economic reforms programme, which has been launched to liberalise the economy and foster closer links with the global economy.

Foreign investment is now very welcome in almost all industries, excepting a few which have been reserved for strategic or other similar reasons. Under new policy regime, a project of any size to manufacture practically any product with foreign equity participation upto 100 per cent can be set up in India. To facilitate foreign investment and technology transfers, the following two channels for approval have been created .

- Automatic channel; and
- Non-automatic channel.

For routing proposals through automatic channel, foreign investors had to accept a couple of minor conditions, namely:

(a) Foreign equity participation could be upto 51 per cent.

(b) Investment is to be made in high priority industries.

(c) The proposal is to be foreign exchange positive or atleast neutral. In other words, the foreign equity should cover foreign exchange requirements for the imported plant and machinery.

Other foreign equity proposals, including proposals involving 51 per cent foreign equity, which do not meet the above criteria can be routed through the non-automatic channel and will require approval of the government. These proposals can be submitted to either Secretariat for Industrial Approvals or the Foreign Investment Promotion Board, which has been constituted to consider foreign investment proposal in totality without any predetermined parameter or criteria.

To integrate Indian economy with the global system, far reaching changes have been made in trade and exchange rates policies in the past three and half years. Import controls through licensing have been virtually done away with. Import duties have been drastically reduced. The peak import duty, which was lowered to 150 per cent in July 1991 was gradually reduced to 50 per cent in March 1995. The exchange rate regime has been progressively liberalised during the post policy period making the rupee fully convertible on current account. In fact, the rupee is fully convertible even on the capital account for overseas and NRI investors, as there is no restriction on repatriation of capital invested, repatriation of dividend, royalty, technical fee, etc.

All these changes, that have been brought about in the last 40 months or so, have helped in creating an investor friendly climate in the country. It would be relevant to mention here the study conducted by Price Waterhouse, a well-known international consultancy organisation, comparing foreign investment policies and fiscal parameters of selected Asian economies. The countries figured in the study were India, China, Indonesia,

Thailand, Singapore, South Korea, Taiwan, Malaysia. Interestingly, according to their findings, Indian policies are more investor friendly than policies of most of the countries selected for the study excepting Singapore and Thailand. Further, it was found that the system of automatic approval for clearing foreign investment proposal, does not exist in any other country than India.

However, recent steps of Indonesian Government particularly relating to deregulation, debureaucratisation and bringing further transparency in Foreign Investment Laws have considerably improved the attractiveness of Indonesia as an investment location.

A well-structured foreign investment policy provides necessary condition, at the same time it does not provide sufficient condition for investment. The FDI policy determines ease of accessing the domestic market and the terms and conditions of entry. Therefore, FDI policy per se is only one of the concerns of foreign investors. In fact, investor has to take into account various other factors for minimising risk and maximising profit. Some of the important factors, which influence investor's decision includes:

- Size of market and its growth potential,
- Political and economic stability,
- Linkages and Proximities with other important markets,
- Availability of trained manpower and wage structure and
- Industrial and institutional infrastructure.

A recent U.N. study on FDI, which found China as the largest recipient of FDI among developing countries, stated that large domestic market, high growth rate and rising incomes are major attractions for oversea investors. In fact size of domestic market has been the single most important factor responsible for the 'China Fever'. With about 1.2 billion population and the economy growing at an average rate of 10 per cent for the past one decade, China has emerged as one of the fastest expanding markets in the world. Hence, a large number of multinational corporations from the U.S.A., Europe, Japan and South Korea have been moving into China to have a slice of investment opportunities.

India is not far behind in terms of the size of market it offers to investors. The size of Indian market, which has over 250 million people in the middle income group, is considered to be the most important factor attracting oversea investors to India. According to an estimate, the middle income group has been growing at the rate of around 10 per cent per annum during the past one decade. It is stated that the rising purchasing power of the Indian middle class has been responsible for boom in demand for consumer goods and consumer durables during this period. The average income of people, belonging to this category, according to purchasing power parity criteria, is calculated to be around $ 2000. Taking 250 million, as the number of people in the middle income group and multiplying it by $ 2000, the average per capita income, the figure we get is $ 500 billion. That is the size of market Indian middle class commands today. A market of $ 500 billion is huge anywhere in the world. Therefore, it is not surprising that practically every multinational corporation is coming to India with an eye on the domestic market.

Political and economic stability of the host country is of paramount importance, as it provides necessary confidence to investors that their capital will not sink. Mexico was on the top of the list of investors till the peso crisis began in December last year. With Peso debacle overseas investors started losing confidence in the economy and that led to flight of billions of dollars from Mexico. The Mexican debacle is the most recent example of economic instability that scared away foreign investors. Such examples are in plenty.

Except for a brief period during the year 1990-91, when the economy suffered serious macro-economic imbalances and shortage of foreign exchange, India has remained politically and economically very stable. During the first two years of reforms programme, foreign investors did ask questions about durability of the new economic policy, now such doubts are things of past. The growing investors confidence in India is reflected in growing foreign direct investment in the country. With deteriorating health of Chairman Deng and overheating of the economy, China has been losing some of its lustre in the recent past. MNCs, who were very bullish on China are now considering other Asian markets, including India, for investment. Political and economic stability has been a common feature in practically all east Asian and

ASEAN countries, and that has helped in attracting large investments into these countries from the USA, Europe and Japan.

Singapore and Hong Kong are island economies and have very liberal FDI policy regimes. In fact, FDI policies of Hong Kong do not differentiate between local and foreign investors. Besides being politically and economically very stable, the strategic location of these island countries provided overseas investors access to fast expanding Asian markets. And this has resulted in substantial flow of foreign capital into these countries.

In terms of location India is very well positioned, having rich West Asian markets on the one side and rapidly expanding east and Southeast Asian markets on the other. The tremendous economic growth that is taking place in ASEAN and east Asian countries are creating substantial markets for manufactured goods and services. The locational advantage India offers to investors is being increasingly recognised. As a result a number of multinational corporations are setting up subsidiaries and manufacturing bases in the country with long-term objective of servicing markets in Asia.

Since the mid 1980's rising labour cost and shortage of skilled and semi-skilled labour forced many companies in Japan and other developed nations to shift business operations overseas. Initially the focus of investment was newly industrialised countries (NIEs) of Asia, which offered ample labour and lower wages. But situation changed due to vigorous industrialisation in these countries as a result there has been substantial rise in wages and availability of manpower had also declined, creating a shortage situation. With these developments in the newly industrialised countries, foreign companies started moving into China and other ASEAN countries, where labour was available at lower wages. With increasing inflow of foreign capital the process of industrialisation got accelerated and it was almost the replay of the NIE scenario in ASEAN countries. Today most of these countries are facing acute shortage of skilled and managerial manpower and wages have also multiplied in past ten years.

As compared to this we have a surplus situation in India. We are known to have third largest pool of scientific and technical manpower in the world. With the result we are net exporter of very high quality human resource to the world. Because of ample availability of manpower , wages in India are one of the lowest in the region. Hence, in view of shortage of manpower and rising labour cost in other Asian countries, India can prove to be most attractive destination for investment.

The infrastructural facilities in most of the developing countries are inadequate. Hence there is a tremendous demand for investment in sectors like power, telecommunications, roads, highways, ports, etc. The Asian Development Bank has estimated that countries in Asia would be requiring an investment of $ one trillion in the next ten years. This clearly reveals the status of physical infrastructure in developing countries of Asia. However, Singapore and Hong Kong have succeeded in creating modern infrastructure facilities and therefore, do not suffer from any major limitation in this area. The availability of modern facilities have attracted a large number of European, American and Japanese corporation to Singapore and Hong Kong and some of them have set up their regional headquarters in one of these countries. Similarly, South Korea and Malaysia have also improved infrastructural facilities in the past one decade or so.

India is not in league with Singapore and requires considerable investment to upgrade its infrastructural facilities. Having realised this the Government of India has announced very attractive policies, in some cases with assured rate of return, to attract substantial investment in infrastructural areas. With the result investment opportunities in India's infrastructure is attracting considerable interest of overseas investors.

Other factors which contribute significantly to India's attractiveness as investment target include existence of well-defined social systems, which are essential for proper functioning of market driven economy. India's legal system, which is based on the British Law, provides full protection to private property. Besides having Asia's oldest functioning stock exchange, existing financial system fully supports the dynamism of the economy. Nevertheless, the financial system is being liberalised to make it more responsive to the changing needs of the economy. Unlike in many Asian countries, entrepreneurship is centuries old and foreign companies interested in establishing strategic alliances have a vast array of Indian firms with proven track record to choose as partners.

In the recent past there has been a total change in attitude towards FDI and factors responsible for this change include the remarkable success of outward oriented policies, particularly in East Asia and disillusionment with traditional strategies. Consequently, perhaps there is no country in the world today which imposes complete ban on FDI.

Not only attitude towards FDI has changed, the key factors determining the location of FDI have also undergone change, over period of time. During the post-war period, the strong demand for natural resources and adoption of import substitution strategies were important factors influencing the location of international production. Over period of time due to innovations in information and communications technologies, growing market competition and move towards internationally integrated production system, location decisions are now being influenced by a combination of factors such as market size and its growth potential, human resources with high degree of technical and managerial capabilities, sophisticated physical and social infrastructure with liberalised investment regime.

There is growing recognition world over that India is one of the most promising and stable destination for investment. During the post liberalisation period, India and her companies have been the subject of favourable attention by foreign investors and the international media.

According to the New York based *Merrill Lynch*, a global securities research and economic group, India's economic reforms are more attractive than similar development in other Asian countries and foreign investors with an eye on new emerging markets will find India more interesting. Recently, other similar international organisations have also ranked India among the best bets for long term investment in emerging markets. Ms Elliot House, President International Dow Jones, wrote in *Wall Street Journal,* dated 24th February, 1995 that "Right now the global market is looking for a new emerging market to replace increasingly unstable China and crisis stricken Mexico. India has the advantage of a stable political system, legal infrastructure and somewhat developed markets, in addition to a large and skilled workforce fluent in English. India has enormous potential-literally". Hence it can be concluded that the feeling in the industrialised countries that India offers possibly the lowest risk environment to do business is getting stronger by the day.

# 6

# Japan's Investment Interest in India and Southeast Asia

K.V. KESAVAN

The expanding role of Japan in the global economy has been a subject of great interest in recent years. Its industrial and technological strength has enhanced its global competitiveness in several vital sectors and thrown a serious challenge to the most advanced western countries. In the past few years, Japan has emerged as the largest aid-giving donor to the developing world, and the total annual volume of its official development assistance (ODA) has amounted to more than $ 11.5 billions.

As Japan's economy has made remarkable strides, its foreign direct investment (FDI) has correspondingly expanded. The cumulative volume of Japan's FDI during 1952-92 amounted to $ 386.5 billion. About 42 per cent of the total volume went to the US and 19.5 per cent to Europe. Asia accounted for $ 64.1 billion or 16.5 per cent of the total volume. The share of the ASEAN group constituted $ 35 billion or 9.05 per cent. The breakdown of the shares of the ASEAN countries is: Indonesia $ 14.4 billion, Singapore $ 7.8 billion, Thailand $ 5.8 billion, Malaysia $ 4.8 billion and the Philippines $ 1.9 billion. Unlike ASEAN, South Asia occupied a very negligible proportion in the overall Japanese FDI. Considering the size of its huge market, India's share of $ 322 million was too meagre. Not only India, but the whole of South Asia had until 1992 received negligible amount of direct investment from Japan. This could be explained by the kind of developmental strategies pursued by them. India in fact gave a lead to other developing countries in pursuing an inward-looking, restrictive policy that placed utmost emphasis on the role of the government. India's economic strategy constituted a pioneering effort marked by political idealism. While placing its stress on the centrality of the role of the state, it considered the private sector as still not capable of managing large-scale industries. One positive aspect of this strategy was that the rate of savings markedly rose from 10 per cent in 1958 to 20 per cent in 1992. But undue emphasis on import-substituting industries resulted in the weakening of export competitiveness. Though some steps were taken in the direction of liberalisation in 1994, the Indian economy needed sweeping reforms.

The inward-looking strategy stressed the importance of foreign economic assistance rather than foreign direct investment from private sources. India was the first Asian country to receive ODA from Japan in 1958. Japan's foreign aid policy was in fact inaugurated with the extension of the first yen credit in that year. Since then India has been a major recipient of Japan's ODA, and in recent years, Japan has maintained its position as the biggest donor country not only to India, but also to all South Asian countries.

Though India has received substantial Japanese assistance, one should take note of the difficulties that are likely to affect the future distribution of Japan's ODA. First, in recent years, the geographical distribution of Japan's aid has become more diversified, and Asia which used to receive more than 75 per cent of the total aid, now accounts for about 60 per cent. Japan which uses aid as a tool in its resource diplomacy has to cope with new demands coming from Africa, Latin America, the former Soviet Republics, etc. Second, the ODA Charter of 1992 has prescribed certain conditionalities for giving its aid and they include sensitive subjects like the recipient country's military expenditure, its attitude to nuclear non-proliferation issues, its system of government, its adherence to human rights, its interest in economic reforms and market economy, etc. Many of these issues are extremely touchy and could act as a constraint on the flow of Japanese aid in the future. Third, South Asian countries, including India, have accumulated huge repayment debts which could create serious difficulties in receiving fresh loans.

The ODA Charter states categorically that Japan will maintain a close linkage between ODA and direct investment and trade. It states that while extending ODA, Japan will endeavour to encourage structural adjustments so that the private sector could fully play its role. Japan believes that close linkages between the ODA and the FDI has been extremely beneficial to the growth of the ASEAN countries. Japan's ODA loans to the NIES and ASEAN countries helped them in building up good infrastructure which in turn attracted foreign direct investment.

Japan's investment in Asia in the initial years was directed towards developing natural resources. This gave rise to criticisms in both the NIES and ASEAN countries that Japan was more interested in exploiting the natural resources for its own interest. But after 1970, it started investing in export-oriented industries. From then on, the Japanese business started shifting from export to local production in overseas markets. Following the 1985 Plaza accords, when the yen started appreciating sharply, several business enterprises found it profitable to transfer their production bases to Taiwan, Hong Kong, South Korea and Singapore. Once the NIES made economic strides, the cost of production rose in those countries necessitating the transfer of these production bases to the neighbouring ASEAN countries.

According to one reliable source, Japanese companies had, by 1991, set up 4299 affiliated companies in Asian countries. Of these, the NIES had accounted for 2490 and the ASEAN for 1469. Only 110 of them were in India and Pakistan. This showed the meagre size of Japan's FDI in India.

Even such small investment as was noticed in the early years was mostly in the chemical industry. Later, in the 1980's, it flowed into automobile sector in a fairly big way. The reasons that held the Japanese away from India included: the restrictive policies of the Indian governments, its insistence on a high degree of local content despite shortage of local skills, high tariff rates, poor infrastructural facilities, bureaucratic red tapism, unattractive equity shares, political instability, absence of proper exit policy, etc.

A major development occurred in July 1991 when the Indian Government embarked on a new policy of economic liberalisation. The reforms that followed were intended to give a new thrust to the global competitiveness of the economy. They cover a wide range of measures such as the relaxation of government regulations relating to foreign investment, technological cooperation, delicensing of industrial activities, reform of public sector enterprises, etc. Though the government will continue to play a critical role, the full potential of the private sector is to be utilised. The private sector can now operate virtually in all sectors except certain strategic spheres like defence, atomic energy, etc. The need for obtaining industrial licences has been removed in all but fifteen industries. Proposals involving foreign equity upto 51 per cent in 36 industries can now be cleared as fast as within two weeks. Foreign equity upto 100 per cent is possible in certain sectors.

The outcome of the reforms could be seen in the dramatic increase in the number of foreign collaborations approved by the government. The number of such collaborations was 666 in 1990, but moved on to register 950 in 1991, 1520 in 1992, and 1476 in 1993. About 80 per cent of these have gone to such sectors as telecommunication, power, oil refineries, electrical equipment, transport, etc. Table 1 gives the figure of foreign investment approved during 1991-93. Japan which figured as the third biggest investor in 1991 and 1992, came to occupy the seventh position in 1993. The sharp decline in Japanese investment could be explained by the traditional cautions attitude of the Japanese business leaders. They are expecting the Indian government to improve the conditions governing equity norms, exit policy, import duties, profits sharing, tax rates, and infrastructure facilities. In the meantime, several official and business delegations have come to India to seek better conditions for investment.

Hashimoto Ryutaro, Japanese minister for International Trade and Industry paid an official visit to India in January 1995. He met the Indian leaders and assured them of Japan's positive support to the reforms programme. He announced a two-way credit line to the tune of $ one billion and lowered the insurance premium on Japanese investments in India. Hashimoto's mission was immediately followed by a delegation of the Keidanren.While appreciating the progress of the reforms, the delegation identified areas where improvement could still take place. It was also around the same time that the US Commerce Secretary Ron Brown visited India, and projects worth about $ 4 billion were cleared. The speed with which the US signed investment agreements with India provided a sharp contrast to the time-consuming consensus-building process of the Japanese.

It would be useful to understand the nature and course of Japanese investment in Southeast Asia. First, there has been effective coordination between ODA and investment in ASEAN. Japan's ODA initially prepared the ground for improving the infrastructure. Improved infrastructure in turn invited greater Japanese private investment. In China, Japan's ODA was almost matched in size by its investment. But in the case of India, the size of the investment was miniscule compared to the massive ODA it received from Japan.

Second, ASEAN countries provided attractive terms for investment in the form of better equity rights, profit sharing, raw materials, cheap labour and so on. In the initial phase, Japanese investment was directed towards exploiting natural resources. But after 1985, Japanese investment was made in setting up production bases in ASEAN. On account of this, ASEAN countries started exporting manufactured goods not only to Japan, but also to the US and Europe. The absolute value of the exports of such manufactured goods from ASEAN to Japan increased by 40 per cent annually during 1986-90. It is also important to note that the growth of the NIES has also started investing in the ASEAN countries in a big way. In 1990, the NIES accounted for 48 per cent of investment in Malaysia as against 29 per cent by Japan. In Indonesia, the NIES invested 30 per cent whereas Japan's share was 26 per cent. In the Philippines, the figures were 40 per cent for the NIES and 32 per cent for Japan. A similar situation was noticed in Vietnam. During 1988-92, the largest overseas investment came from the NIES. Taiwan invested $ 789 million, followed by Hong Kong with $ 606 million. Japan figured 6th in the list with $ 305 million. With the resumption of full diplomatic relations, the US will also participate in Vietnam. This is perhaps the right time for India to attract more investment not only from Japan and the US but also from the NIES and ASEAN.

**Country-wise breakup of foreign investment approved**

*(Value in Rs. Million)*

| *Sl. No.* | *Country* | *1991* | *1992* | *1993* |
|---|---|---|---|---|
| 1. | U.S.A. | 1858.5 | 12315.0 | 34618.8 |
| 2. | U.K. | 321.0 | 1176.7 | 6227.3 |
| 3. | Oman | — | — | 5429.8 |
| 4. | Switzerland | 355.0 | 6897.6 | 4268.0 |
| 5. | U.A.E. | 22.0 | 64.5 | 4044.9 |
| 6. | Thailand | | 19.2 | 3684.2 |
| 7. | Netherlands | 559.2 | 967.9 | 3216.5 |
| 8. | Japan | 527.1 | 6102.3 | 2574.3 |
| 9. | Mexico | | 52.8 | 2389.8 |
| 10. | Germany | 418.0 | 862.7 | 1759.3 |
| | Total | 5341.1 | 38875.4 | 88593.3 |

# IV

# TRADE, SERVICE AND FINANCE

# 7

# Indo-ASEAN Trade Relations

INDRA NATH MUKHERJI

Five years since the end of the Cold War, the Asia-Pacific region has been showing a pace of rapid economic growth at a time when most of the industrial world has been having sluggish economic performance.

The political constraints to India's relations with South East Asian countries having recede, India's Look East policy is being strengthened.

The first landmark reflecting the stabilizing of Indian economic ties with ASEAN countries was the meeting of ASEAN and Indian senior officials on the establishment of sectoral dialogue relations between ASEAN and India which was held in New Delhi on March 16-17, 1993. The meeting identified trade and investment, science and technology and tourism as possible areas for strengthening cooperation. In the area of trade, India proposed four areas of co-operation which could form the basis for discussion in future dialogue meetings.

These proposals included:

(1) holding regular trade between India and ASEAN;

(2) establishment of a mechanism for the exchange of trade and commercial data;

(3) regular interaction between the business communities of India and ASEAN and

(4) establishing a mechanism for interaction on industrial standards and quality control.

A notable development in Indo-ASEAN relations was the decision by ASEAN to accept India as a full dialogue partner. This decision was taken at the ASEAN summit meeting of December 14-15, 1993 in Bangkok.

As a dialogue partner, India can attend and participate in the meetings of ASEAN and its member countries regularly and project her views on the issues of internal security in the Asia-Pacifics to facilitate herself in gaining the membership of APEC. (*Economic Times*, 1995)

The objective of this study is:

(1) to analyse trends in India's trade with member countries of ASEAN;

(2) to examine the structure of India's trade in terms of high tech and non-high tech products; and

(3) to identify the top ten products traded by India as also commodity concentration in bilateral trade;

(4) to assess the incidence of India's customs tariffs on principal identified imports.

**Indo-ASEAN Trade**

India's export to the ASEAN region has been growing quite rapidly since 1989 as will be seen in Table 1. From US $ 733 million in 1989, the value of exports increased to US $ 1534 million in 1993. There was however a decline in India's imports from the region from US $ 1670 million in 1989 to US $ 991 million in 1993. As a consequence of these trends, India's balance of trade which was negative to the tune of US $ 737 million in 1989, became positive to the extent of US $ 543 million in 1993.

In relation to India's world exports, the share of ASEAN countries increased from 4.6 per cent in 1989 to 7.7 per cent in 1993. However, the share of these countries in India's global imports declined from 8.2 per cent to 4.2 per cent during the same period. These trends underline the growing importance of ASEAN particularly as a growing market for India's exports.

Looking at India's trade with individual member countries of this region, one may notice that in 1993 Singapore and Malaysia were India's largest trading partners followed by Thailand and Indonesia. It will be further observed that India's trade with the larger trading partners, viz., Malaysia and Singapore was well balanced. India had a larger trade surplus with Thailand and Indonesia. This picture is thus quite different from the one prevailing in 1989 when India had a trade deficit with all ASEAN member countries except Thailand.

### TABLE 1
### Trade with ASEAN member countries (US $ mn)

| *Countries* | *1989* *EXP* | *IMP* | *BOT* | *1990* *EXP* | *IMP* | *BOT* | *1991* *EXP* | *IMP* | *BOT* | *1992* *EXP* | *IMP* | *BOT* | *1993* *EXP* | *IMP* | *BOT* |
|---|---|---|---|---|---|---|---|---|---|---|---|---|---|---|---|
| Brunei | — | — | — | — | — | — | 1 | — | 1 | 1 | — | 1 | — | — | — |
| Indonesia | 50 | 76 | -26 | 92 | 173 | -81 | 145 | 67 | 78 | 167 | 67 | 100 | 203 | 90 | 113 |
| Malaysia | 139 | 628 | -489 | 126 | 658 | -532 | 203 | 546 | -343 | 246 | 391 | -145 | 240 | 228 | 12 |
| Philippines | 41 | 81 | -40 | 21 | 4 | 17 | 64 | 31 | 33 | 77 | 11 | 66 | 53 | 7 | 46 |
| Singapore | 371 | 834 | -463 | 308 | 689 | -381 | 386 | 311 | 75 | 535 | 367 | 168 | 700 | 612 | 88 |
| Thailand | 132 | 51 | 81 | 201 | 62 | 139 | 199 | 49 | 150 | 257 | 65 | 192 | 338 | 54 | 284 |
| ASEAN Total | 733 | 1670 | -937 | 748 | 1586 | -838 | 998 | 1004 | -6 | 1283 | 901 | 382 | 1534 | 991 | 543 |
| World Total | 15839 | 20264 | -4425 | 17813 | 23990 | -6177 | 17872 | 19509 | -1637 | 18528 | 24206 | -5678 | 19964 | 22493 | -2529 |
| ASEAN as % of World | 4.627 | 8.241 | | 4.199 | 6.611 | | 5.584 | 5.146 | | 6.924 | 3.722 | | 7.683 | 4.405 | |

*Source :* IMF, Direction of Trade Statistics Yearbook, 1994.

### Structure of Trade: Methodology

The structure of India's trade with ASEAN member countries has been classified into two categories, viz., high technology and non-high technology products. For this purpose about 40,000 records were scanned over two years, viz., 1987-88 and 1992-93 in terms of most highly disaggregated data available from computerised data base of DGCI'S. The data was sorted in both the years to rank the products in terms of ascending order for commodity code to facilitate classification of products in terms of high tech and non-high tech products. Footnote to Table 2 lists the sections from which the products were included under high tech and non-high tech categories which is based on the researcher's best assessment of description of products. Non-high tech products were drawn from Sections I-XIV (including chapters 1-71) and high tech products were drawn from Sections XV-XXI (including chapters 72-99) of the H.S. coding system. Since the products run in several thousands, it is not feasible to include all the products in the list. We thus included only the top 50 products in terms of value traded by India (exports and imports) with member countries of ASEAN. The data set for Brunei could not be obtained because of India's negligible trade with this country. Since trade among the developing countries is typically characterised by the preponderance of a few products, the top 50 products, even though highly disaggregated, was expected to cover a large proportion of India's bilateral trade with the ASEAN member countries. This has been demonstrated to be so (except for India's imports from Singapore in 1992-93) as we shall presently see.

India's bilateral trade with ASEAN member countries was sorted in descending order of importance in value both in 1987-88 and in 1992-93 to ascertain their order of importance. In this study only the top ten products traded in 1992-93 has been presented.

### High Tech and Non-High Tech Products

When analysing the composition of bilateral trade, the shares of high tech and non-high tech products indicate to what extent the bilateral trade is dominated by higher value added products in relation to traditional and simpler manufactured products.

Table 2 gives us this picture with respect to India's exports. It will be observed that by and large, India's exports were dominated by non-high tech products, generally accounting for more than three-quarters of India's bilateral exports to member countries of ASEAN. However, the share of high tech products had increased in 1992-93 as compared to 1987-88 in respect of India's exports to Malaysia, the Philippines and Thailand. The converse could be noticed in respect of India's exports to Indonesia and Singapore.

The composition of India's imports from ASEAN member countries has been presented in Table 3.

The table again reveals the preponderant share of India's non-high tech imports from all member countries of ASEAN in relation to high tech products, with the exception of Singapore. It may be observed that the dominance of non-high tech products in respect of India's imports is more pronounced than in case of its exports to the region. Among all the ASEAN member countries, Singapore stood out in marked contrast since high tech products account for more than 70 per cent of India's imports from that country during both the years under study.

Looking at India's trade with ASEAN member countries, we notice that the proportion of high tech products was increasing both for imports from and exports to Malaysia and Thailand. Another observation which we may make is that the preponderance of non-high tech products in India's trade with ASEAN member countries is more marked in case of imports, rather than with respect to export suggesting that India exports relatively more high tech products to ASEAN member countries as compared with the exception of Singapore.

**Product Concentration in Bilateral Trade**

When trade is dominated by a few products, then a smaller number of products would account for most of the bilateral trade. Conversely when trade is diversified, no single product or group of products would dominate the trade basket. Table 3, apart from listing the top ten products exported to the region, shows what percentage of India's bilateral exports are accounted for by the top ten and fifty products exported to the region during 1992-93. It will be seen that India's exports to Thailand is most highly concentrated followed by the Philippines. The top ten products cover more than half, and the top fifty more than

**TABLE 2**

**India's export of high technology and non-high technology products to member countries of ASEAN (percentage distribution)**

| Indonesia | | | | Malaysia | | | | Philippines | | | | Singapore | | | | Thailand | | | |
|---|---|---|---|---|---|---|---|---|---|---|---|---|---|---|---|---|---|---|---|
| 1987-88 | | 1992-93 | | 1987-88 | | 1992-93 | | 1987-88 | | 1992-93 | | 1987-88 | | 1992-93 | | 1987-88 | | 1992-93 | |
| HT | NHT | HT | NHT | HT | NHT | HT | NHT | HT | NHT | HT | NHT | HT | NHT | HT | NHT | HT | NHT | HT | NHT |
| 55.27 | 44.73 | 22.14 | 77.86 | 17.57 | 82.43 | 28.46 | 71.54 | 20.38 | 79.62 | 31.04 | 68.96 | 31.20 | 68.80 | 25.90 | 74.10 | 14.60 | 85.50 | 19.92 | 80.08 |
| (67.28%) | | (73.15%) | | (74.68%) | | (64.25%) | | (86.95%) | | (77.34%) | | (54.68%) | | (64.33%) | | (79.43%) | | (78.37%) | |

*Source* : Estimated from computerised data base, Director General of Commercial Intelligence and Statistics, Ministry of Commerce, Government of India, Calcutta.

Notes : 1. NHT (Non-High Technology) includes all products under Sections I-XIV and chapters 1-71 of Indian Trade Classification Based on Harmonised System. (Section I : Live Animals, Animal Products, Section II: Vegetable Products; Section III; Animal or Vegetable Fats and Oils and their Cleavage Products; prepared Edible Fats; Animal or Vegetable Waxes; Section IV: Prepared Foodstuffs; Beverages, Vinegar and, Tobacco and Manufactured Tobacco Substitutes; Section V: Mineral Products; Section VI : Products of Chemical and Allied Industries; Section VII: Plastics and Articles thereof; Rubber and Articles thereof; Raw Hides and Skins, Leather etc.; Section IX: Wood and Articles of Wood etc.; Section X: Pulp of Wood etc.; Section XI: Textile and Textile Articles; Section XII: Footwear, Headgear. Umbrellas etc.; Section XIII: Articles of Stone, Plaster, Cement, etc.; and Section XIV: Natural or Cultured Pearls, Precious or Semi Precious Stones, etc.

2. HT (High Technology) includes Section XV: Base Metals and Articles of Base Metal; Section XVI: Machinery and Mechanical Appliances; Electrical Equipment, etc.; Section XVII: Vehicles, Aircraft, Vessels, etc.; Section XVIII: Optical, Photographic, Cinematographic, measuring, etc.; Section XIX: Arms and Ammunition etc.; Section XX: Miscellaneous Manufactured Articles; and Section XXI: Works of Art, etc.; For Complete Description of Items, refer to Indian Trade Classification (Based on Harmonised Commodity Description and Coding System), DGCIS, Calcutta.

3. Figures in brackets indicate the percentage of total exports to ASEAN member countries covered by the top 50 products under eight digit H.S. products classification.

**TABLE 3**

**India's import of high technology and non-high technology products from member countries of ASEAN (percentage distribution)**

| Indonesia | | | | Malaysia | | | | Philippines | | | | Singapore | | | | Thailand | | | |
|---|---|---|---|---|---|---|---|---|---|---|---|---|---|---|---|---|---|---|---|
| 1987-88 | | 1992-93 | | 1987-88 | | 1992-93 | | 1987-88 | | 1992-93 | | 1987-88 | | 1992-93 | | 1987-88 | | 1992-93 | |
| HT | NHT | HT | NHT | HT | NHT | HT | NHT | HT | NHT | HT | NHT | HT | NHT | HT | NHT | HT | NHT | HT | NHT |
| 10.56 | 89.44 | 9.40 | 90.60 | 1.97 | 98.03 | 5.98 | 94.02 | 9.53 | 90.70 | 18.35 | 81.65 | 76.08 | 23.92 | 72.69 | 27.31 | 2.94 | 97.06 | 12.93 | 81.07 |
| (82.11%) | | (92.52%) | | (100.0%) | | (94.04%) | | (43.46%) | | (98.6%) | | (57.34%) | | (26.79%) | | (94.71%) | | (84.22%) | |

*Source* : Same as Table 2

*Notes* : 1. Same as Notes 1, and 2 in Table 2.

2. Figures in brackets indicate the percentage of total imports from ASEAN member countries covered by the top 50 products under eight digit H.S. products classification.

three-quarters of India's total exports to these countries. The Product concentration in respect of India's exports to Indonesia, Singapore and Malaysia, even though somewhat lower, still remains quite high. It may be said that generally, India's product concentration in bilateral exports exceeded 40 per cent for the top ten and 64 per cent for the top fifty to all ASEAN member countries.

India's imports of top ten and fifty products from ASEAN member countries in 1992-93 has been presented in Table 5. It will be easily observed that India's product concentration of imports from ASEAN member countries is much higher than those for exports, the only exception being Singapore. Except for Singapore, India's top ten and fifty products imported from the region accounted for more than 50 per cent and 84 per cent respectively during 1992-93. As to some extent in case of exports, India's imports from Singapore is even much more diversified.

**Identification of Top Ten**

In this section we examine the product specific exports to and imports from ASEAN member countries. The product analysis is based on the highest available level of disaggregation. The product coverage, however, relates to the top products traded by India with these countries.

In order to examine the characteristics of the top ten products and their percentage shares in total exported to and imported from ASEAN member countries, we need to revert to Tables 4 and 5 respectively. Since these tables list only the product codes, their respective product descriptions need to be matched from Annexure-1 containing the product descriptions arranged in ascending order for their corresponding codes.

Our objective here is to examine some of the important products, both high tech and non-high tech, traded by India with the member countries of this region. While identifying, we may refer to products that are among the very top in the list, and particularly those that are traded by more than one country with India.

A look at Table 4 which indicates the top ten products exported by India, reveals that among non-high tech products the most important are "oil cake... meal of soya bean, solvent extracted" (code: 2304003, exported to all the member countries of ASEAN); oil cake and oil cake meal, of groundnut (code: 23050002,

## TABLE 4

### Top ten products exported by India to member countries of ASEAN (1992-93)

*(Percentage of Total Exports)*

| *Indonesia* | | *Malaysia* | | *Philippines* | | *Singapore* | | *Thailand* | |
|---|---|---|---|---|---|---|---|---|---|
| *H.S. Code* | *%* | *H.S. Code* | *%* | *H.S. Code* | *%* | *H.S. Code* | *%* | *H.S. Code* | *%* |
| 23050002 | 10.96 | 20233000 | 12.16 | 23040003 | 37.66 | 23040003 | 19.11 | 71023901 | 22.85 |
| 23040003 | 10.81 | 23040003 | 7.11 | 84292000 | 5.72 | 76011001 | 8.80 | 23040003 | 14.64 |
| 26011201 | 5.44 | 02013000 | 4.49 | 87149307 | 3.50 | 71023901 | 6.94 | 76011001 | 5.75 |
| 02818200 | 4.89 | 07031001 | 4.43 | 40112001 | 3.06 | 40112000 | 2.64 | 52010013 | 5.41 |
| 52010013 | 4.52 | 10063001 | 3.94 | 73089007 | 1.61 | 84733001 | 2.55 | 72281009 | 3.84 |
| 76011001 | 3.98 | 72082000 | 2.39 | 72044100 | 1.45 | 27111100 | 1.68 | 71039101 | 3.43 |
| 23064002 | 3.68 | 02305002 | 1.79 | 85451901 | 1.38 | 73269015 | 1.34 | 71023909 | 2.31 |
| 13011002 | 2.51 | 52083101 | 1.75 | 55032000 | 1.36 | 07031001 | 1.25 | 23064002 | 1.48 |
| 87149309 | 1.59 | 08706009 | 1.74 | 87149209 | 0.99 | 23064002 | 1.12 | 23069008 | 1.33 |
| 07201300 | 1.46 | 03061301 | 1.34 | 76011001 | 0.96 | 08013002 | 1.04 | 23050002 | 1.22 |
| Top Ten | 40.85 | Top Ten | 41.14 | Top Ten | 57.69 | Top Ten | 46.47 | Top Ten | 62.26 |
| Top Fifty | 73.15 | Top Fifty | 64.25 | Top Fifty | 77.34 | Top Fifty | 64.33 | Top Fifty | 78.37 |

exported to Indonesia and Thailand); oil cake and oil cake meal, solvent extracted (code: 23064002; exported to Indonesia and Thailand) and cotton not carded or combined... Indian cotton... (exported to Indonesia and Thailand); one of the important high tech products exported by India include: unwrought aluminium, ... ingots (code: 76011001), exported to Indonesia, the Philippines, Singapore and Thailand); Some other high tech products exported by India include: self-propelled bulldozers... graders and levellers. (code: 84292000) and parts and accessories of vehicles, hubs (code: 87149307) exported to the Philippines.

It may be observed from Table 5 that some of the important non-high tech products imported by India include coconuts... raw cashew nuts (code: 08013003, from Indonesia and the Philippines) ash and residues — other, (code: 26201900 from the Philippines and Thailand) and chemical, wood pulp, soda or sulphate... non coniferous (code: 47032900 from Indonesia and Thailand). Some of the high tech products imported by India include: Ferrous waste and scrap... other (code: 72044909, from Malaysia and Thailand); copper waste and scrap ... of copper (code: 74040001 from Indonesia); automatic data processing machines.... winchester/hard disc drives (code: 84719302 from Thailand and Singapore); and electronic integrated circuits — others (code: 85421900 from the Philippines and Singapore).

### Tariffs on India's Imports

The details relating to India's customs tariffs on the top ten products imported from the ASEAN member countries has been presented in Table 5. A look at the table clearly reveals that in respect of none of the top products imported by India from these countries exceeds 50 per cent the maximum ceiling on tariffs that has been imposed under the Union Budget, 1995-96. There are some products in respect of which the tariff rates are even lower. It may added here that a look at the prevalence of non-tariff barriers also needs to be looked into for a proper assessment of India's trade barriers on imports from ASEAN member countries.

### Conclusions

Member countries of ASEAN belong to the Asia Pacific Community which is the most dynamic region in the world today.

**TABLE 5**

**Top ten products imported by India from ASEAN (1992-93) and customs tariffs (1995-96) thereon**

*(Percentage of Total Imports)*

| Indonesia | | | Malaysia | | | Philippines | | | Singapore | | | Thailand | | |
|---|---|---|---|---|---|---|---|---|---|---|---|---|---|---|
| H.S. Code | % | Tariff | H.S. Code | % | Tariff | H.S. Code | % | Tariff | H.S. Code | % | Tariff | H.S. Code | % | Tariff |
| 08013003 | 17.97 | 50 | 27090000 | 49.83 | 35 | 2809200 | 65.12 | 50 | 08473309 | 2.35 | 50 | 29419001 | 10.81 | 50 |
| 28141000 | 16.63 | 50 | 44039929 | 18.77 | 25 | 91149001 | 11.71 | 50 | 72044909 | 1.79 | 50 | 71031001 | 8.53 | 50 |
| 15191900 | 7.40 | 50 | 44033309 | 8.94 | 50 | 8013003 | 2.84 | 50 | 85421900 | 1.76 | 50 | 40012100 | 7.10 | 50 |
| 29031500 | 5.65 | 50 | 15119000 | 2.54 | 50 | 85421900 | 1.78 | 50 | 8528000 | 1.47 | 50 | 98010003 | 5.48 | 50 |
| 47032900 | 5.43 | 25 | 15191900 | 2.28 | 30 | 26201900 | 1.26 | 50 | 99930002 | 1.32 | 50 | 28030002 | 5.42 | 50 |
| 29024300 | 3.89 | 50 | 80011009 | 1.16 | 10 | 25301009 | 1.22 | 35 | 74040002 | 1.07 | NA | 40012909 | 4.58 | 50 |
| 74071001 | 3.76 | 50 | 26011209 | 0.73 | 50 | 61178049 | 1.13 | 50 | 84719302 | 0.96 | 50 | 26201900 | 3.36 | 10 |
| 27011909 | 2.93 | 40 | 74040001 | 0.69 | 30 | 61179000 | 1.06 | 50 | 74040001 | 0.81 | 50 | 470322900 | 2.79 | 25 |
| 29022000 | 2.40 | 50 | 80011001 | 0.68 | 50 | 85412900 | 0.82 | 50 | 39012000 | 0.69 | 50 | 84719302 | 2.34 | 50 |
| 38051002 | 2.17 | 50 | 72044909 | 0.65 | | 61169909 | 0.82 | 50 | 38112900 | 0.64 | 50 | 71023100 | 2.20 | 50 |
| Top Ten | 68.23 | | Top Ten | 86.27 | | Top Ten | 87.74 | | Top Ten | 12.86 | | Top Ten | 52.61 | |
| Top Fifty | 92.52 | | Top Fifty | 94.08 | | Top Fifty | 98.62 | | Top Fifty | 26.79 | | Top Fifty | | |

Also taking note of the post Cold War scenario, it is but natural for India to 'Look East'. One of the best ways of doing this is to further widen and deepen India's trade linkages with the ASEAN member countries. The ASEAN market has been becoming of increasing importance for India's exports in recent years. But the result achieved is far below the potential.

India has high commodity concentration of trade with member countries of ASEAN, more so for imports. More diversified trade with ASEAN member countries could be a desirable objective.

The product characteristics of India's trade with ASEAN member countries reflects the predominance on non-high tech products, particularly with respect to imports. Thus one significant result of this study demonstrates that not only in India's exports are relatively more diversified as compared to India's imports from the region, but further, India's exports are relatively more high tech in its characteristics as compared to its imports from the region. This possibly reflects India's relatively advanced technology. To what extent trade policies contributed to this pattern of trade, we are unable to make an assessment without ascertaining the trade regimes in both India and in the ASEAN member countries. In this study we have merely examined the incidence of nominal customs tariffs on import of top products supplied to India. Thanks to the process of ongoing liberalisation in India, the incidence of customs tariffs is on the decline. In the years ahead further declines are envisaged as India braces for entry to any larger organisation in the larger and most dynamic Asia Pacific region. India's legitimacy as also eligibility for entry would depend very much on to what extent it has brought down its protectionism to a level comparable to the countries of this region.

## REFERENCES

*Economic Times* (1995), "ASEAN Accepts India as Dialogue Partner", 29 December, 1995.

Meeting of ASEAN and Indian Senior Officials on the Establishment of Sectoral Dialogue Relations between ASEAN and India, (Meeting 1993), Joint Press Release, New Delhi, 16-17 March, 1993.

Jain R.K., *Customs Tariff of India, 1995-96* (1995) Centax Publications Pvt. Ltd., New Delhi, 1995.

# ANNEXURE 1

## Description of top ten products traded by India with member countries of ASEAN

| *ITC (H.S.)* | *Product Description* |
|---|---|
| 2013000 | Boneless meat of bovine animals, fresh or chilled |
| 2305002 | N.A. (Not Available) |
| 2809200 | N.A. |
| 2818200 | N.A. |
| 3061301 | Shrimp (Scampi) macrobactium frozen |
| 7031001 | Onions fresh or chilled |
| 7201300 | N.A. |
| 8013002 | Cashew carnels whole |
| 8013003 | Cashew nuts raw |
| 8473309 | N.A. |
| 8528000 | N.A. |
| 8706009 | N.A. |
| 10063001 | Rice parboiled |
| 13011002 | Shellac machine made |
| 15119000 | Refined palm oil and its fractions |
| 15191900 | Other industrial monocarboxylic fatty acid |
| 20233000 | N.A. |
| 23040003 | Meal of soyabean solvent extracted Defated |
| 23040003 | Meal of soyabean solvent extracted Defated |
| 23050002 | Oil-cake & oil-cake meal of groundnut solvent ex |
| 23064002 | Oil-cake & oil-cake meal solvent extracted variety |
| 23069008 | Oil-cake & oil-cake meal of seasamum seeds solvent extract |
| 25301009 | Others (including powder) |
| 26011201 | Iron ore pellets |
| 26011209 | Others (sinters briquettes etc. agglomerated) |
| 26201900 | Other ash & residue counting mainly zinc |
| 27011909 | Others coal |
| 27090000 | Petroleum oils and oils obtained from bituminous mi |
| 27111100 | Liquefied natural gas |
| 28030002 | Carbon black for rubber industries |
| 28141000 | Anhydrous ammonia |
| 29022000 | Benzene |
| 29024300 | P-xylene |
| 29031500 | 1,2D Chloromethne cethylene dichlorde, saturated |
| 29419001 | Antibiotic - other |
| 38051002 | Spirit of turpentine (gum & sulphate) |
| 38112900 | Other additives for lubricating oils |
| 39012000 | Polyethylene having a specific gravity 0.94/more |
| 40012100 | Natural rubber in SMKD sheets |
| 40012909 | Other natural rubber non-latex |
| 40112000 | New PNMTC tyres used on buses/lorries |
| 40112001 | New pneumatic tyres of rubber-used on buses and lorries |

| | |
|---|---|
| 44033309 | Others |
| 44039929 | Other |
| 47032290 | Chemical wood pulp - coniferous |
| 47032900 | Bleached or semi-bleached non-coniferous chemical wood pulp |
| 52010013 | Indian cotton of staple length over 24.5 mm (30/32 inches) & AB |
| 52083101 | Lungi, handloom |
| 55032000 | Staple fibres of polyester NT CRD/CMBD |
| 61169909 | Other gloves etc of other textile fibres |
| 61178049 | Other accessories of other fibres |
| 61179000 | Parts of garments, knitted/crochetted |
| 71023100 | Non-industrial diamonds unworked/simply sawn, cleaved or broken |
| 71023901 | Diamond (other than industrial diamond) cut or otherwise worked |
| 71023909 | Others |
| 71031001 | Emeralds, uncut |
| 71039101 | Emeralds, cut |
| 72044100 | Turnings, shavings, chips, milling west, sawdust, fillings, trimmings, & stampings |
| 72044909 | Ferrous waste & scrap - other |
| 72082000 | Flat-rolled products of iron ..... of thickness > 10 mm |
| 72281009 | Others |
| 73089007 | Tubular steel poles for electric transmission and distribution |
| 73269015 | Finished & semi-finished STL forgings, N.E.S. E.G. flanges for studs |
| 74040001 | Waste & scrap of copper |
| 74040002 | Waste and scrap of copper alloys (e.g. brass, bronze, etc.) |
| 74071001 | Electrolytic copper rods or black copper rods (including coils) |
| 76011001 | Aluminium ingots - not alloyed |
| 80011001 | Block tin |
| 80011009 | Anodes cathodes ingots pigs slabs and other primary form |
| 84292000 | Graders and levellers |
| 84719302 | Winchester/hard disc drives |
| 84733001 | Parts & accessories of the machines of heading no. 84.71 |
| 85412900 | Other transistor, other than photosensitive transistor |
| 85421900 | Other monolithic integrated circuits |
| 85451901 | Electrodes of graphite |
| 87149209 | Others |
| 87149307 | Hubs - bicycle free wheels, others |
| 87149309 | Others |
| 91149001 | Other parts for watches |
| 98010003 | Power project |
| 99930002 | Returned goods |

*Source:* Indian Trade Classification, DGCI&S, Calcutta

*Note:* In some cases abbreviations have been used. Researchers interested in complete description may refer to above source.

# 8

# India and SEA: Cooperation in Service Sector

M.C. VERMA

The Southeast Asia covers the ASEAN-seven, it also includes the three countries of Indochina. Out of this the countries of Indonesia, Thailand, Malaysia and Singapore have established themselves as an important economic grouping with fairly close relations with India. The Philippines and Brunei are the other two countries of ASEAN. India as the sectoral dialogue partner of ASEAN has been steadily developing its economic relations with the group, though it has not succeeded in becoming a member of the newly formed ARF (ASEAN Regional Forum) for security cooperation among Asia-Pacific countries. India also has large numbers of world class engineers, doctors, managers, technocrats, academics and skilled labour of all variety. Furthermore, the people of this region are already familiar with the work of high level/skilled man-power from India and have confidence in the abilities of the same. It is in this context that cooperation in service sector between the region and India should be envisaged.

## General

It is necessary to understand the scope of service sector discussions. Services have a huge variety but they can be classified into two major groups for simplicity namely, marketed services of the following kind: (a) Producer services; (b) Distributive services; (c) Communications and (d) Personal services. In the non-marketed services the following are generally included: (i) Health; (ii)Education; (iii) Public welfare; (iv) Public administration, legal and military services. Even this classification is neither universally accepted nor is static. For example, under some definitions public utilities including electricity, water and sewage are also included under services. It is also a fact that some of the non-marketed services of the earlier time are becoming marketable and can be delivered to non-nationals. This includes health, education, legal and even military services since some of them can be transmitted through the telecom network while others can be transported to other countries through the means of personal visiting and short stay, something which has been especially used in the case of computer software aptly called body-shopping. Further, the older style provision of support in the case of emergency or military always existed.

A special feature of trade in services has been lack of disaggregated data on them. In the balance of payment statistics or those of IMF and other international organisations, services get classified as a separate item outside merchandise and form part of the current account statistics. It is however clear that a total of imports or exports of services does not help in any analysis because of the huge variety which is clear from the classification attempted above. This disability is even more pronounced in the case of developing countries and hardly any data is available on the services transactions between India and the SE Asia region, either as individual nation or even as a regional grouping. The only exception is data on tourists exchange where number of tourists visiting India (or those going from India) from several countries can be obtained through trade associations.

The UNCTAD has done commendable service to the developing countries in general in this field and has been able to convince all of them including India of the need for improving data base. However, as on date there is no way disaggregated data on flow to and fro of individual services can be valued in dollar terms for any international comparison. In some ways this is not absolutely crucial for our propose, since we propose to focus on prospects of services trade in the future, something which does not necessarily flow from the poor exchange of such services in the recent past. In fact, the signing of the Uruguay Round Agreement and the start of the WTO (World Trade Organization) from 1st Jan., 1995 is bound to assist liberalisation of services and improve services flow between India and SE-Asia region. Taking the WTO as the water-shed and the fact that all members of ASEAN are already members of WTO, we should all look forward to increased exchanges within ourselves in the short to medium term.

The GATT publications give some statistics on international service transactions. Under the definition of commercial services, GATT provides data on an annual basis and this includes transportation, travel and other private services and income. While providing such data however, GATT does point out that recorded figures on trade in services are subject to significant overall downward bias for several reasons, applicable to developing countries like India and the ASEAN. First, most countries do not report statistics of specific service items. Second, many service transactions simply are not registered. If central bank records are used, this is often the case when any financial intermediaries are employed. In the case of surveys, the coverage on trading establishments is often incomplete. Services transmitted electronically are frequently not registered, specially when such transactions are between affiliates and present multinational firms. Thirdly, in many cases statistics are reported on a net (exports-imports) basis rather than on a gross basis required for our purpose. Finally, many transactions are declassified, e.g., some are registered as income, remittance (transfers) or trade in merchandise rather than as trade in services. Despite these limitations, the recent data compiled by the GATT shows that world exports of commercial services reached one trillion dollars (US) in 1992 and their share in the total exports reached 21 per cent. The growth in exports of commercial services registered in 1992 was as high as 12 per cent compared to only 6 per cent for merchandise.

GATT also compiles the list of leading exporters and importers in the world trade in commercial services. Based on the 1992 data, Singapore was listed as number 12 in the list of exporters and 21 in the list of importers but was on top as far as other countries covered here. Next in rank comes Thailand, both in exports and imports. Philippines comes next in the list of exporters followed by Malaysia, India and Indonesia. The ranking in terms of imports changes with Malaysia following Thailand, followed by Indonesia, India and Philippines. The interesting point is that Singapore exports much more of services than some developed countries like Sweden, Canada, Denmark, Norway or Australia. Similarly, it ranks higher than some developed countries in respect of imports like Denmark, Finland and New Zealand. India's rank and share in imports of commercial services is higher than its corresponding rank and share in merchandise trade. The tiny Sultanate of Brunei does not figure much in the list of traders in commercial services however.

Looking closely at services exports (for 1992) we find that Singapore has a very well diversified services base with shipping, air- travel, professional services, trading, tourism and financial services all contributing to its high rank in exports. Thailand's high ranking is mainly due to tourism and air-travel while that of Philippines is perhaps more due to exports of labour services. Malaysia has good ranking compared to its size, thanks to tourism, air-travel and other services. As against this, India has a relatively balanced portfolio of services including travel, tourism, shipping, labour services, computer software, professional services, financial services and even some social services like health and education.

Looking at the imports picture (1992), Singapore again has a strong appetite for tourism, travel, shipping, financial services, professional services, labour services, communications, etc. Thailand's imports of services is dominated by travel, shipping , communications, professional services, financial services and some social services. The picture about Malaysia is largely similar. As against these, India's imports of services again display a wide range of areas covering practically all the sectors and as per GATT data both India and Indonesia show a substantial deficit in commercial services. On the other hand, Singapore and Philippines have been maintaining substantial surpluses in their trade in commercial services.

**Impact of the New GATS**

Since trade in services has been growing in an explosive manner amongst nations due to revolutionary technical changes, the past patterns of imports and exports of services are not likely to remain valid in the future. This is specially so for our group of countries since liberalization has been accepted almost everywhere and the detailed agreements under the GATS (General Agreement on Trade in Services) are in the process of being finalised under the new WTO. In fact, GATS establishes an entirely new contractual framework for the WTO members, applicable to all the countries under discussions, which contains new concepts including different modes of supply of services across national borders. These possible modes are: supply through cross-border movement, movement of consumers, commercial presence and the presence of natural persons. GATS also provides for such important principles as national treatment and unconditional MFN (Most Favoured Nation) treatment. Of course, specific derogations from the MFN have been permitted, as notified by individual countries. Such derogations would be subject to review and justification after 5 years. All the countries under discussions have made various offers in the GATS negotiations, conditional or unconditional, though the offers may cover only some sectors. In particular, the GATS covers in detail three important services namely, maritime transport services, telecommunications and financial services each of which gets a separate annex covering that service and defining in more precise terms the concepts of provisions involved.

All the countries under discussion have the possibility of getting exemptions from the rigorous commitments envisaged under the GATS which includes possibility of liberalization to a lesser degree and make market access conditional upon measures to assist them in strengthening their respective services sectors, for example, through availability of information networks/distribution channels/access to technology, etc. The position of different countries in this respect differs. For example, Singapore with a strong base in many sectors does not need exemptions to the same extent as other countries under discussions. In any case, the negotiations in the case of maritime transport services, financial services and telecommunications are as yet incomplete. It is difficult to say whether the upcoming Council for Trade in Services would agree to all the exemptions sought by the various countries or whether these will be brought down now or after 5 years. In any case, it is expected that exemptions should not exceed a period of 10 years and would have to be negotiated again in subsequent trade liberalizing rounds.

Since there are 96 schedules of specific commitments and since most of the offers (61) accompany an MFN exemption lists which vary widely, it is difficult to assess how these would affect the services trade between India and the ASEAN. The impact of specific commitments on market access and national treatment will be a function of the extent to which (i) services sectors were included in individual schedules; (ii) the four modes of supply are included; (iii) terms of market access and national treatment in the transactions listed are limited or qualified; (iv) requirements for an "economic needs test" are included without specifying objective criteria and (v) the number of MFN exemptions. Because of the great variety and complexity of such discussions and commitments, it is necessary to look at existing domestic regulatory frameworks and assess whether each country has introduced legislative changes to implement the commitments it has undertaken. Furthermore, since disaggregated statistical data on trade in services through different modes of supply is not yet available, a meaningful assessment of the impact of the Uruguay Round Agreement on the countries under discussions here is not feasible at this stage.

Despite the problems mentioned, it is a fact that GATS extends the scope of multi-lateral trade rights and obligations to cover measures affecting such diverse aspects as FDI, professional qualifications and the movement of persons and electronic data movement across national frontiers, thus making these items a subject matter for future trade commitments under GATS or other agreements like the AFTA. Reference can be made here to the annex on telecommunications which includes a new "users" right to ensure that enterprises benefiting from market access commitments have the right to plug into national telecommunications systems. This is relevant to our group of countries. Similarly, GATS covers travel, transportations and other services out of which the earlier ICAO agreement was able to adjudicate only on air-traffic rights. GATS also has an understanding of commitments on financial services subscribed to by the OECD countries which should be finalised like the other two areas of maritime transport and telecommunications before July 1995. In this area, the majority of commitments involve commercial presence mode of supply, reflecting the desire of countries to attract investment rather than have services supplied from abroad. Finally, the commitments included in the GATS about natural persons' movement are on a horizontal basis, i.e., relating to the position of an individual person within a firm (such as executives and expert technicians) and not to specific economic sectors. These general commitments make it difficult to assess their value for our group of countries but they are still very important in the process of liberalization of movements of natural persons, especially for countries with volumes of skilled, technical and high level manpower like India and Singapore.

The countries under discussions have no doubt taken the Uruguay round negotiations very seriously and have actively participated in them. Under the continuing sub-committee on services of the new WTO the negotiating groups on mari-time transport, natural persons' movement and telecommunications are continuing to work with active participation of our group of countries. Our group has also participated actively in the discussion on financial services even though none of the countries except Singapore has any sizeable revealed advantage in them. This is reasonable, even logical in the context of services acquiring a higher and higher share in each country's GDP. As of 1992, Singapore's service sector output had already reached 65 per cent while that of Thailand was close to 50 per cent. Philippines' share of services output was close to 45 per cent while Malaysia, Indonesia and India had their services sector output close to 40 per cent and in any case higher than either the primary or secondary sectors of the economy. There has been a specially interesting transformation for the countries of Thailand, Philippines, Malaysia and Indonesia whose export success so far had been almost entirely based on low-wage manufacturing. In fact, the people of the region are discovering that the low-wage, low-skilled jobs are usually found in manufacturer's production lines while services are continuing to go upscale both in terms of wages and skill levels. The transformation has obviously gone farthest in Singapore which has been able to open up its service industry to foreign competition as much as its manufacturing industries. Other countries are now waking up to the need for liberalising their service industries as well to make them world class competitive and on the face of it, there appear to be complementarities between India on the one side and the ASEAN on the other to take advantage of relative strengths of each for mutual benefit.

**Indian Scene**

The famous NRI economist, Dr. Jagdish Bhagwati had in his research found that the developing countries have potential comparative advantages in the services sector. Also most services use a lot of labour, barring financial services which use relatively large capital, which is surplus in India both at the unskilled low end and the skilled upper end. Theoretically, therefore India has potential comparative advantages in most services provided it improves the productivity of its labour, something dependent on the pattern of development followed including competition both from domestic and international sources. Since India has been opening up significantly since July 1991— more in manufacturing than in services— it can start developing the comparative advantages now. Interestingly even in a study of competitiveness of US services, Mc Kinsey had found that it was not the volumes of capital which mattered in the competitiveness of US in retail banking but the organization of labour which mattered. This implies the necessity of taking actions to improve labour productivity in the entire services sector and liberalisation of various regulations to enable competition to be provided in each sector.

India has been providing services to most developing countries in the last few decades which includes all professional services, computer and related services, R&D services, various consultancy services, printing and publishing services, postal services, telecom services, audio-visual services, construction services, educational and health services, environmental services, tourism, recreational and cultural services, transport services and even financial services. It is however, clear by now that it has not excelled in any of them. Part of the reason lies in the Government interventions in practically all the services directly or indirectly and massive body of arcane rules or regulations for the same. Thus we have the funny situation of individual Indians being highly valued for their services but no worthwhile firms or companies providing world class services. As the ASEAN countries have grown rich and achieved high rates of economic growth, they look forward to developing and obtaining quality services. There are doubters in the Indian Government and even academica about the potential of India's services sector and this pessimism is not different from what was called export-pessimism, relevant to goods sector. Since human capital formation has not been attended to in India as seriously as in most ASEAN countries, its literacy level has been lower, the average years of the schooling also lower and the average skill formation deficient despite the fact that Indian workmen are great improvisers and can survive in very difficult situations. It has been noticed that in comparison to the NICs, India did not make its labour efficient through intensive use of capital but with the coming of competitive multinationals and significant capital amounts through FDI, this is also changing. India has in any case, three basic advantages namely, knowledge of English, computer literacy and mastery of mathematics. Various international companies have relocated accounting, computer programming, software development, insurance claims adjustment and other labour intensive work involving English, mathematics and programming to India in the last couple of years. This may not be significant compared to Singapore but is nevertheless an important vote of confidence in the capability of India service providers.

The Indian Government has already started an export promotion capital goods scheme for the services sector wef 1st April 1993, permitting import of capital equipment by specified categories of professionals, hotels and restaurants and other services providers at a nominal duty. The government has also taken other steps to open up hitherto closed sectors to competition like banking, higher education, telecommunications, courier services, advertising, TV transmission, franchising, value added telecommunications, energy distribution, shipping and transport, ports, roads and inland water transport, rail transport, some insurance services, tourism, pipelines, etc. Some studies in India indicate its revealed comparative advantage mainly in labour related services but these studies were based on pre-92 data and therefore need to be reviewed in the light of new developments.

Some of the revolutionary changes already set in motion relate to shipping and transport sector. The regulatory changes in the case of shipping refer to almost free acquisition of all kinds of ships except crude tankers, sale of ships for further trading/ scrapping to Indian companies within India or abroad and encouragement to improve their efficiency. These include steps to time charter out to foreign shipping companies, acquisition of vessels by charter-cum demise method, foreign exchange permissions for ship repairs, etc., relaxation of carriage laws for five years for container traffic, leasing of unused and new facilities like dry docks, issue of dedicated berths to private companies, permission to use private mobile equipment, advanced reservation of berths, priority berthing and other practices to improve labour productivity. Similarly, government vessels have been handed over to some private operators in inland waterways transport and private sector permitted to invest in new jetties, crafts and other facilities, etc. In the road sector, toll roads have been permitted in almost all the states and multi-modal transport facilitated. All India permits for tourist transport operators have been introduced to by-pass state regulations, foreign operators have been invited to build roads and bridges on BOT basis of international standards and State Governments have been delegated more powers and work to facilitate quick decisions. Similarly, large number of domestic and foreign proposals are under process in the development of ports facilities and government is examining equipment leasing, terminal leasing and even management leasing to private companies interested in sharing revenue and profits with the ports.

In the financial sector, government has already opened up banking and capital markets to private operators, both Indian and foreign, under certain conditions. Recently the minimum capital requirement for opening bank branches in the country has also been reduced considerably. The government has already taken various measures to ensure safety of the financial sector and thus there is no fear for either Indian banks or insurance companies to be wiped out if opened up to foreign competition, especially from the US. Indian regulatory measures are certainly considerable but then even countries like the US and our ASEAN friends also have several kinds of restrictions on foreign insurance and banking companies. Some Indian counterparts operate profitably in some of the ASEAN countries and have experience of those markets, it is felt that India can do well in these areas, if there is mutual removal of restrictions in this sector. In the most recent round of clearances, the Reserve Bank of India has already permitted some more companies of ASEAN to set up shops in India. The same would be true of Indian mutual funds and other capital market operators who have acquired a lot of experience in the newly liberalised set up in the country in the last three years including that of how to handle financial scams. A few years back Indian banks abroad were in deep trouble and were losing money practically everywhere. This has been reversed in 1993-94 and the Indian banks should be making sizeable operating profits in 1994-95. The reasons for the losses and the steps taken for coming out of the same lie in poor or good management and with the opening up of the sector to competition the public sector banks had no option but to tighten their supervision abroad and learnt how to make use of the latest technology for their benefit. Computerisation of branches has therefore proceeded at a fast pace and provisioning for the losses has been done without waiting for long. The Ministry of Finance has also found some money for the loss-making public sector banks to improve their capital adequacy and insist on efficiency improvements.

As regards insurance sector, the government has yet to take decisions on Malhotra Committee recommendations. This Committee has recommended wide ranging liberalisation including privatisation or 50 per cent government holding of existing government owned insurance companies and allow foreign companies through the joint venture route. It also recommended strong regulatory framework to supervise such companies. Though, India is relatively poorly served in insurance, the insurance density being only 1.2 in recent years. Life insurance reached even the small man in the remote and rural areas through the government directed expansion of Life Insurance Corporation of India. The experience of dealing with the small consumers and the small policies is certainly an advantage for Indian companies and in fact, they have not lost money abroad where they have operated, e.g., Singapore, Thailand and Malaysia. It is expected that when the ASEAN countries open up their markets further Indian companies would be able to extend themselves there both directly and through joint ventures, which will be helpful in developing the expertise of the local insurance companies as well. So far, ASEAN countries have been served mainly by insurance companies from the West which may have provided them new technology for the sector but not necessarily training in human resources required for this specialization.

There has been liberalization in the audio-visual sector also with government permitting producers of software and increased access of private sector to the government channels. Advent of Star TV and other satellite based TV transmissions have also been helpful in opening up this sector. Government has also opened up to foreign motion pictures and videos. Such films may receive certification of import under certain conditions and prohibition against dubbing foreign films into local languages has been abolished. Foreign film companies can now set up offices in

India for importing and distributing films and videos. Competition from foreign films has helped Indian producers but Indian films, especially Hindi, were always having a huge market abroad. Such films were welcomed in all the ASEAN countries except for Singapore which follows a very tight certification/censoring policy. It is expected that as ASEAN countries open up their markets further to audio-visual products, India can export a considerable larger quantity to each of them. This could be in the form of films, videos, serials, news, audio-cassettes of various formats, etc. The on-going liberalization in this field will diversify Indian audio-visual products and make them available to various audience both in India and abroad. Furthermore, new training institutions to deal with TV software, multi-media and other audio-visuals production and processing have come up in the private sector to meet the exploding demand. These training centres would certainly be useful to the ASEAN members except possibly Singapore.

While there have been no new deregulatory efforts in the case of newspapers and print media, a number of foreign papers have developed linkages with Indian newspapers. This has happened especially in the case of economic journals, all in English language. The quality of economic journalism has also improved considerably due to exploding audience numbers and due to competition among economic journals which cover all streams of economic activity from macro economic to habitat and construction. Though the ASEAN nations also have access to English language, India can surely help ASEAN in improving journals through human resource development and other linkages. The same cannot however be said about trade in books where India should have developed a big advantage, what with huge market and English speaking people. The quality of printing and publishing has to improve sufficiently to attract foreign interest in making India, a base for printing and publishing as it has done at Singapore. However, the ongoing competition in the sector should help in improving the quality and make it world class competitive. In the meantime, India can learn from the experience of Singapore where wages rates have gone up considerably, and go for joint ventures and other tie-ups.

In the telecommunications sector, the monopoly of government owned Department of Telecom is being dismantled both for basic and value added services. Private providers of various services have already been competing for different permissions to cover the entire country and are likely to bring large new capacities so badly required in a country with the lowest telephone density in the group of countries under discussion. However, it does not mean that niche markets for some services have not been developed through TCIL, a consultancy firm, and other companies. In fact, India has also surplus capacity on its satellite transmission for telecommunications which can be useful to ASEAN countries. Furthermore, Indian postal services are almost world class competitive and liberalization of courier service has meant better services, especially for corporates. Large number of new courier service operators are now competing with government owned courier services and more competition is on the way. This may be of some interest to under-serviced countries in the ASEAN region and India could provide human resource development facilities for the purpose.

There has been liberalization in the environmental services, education services and health related services as well. While Singapore has excellent services on both these accounts, other countries in the region can perhaps afford to learn from Indian experience. Similarly, Indian higher education facilities though already in use by ASEAN nationals, are likely to be further developed for higher quality . The government has already deregulated the higher education sector though so far no new private universities or colleges have come up. A number of training institutions for computer programming, medical and engineering education, audio-visual and other sectors are already existing in the private sector and are getting expanded. So far, the ASEAN nationals were encouraged to go to the UK or the USA for higher studies at rather high cost. On the other hand, if world class universities from Europe or America develop formal linkages for providing dual degrees through Indian higher education institutions, these should be welcome to the ASEAN nationals. In any case, they are already familiar with the Indian higher education scene.

In the case of travel and tourism the on-going liberalization now encourages the private airlines within the country and private hotels, tour operators and other services. The Government monopoly on internal travel has gone and the foreign companies have been allowed to increase their services to India on reciprocal basis. Unfortunately, GATS did not cover air traffic rights and the ICAO supported agreements are still restrictive and favour links with the West rather than South-East Asia. It is necessary to redress this historical imbalance in view of much higher growth of air traffic in the Asia-Pacific region now and also in future. The airlines of Singapore, Malaysia and Thailand already have very lucrative connections with India and are likely to be expanded soon. The existing capacities of India owned airlines are not however, sufficient to increase their coverage of ASEAN but the Government of India should be ready for unilateral liberalization with some friendly countries which should help the ASEAN members with their own expanding airlines. Furthermore, there should be linkages in chartering of tourists for India especially because of its Buddhist and Muslim base and Indian tour operators can team up with some countries of the ASEAN for developing common tourist packages.

**ASEAN Services Industries: Prospects for Co-operation**

As mentioned earlier, ASEAN economies have been growing very fast except for the Philippines but even that economy has now picked up. Each of these economies is now engaged in deepening of the service sector industries so that they also become more efficient and improve their international rankings. It has also been mentioned earlier that the current co-operation in the sector between India and the ASEAN countries has been rather small (except possibly Singapore) but this is also a reflection of the overall inadequacy of the two-way economic relations. For example, the total Indo-ASEAN trade crossed $ 1 billion only in 1990 and has been dominated by bulk commodities like edible oil, chemicals, coal, fertilizers, gems and jewellery, marine and agricultural products.

A survey made by RIS in 1993 on Indo-ASEAN economic relations could cite only a few items of existing co-operation in the services sector. In the field of electrical goods, an Indian company is venturing in a big way into power transmission and other projects in Indonesia which might involve some services components. Another Indian telephone company has a joint venture in Singapore, whose initial thrust was rural telecommunications in Indonesia, Malaysia and Vietnam. Similarly, there has been co-operation in the field of export credit insurance with Malaysia, Singapore and Indonesia. Tata Energy Research Institute (TERI) had conducted a study on energy conservation in hotel management, of relevance to ASEAN. Some other items of co-operation in tourism sector have also been mentioned in this survey, but tourism sub-sector is being covered elsewhere.

In the general field of human resource development, there were several efforts by India at providing training to the railway personnel from Indonesia, small industry personnel from Philippines and implementation of a quality system based on ISO 9000 standard in Indonesia, high-tech tool-room work with Malaysia, training materials on information technology to Singapore, computerised maintenance management system to Indonesia and modular training programmes for energy managers, auditors and trainers of ASEAN. CSIR in India has also provided support to Thailand in technology development in various fields, while another regional research laboratory is co-operating with the Malaysia Palm Oil Research Development Board. In the case of construction, there have been instances of co-operation with Malaysian railways as well as with that of Indonesia. However, taking all the instances together we get the impression that the current linkages have been rather marginal and there is much greater scope for the future.

Apart from the RIS study, various organisations and economists as well as economic journalists have made their own studies covering one or more services subsectors focussing on future prospects. We may start with human resource development. Malaysia already had a twinning system of linking local higher educational institutions with foreign institutions for preparing a student for final year examination abroad. Malaysia as well as other ASEAN countries, except Singapore, tried to develop their higher education system on local languages, which was not found to be the most effective for international competition. Malaysia has already reverted to greater use of English and has the ambition of setting up branch campuses of well-known private institutions of London or elsewhere and attract ASEAN students to come to Malaysia rather than go to North America or Europe. Asian level institutions like the Asian Institute of Technology are not very many and since India already has a large number of famous educational institutions of its own, there are various possibilities of co-operation. With some foreign universities setting up joint ventures in India while others may set-up elsewhere in the ASEAN, there could be sizeable exchange of students and faculty.

In the case of publishing and printing also, while the existing exchange is marginal, a large number of printing units in India are coming up with the latest technologies. With Singapore currency having appreciated, a lot of printing which used to go to Singapore could now be diverted to India in collaboration with Singapore parties. The existing co-operation in software development, audio-video programmes development and media could go up fast with the coming of satellite transmissions, satellite based printing, publishing and greater use of English where India has a comparative advantage. The ancient cultural links between India and ASEAN should come in handy in this regard, since the variety of Indian culture allows for linkages with practically all countries in ASEAN.

In the field of air transport and system it is now clear that Asia is going to be the biggest air travel market in the 21st century and ASEAN countries would have a significant part of that. Already Singapore as the largest air traffic hub has developed capacities for handling over 24 million passengers annually. Thailand, Indonesia, Singapore and even India all are projected to grow fast in the coming years. Since tourists have discovered new places of interest in the region, tourism and related air travel is expected to grow as fast as before but an important change is that out-ward travel from the region is also expected to explode. With current account restrictions in India almost insignificant, Indian tourists are also likely to go out in large numbers, along-side those of ASEAN countries. It is, however, necessary to ensure that visa and another immigration formalities are reduced to ensure that the potential is realized.

In the case of mari-time transport, it is difficult to say how quickly India and ASEAN countries would develop the same since it would depend more on growth of merchandise trade within the region. It is, however, useful to note that Indian shipping industry has liberalized recently and is hopefully moving towards higher efficiency. India has a large fleet compared to other ASEAN countries, barring possibly Singapore, but the inter-change between ASEAN and India has been marginal. Singapore based facilities are however, being used by Indian vessels also including for repairs. In view of appreciation of Singapore currency and opening up of India, it's likely that more shipping facilities would get concentrated in India, especially if merchandise trade between India and ASEAN really moves fast. In this regard, Singapore's liberalization initiatives have already yielded rich dividends while other countries of ASEAN have yet to liberalize their mari-time sector significantly.

Financial services have also been exploding in the ASEAN and India has already liberalized significantly. While Thailand got its stock market in 1974, the new stock market in Jakarta opened only in 1992. In contrast, Indian capital markets have experience of almost a century and though they may be behind Singapore currently, they are expanding rather fast. An IMF study in 1991 found that like India ASEAN countries also had significant restrictions in financial sector and consumers were poorly served by monopolistic practices and lack of competition. Share processing takes a long time in a number of countries and a powerful Security's Commission is yet to develop in several countries. With the 1992 stock market scam behind it, Indian capital markets and their regulators have a lot to share with others in the region. But a country like Thailand now has significant new services like use of ATMs for trading mutual funds. Home mortgages were underdeveloped in several countries but mortgage growth is exploding almost everywhere along-side growth of credit cards and other new financial instruments as global. Since Indian banks as well as insurance companies already have experience of ASEAN and are in the process of modernizing themselves, significant prospects for co-operation should be available in the near future. Note should be made, in this connection, of the ambition of Thailand to make Bangkok as a regional financial centre in addition to the existing centre at Singapore. However, Bombay is already a significant financial centre with an increasing regional as well as global reach. If paperless trading of shares get implemented in India, e.g., through the National Stock Exchange (NSE) and otherwise the foreign institutional investors do not lose their interest in Indian economy, a number of ASEAN countries would be able to make use of India/Bombay-based financial service facilities. In return India could make use of Singapore based facilities for deepening its financial system.

It is not possible to survey every sub-sector under services in this brief study and try to locate items of possible co-operation but mention must be made of tele-communications, environmental services and even retail trading. In most recent tenders for Indian telecommunications, companies from Singapore and Malaysia have participated. Even Philippines has significantly liberalised telecommunications sector and has allowed foreign firms from Singapore, Thailand and UK. There is no reason why more exchange of telecom services would not take place in the near future between India and ASEAN. Similarly, while Singapore has strong technology and environmental services companies of its own as well as those of trans-nationals, the same is beginning to happen in India with tightening environmental regulations. Since other ASEAN countries have already been suffering from severe problems of pollution due to very fast industrialisation and rise of vehicular traffic, significant opportunities of exchanging expertise of each other exist. Finally, retail trading is something which comes naturally to Indian and Chinese population, both of which are active in the ASEAN countries and India. However, modern large scale retailing is rare in India as well as other countries though Singapore and now Thailand is getting experience of such large outfits. It is time for India and other ASEAN countries to also open up their retail trading sector and develop efficiency in this area. India can also learn from the experience of other ASEAN countries which have built up powerful brands in such significant areas as fast foods, hotels and airlines. Now that India has improved its trade mark legislation and developed brand awareness, experience of other ASEAN countries and joint ventures with the same would be useful to Indian retail trade, hotels, fast food joints and other consumer products.

**Conclusions**

India has significant number of NRIs already working in each of the ASEAN countries who are distributed in different professions and economic sectors. A few of them have already learnt from fact liberalization of many ASEAN economies and developed niche markets for themselves in the host countries which could be transferred to India. This significant pool of human resources is already making its presence felt via Singapore and Hong Kong. In the development of Indian infrastructure through private sector, now well under way, several companies of the region are already involved. Many of them are interested in bringing not only their expertise/experience of infrastructure projects but also capital and this should be certainly welcome to Indian policy-makers and Indian markets. The already existing links in air travel, tourism, software, media, printing and publishing, telecommunication, have chances to become bigger and deeper. Unfortunately, it is difficult to place a figure on the projected increase in these services sector exchanges because of poor data base. However, even this could be a point of co-operation since Indian statisticians are known to be rather good.

Whether the two-way co-operation and exchanges grow at a good rate or whether they explode, would depend on India's relations with ASEAN as sectoral dialogue partner and whether India can join the new grouping APEC. In recent discussions India has perhaps been told to wait for a couple of years before compete for APEC membership, which is certainly disliked by a number of Indian trade analysts and policy-makers. Since the centre of economic gravity of the global system is shifting towards Asia, there is no way India can avoid improving and deepening its relations with ASEAN and other nations of the Southeast Asia. This would include the three Indo-China countries out of which Vietnam is already growing very fast while the other may follow the Vietnam's growth path soon. Each of these countries have had close political and economic relations with India in the last couple of decades and is expected to join ASEAN. It is therefore, likely that India may have better opportunity of co-operation with them as well. Again, it is difficult to put a number at this stage since India is not an exporter of capital and in some ways is competing for the same global capital as other countries of the South East Asia region. A lot will therefore, depend on the pace of Indian structural reforms and its ability to hold the attention of TNCs from Europe, North America or Japan. It will also depend on whether the momentum of liberalization exhibited in the merchandise trade sector is carried forward in India to the service sector. It will suffice to say at this stage that the prospects for such liberalization are good, and to that extent, following on the GATS, India and ASEAN can extend and deepen their service sector relationship in the medium term.

# 9

# Financial Reforms in India and the ASEAN

V.L. Rao

Several developing countries, including India and the ASEAN countries, have undertaken reform and liberalization of their financial sectors as part of their overall economic liberalization process. Most developing countries till the 1980s had highly regulated financial sectors. Some common characteristics of the controlled regimes included: restrictions on interest rates, controls on domestic credit, high reserve requirements, segmented financial markets, underdeveloped money and capital markets, and tight exchange control systems. The need for financial sector reforms and liberalization arose from the capital requirements for funding developmental projects from domestic savings and external savings, and also from the fact that generally there was over-regulation and control of their financial sectors.

The general criticism against the developing countries' financial sectors is that they are highly 'repressed', i.e., the governments of the respective countries heavily controlled and intervened in the domestic financial system and interest rates and credit allocation are highly regulated.

However, the experience of several developing countries, and even of the industrial countries, has shown that prudential supervision and regulation of the financial markets is not only necessary but also beneficial for maintaining public confidence in the financial instruments and markets, and ensuring systemic stability.

In this context, the experiences of individual countries will be of interest to others in strengthening the financial service sectors on their own and in cooperation with other countries.

The purpose of the present study is to discuss the liberalization and reform measures undertaken in the financial service sector by India and select ASEAN countries and suggest various possible avenues of cooperation between India and the ASEAN in the sector. India has been a sectoral dialogue partner of the ASEAN since 1992. The sectors include trade, joint ventures, tourism, science and technology, and human resource development[1]. In December 1995, India has been accepted by the ASEAN as a full dialogue partnership. Therefore, it can be envisaged that cooperation between India and the ASEAN will be strengthened in various sectors including the financial service sector.

### Liberalization and Reform

The financial and capital markets in different developing countries are at different stages of maturity, depth and sophistication. Financial liberalization and reform in different countries is varied but some common characteristics are :

- interest rates have been deregulated;
- direct controls on credit have been reduced or eliminated;
- entry barriers have been reduced for domestic as well as foreign financial institutions;
- exchange rates have been made more flexible;
- exchange controls have been relaxed; and
- domestic securities markets have been opened to foreign investors.

There is hardly any country which has gone in for total deregulation of its financial markets. Most countries, as is the case with the situation obtaining in the developed countries, have set in place prudential supervision and control, dictated by the consideration that a fully deregulated financial system gives rise to speculative activities and also makes the conduct of monetary policy and balance of payments management difficult.

### Interest Rates and Priority Sector Lending

Regulatory measures on commercial banks such as control of interest rates and directed credit to selected sectors have been motivated by the individual countries' objective of providing low cost finance to encourage investment, particularly in priority sectors.

Some of the consequences of directed credit were: adverse impact on allocative efficiency; low rates of return on investments leading to banks' having large non-performing loans; limited competition in provision of financial services; and stunted development of new services and instruments.

Several countries have liberalized interest rates and reduced of eliminated overall direct controls on bank lending. After liberalization, in most countries, the nominal interest rates rose sufficiently, to make real interest rates positive. However, individual countries, while maintaining the general trend of liberalization, introduced changes from time to time to meet specific objectives.

For example, in 1990, most subsidized credit programmes in Indonesia were abolished including small investment credit, permanent working capital credit, and all other credits for small scale enterprises, except small credit programme for cooperatives. Also banned with this policy was credit for university students. In place of the banned credit programmes for small scale enterprise, the monetary authority required all banks to extend 20 per cent of their credit portfolio to the small-scale companies with certain stipulations.

In 1992-93 Bank Indonesia gradually eased domestic liquidity. The domestic interest rates were brought down. Following this the three-month time deposit rate came down. However, the spread between the deposit and lending rates widened.

In Thailand the bank rate and the refinancing rate on finance companies promissory notes arising from business in agriculture, manufacturing and commerce were reduced by one per cent in 1993, taking the underlying monetary conditions into account and to serve as a signal to financial institutions to lower their lending rates.

The target for priority sector lending (which includes agriculture and small-scale sector) in India is 40 per cent of gross bank credit plus an additional 10 per cent of total advances towards export credit ( agriculture has a sub-target of 18 per cent).

As part of the reform process of the Indian financial sector, the number of lending categories was brought down from over 50 in 1989 to only 3 in December 1993.

The minimum lending rate was brought down, in four stages, from 20 per cent in October 1991 to 15 per cent in October 1993. The high lending rate in 1991 was justified on the grounds of high inflation and the deterioration in the overall macro-economic situation. With improvement on both the fronts, the reduction in interest rates was effected. With effect from March 1, 1994 the minimum lending rate of scheduled commercial banks on term loans of three years and above was lowered from 15 per cent to 14 per cent. In October 1994, lending rates of scheduled commercial banks for credit limits of over Rs. 0.2 million were freed. However, rates have been prescribed for credit limits below this level to protect small borrowers.

As can be expected from its extremely open nature, Singapore's interest rates are dependent mainly on the US interest rates and domestic demand for finance. Singapore, however, uses interest rates for fine-tuning of its economy, e.g., in 1990-91 interest rates were brought down when its growth rate fell.

Because of excess liquidity, interest rates in Malaysia moved downwards during 1993. These lower rates were envisaged to maintain interest differentials which otherwise would widen further and make capital inflows unmanageable. As a result, the fixed deposit rates of both the commercial banks and finance companies also declined during 1993.

Thus it can be seen that individual countries have been taking specific measures for specific objectives though the general trend has been towards financial liberalization.

**Rural Finance**

A controlled financial regime means inefficient allocation of resources. However, in several developing countries, the expansion of branch-network in rural areas and lending at concessional rates to priority sectors such as village and small-scale units have helped in fostering banking culture and reduced reliance on unorganized (informal) sector. Though priority-sector lending usually meant that recovery rate is very low, there are some success stories which could be strengthened and adapted by other countries.

Commercial banks have traditionally set up branches in urban areas catering to the manufacturing and service sectors. It is after nationalization of banks in several Asian countries that, as a social objective, these banks were directed to open branches in rural areas. For example, two-thirds of increase in branches of all Indian public sector banks (from 7,015 in 1969 the year of nationalization of banks, to 60,650 at end-June 1992) was in rural areas. The important contribution of the rural branch network is the availability of financial services in the rural areas which were earlier dependent on informal finance, e.g., on money-lenders practising usury. However, over time, rural banking has been characterized with problems such as leakages, loans not being given to the most needy, non-recovery of loans, etc.[2]

A success story often cited in the area of rural banking is that of the Grameen Bank of Bangladesh. The Grameen Bank was set up in 1983. Its branches increased from 86 in 1983 to 823 in 1991, and loans and advances increased from TK 14 million to TK 2,133 million during this period. By 1994 the number of branches increased to 1,045 (in 35,000 villages) with 2 million borrowers. The volume of loans was $ 385 million. Financial services are brought to the target borrowers by field workers who go to villages, help arrange groups of five "like-minded" prospective borrowers; and train them in the Grameen Bank procedures. The groups are organized into centres each with an elected officer. Those deemed viable are recommended for loans by the bank worker, who also disburses the loan and collects the payments during weekly meetings.[3]

The bank has a repayment rate of over 98 per cent. The reasons for the high recovery rate are the appropriate system of identifying viable projects, and proper monitoring of the loan disbursal and recovery.

The other developing countries where this concept has been replicated include Bolivia, Burkina Faso, Colombia, Guinea, Indonesia, Kenya,Malaysia, Mali, Malawi, Nepal, Pakistan, Peru, the Philippines, Sri Lanka and Zambia.

Rural banking in individual countries, however, is beset with several constraints such as inadequate capital base and lack of experience in operation of rural branches. One of the objectives of the first Indo-Nepal joint venture bank, the Nepal-SBI Bank Ltd., is that the State Bank of India (SBI), which has experience in rural banking, would develop the same in Nepal. Rural and agricultural borrowers in Nepal do not easily avail of formal credit because of complicated lending procedures and unavailability of loans of time.

Another important point regarding small borrowers is that in addition to finance, they require a package of services including management, skills, marketing, etc. For example, recent gains in agricultural production in Nepal have been ascribed to expanded acreage of cultivation rather than higher productivity. Extension units lacked coordination with financial institutions and lagged in teaching farmers the use of modern production technology and facilities that could be obtained through credit.[4]

The select examples show that the experience of rural banking is quite varied as between countries and countries could learn from each other's experience.

**Commercial Banking**

Cooperation in this area would include: (i) assisting projects; (ii) setting up joint venture banks; (iii) opening of branches in each other's territory, exchange of information, e.g., relating to trade and investment opportunities, creditworthiness of clients, particularly through computerized telecommunication network, (v) training of personnel in specialized fields such as trade, financing, international banking, etc., and (vi) holding of seminars and conferences to discuss banking issues of common interest[5].

**Financial Derivatives**

Financial institutions in many of the developing countries have not acquired the expertise to handle new instruments in the international financial markets such as swaps, forward rate arrangements and options, now referred to as financial derivatives.

The reasons why the developing countries did not utilize international bond markets in a big way in the past are :

(a) the easy availability of concessional aid through bilateral and multilateral channels;

(b) the more stringent requirements of creditworthiness in bond markets compared with syndicated loans. (An oft-repeated example is that the creditworthiness of agents issuing bonds has to be established with the Belgian dentist for him/her to invest in the bonds.)

(c) availability of bank loans for general purpose uses rather than specific uses.

Lessard and Williamson suggested that the little use of the exploding swap markets by the developing countries may in part be due to a lack of interest on their part. This does not seem to be an adequate explanation. The more appropriate reasons are that the developing countries are not fully aware of the complexity of the emerging markets and are not fully equipped with the expertise to participate more actively in these markets. Secondly, developing countries may be considered high-risk counterparties.

What is required is analysis of the experience of individual countries with regard to the new financial instruments and financial engineering and draw the lessons especially for the developing countries.

One way of developing this expertise is through the operations of the branches of the banks of individual countries in foreign countries. The experience of Indian banks abroad, e.g., in comparison with other international banks, that the former have developed some expertise in the new international financial instruments, but the branches often operated in areas of corporate finance and trade finance without following prudential norms. Also, they have been keen on entering high-risk areas like futures and options which require a large capital base. Instead, they should develop niche areas such as new forms of trade financing, e.g., financing offshore trade and financing trade in third countries in collaboration with export- import banks and export credit guarantee institutions[6].

These new financial instruments have proliferated in international capital markets primarily to facilitate hedging against risks, e.g., hedges for export receivables. However, derivatives have been used for speculative purposes by some financial institutions resulting in huge losses.

Financial innovations do not normally reduce risk but redistribute them. The objective of short-term gains may lead to overlooking of credit quality . For example, Kashima Oil, a Japanese firm, lost US $ 1.5 billion in trading in foreign exchange derivatives. The company entered into a large number of forward contracts to buy US dollars. When the currency moved against it, the company was rolling over losses instead of making provision for loss.

Another example is the US $ 6 billion loss in currency-trading by Malaysia's Central Bank in 1992 and 1993. The bulk of the losses arose from forward contracts brought by the currency traders of Bank Negara on the assumption that the British pound would stay in the European Exchange Rate Mechanism (ERM) in 1992. However, the significant changes in the ERM in 1992 showed how difficult it is to predict exchange-rate changes.

The most recent example is that of the collapse of the Barings Bank which underlines the need for streamlining the monitoring system within individual banks and prudential supervision of the financial institutions.

If companies are interlocked in a derivatives contract, default by one affects the other companies resulting in "systemic risk", i.e., the whole financial system will be adversely affected.

The experience with financial derivatives shows that they need to be handled with care, as they can be used both for limiting as well as taking risks. The above examples show how miscalculation is possible even in cases of attempts to limit risks. Use of derivatives for risk-taking would be even a more difficult task.

If it is asserted that 'derivatives are not the problem' but 'risk-management is the problem'. Those who consider that the problem is with the derivatives themselves would favour tight regulations on them. Those who consider that risk management is the problem suggest alternatives such as seeking outside help by firms for risk-management. The latter is neither a panacea nor tight regulation, the only solution. Prudential regulation of the markets coupled with prudential self-regulation by the market participants themselves will be needed to meet the adverse impact of the derivatives on individual companies and on the financial system. In this context, the long-standing demand of the developing countries to convene an international conference on money and finance needs to reiterated. Such a conference could suggest ways to stabilize the world financial system.

Cooperation among regulators can take the forms of exchange of information, and harmonization of standards. The objective is to limit the use of derivatives to hedging activities and prevent trading of derivatives for speculative purposes. It is necessary to relate derivatives with actual goods and underlying transactions to avoid speculation.

In Malaysia, priority is given to financial innovation and modernization of financial markets. The country is preparing the legal and institutional infrastructure for trading in financial derivatives (i.e. stock index and interest rate futures) at the Kuala Lumpur Futures Market (a wholly-owned subsidiary of the Kuala Lumpur Commodities Exchange) and proposed the Kuala Lumpur Options and Financial Futures Exchange[7].

In Thailand, the government would act as a guiding hand in the development of the market which includes the establishment of an over-the-counter (OTC) and a futures market. Mutual Funds in Thailand are not allowed transacting in derivatives. The government is cautious that the derivatives do not lead to systemic risk. To start with, it proposes to allow futures and options that relate to actual goods and underlying transactions.

From the above discussion, it can be concluded that it is better, at least for the developing countries to stress the linking of derivatives to actual goods and underlying transactions to control speculation. The huge losses suffered by some countries in dealing with financial derivatives are indicative of the extent of damage, that can be expected if derivatives are misused.

**Development Banking**

Funding of projects may require active participation of development financial institutions (DFIs) in individual countries and regional development banks. Regional projects may be set up in specific countries due to non-economic reasons, though economic criteria would have suggested the setting up of a project in another member country in the region catering to the whole region.

Many regional projects did not succeed due to lack of proper feasibility studies, lack of information and administrative delays. For example, ASEAN had schemes such as the ASEAN Industrial Projects (AIP) and ASEAN Industrial Complementation (AIC) the former for creating new projects and the latter, to promote complementarity among the existing projects. AIP projects did not succeed because they were implemented without proper feasibility studies. Problems arose in respect of location, infrastructure, availability of raw materials and labour, etc.

The AIC packages were intended to succeed, while the AIP did not. Even in the AIC packages several problems arose, e.g., the requirement of at least four members' participation in each package. To avoid this problem, in 1981 ASEAN Industrial Joint

Venture (AIJV) proposal was introduced under which even two or three ASEAN partners from the private sector could launch a project.

The experience of SAARC in this respect should be useful to the ASEAN. The SAARC Fund for Regional Projects (SFRP) with a DFI from each member country acting as a focal point is functioning well. It is identified some regional projects and feasibility studies are being undertaken.

**Venture Capital Funds**

Venture capital companies are established to meet the requirements of equity capital in new and somewhat risky but desired economic activities. In some developed countries, venture capital companies are subsidiaries of high profit-making parent firms.

In Southeast Asian countries, Build-Operate-Transfer (BOT) and Build-Own-Operate-Transfer (BOOT) schemes have been working satisfactorily. In India, the DFIs and others have set up venture capital companies.

Small and new companies not only require finance, but a whole range of services as a package including technical and marketing assistance for them to gain a foothold and operate efficiently. The BOT and BOOT schemes incorporate various mixes of equity participation (by interested companies, commercial banks and export-import banks, etc.), management, and possible gradual withdrawal from both.

India and the ASEAN countries would gain more by learning from their mutual experience.

**General Agreement on Trade in Services (GATS)**

Article IV of the GATS states that increasing participation of developing countries in the world trade shall be facilitated by strengthening their domestic services capacity and its efficiency and competitiveness, inter alia, through access to technology on a commercial basis. Not all the developing countries will be able to access technology on a commercial basis. It is essential for the individual developing countries to identify the niche areas in the services sector and attempt to strengthen them through cooperation with others besides measures to achieve this objective.

Article V 3(a) of GATS gives good scope for cooperation in the services sectors among the developing countries at different levels of development. Flexibility has been provided for in the conditions set out for agreements to liberalising trade in services between or among the parties to such agreements.

India and ASEAN should be able to utilise suitable provisions to foster cooperation in the services sector including that of financial services.

**Clearing and Payments Arrangements and Trade Finance**

The main purpose of these arrangements is to clear current transactions in the currencies of the member countries and use convertible currencies only to settle the payment of debtors' balances arising from the periodic settlements. Thus there is saving of convertible currencies for settling intra-regional trade. CPAs (Clearing and Payments Arrangements) are especially of help to regional groupings among the developing countries which are facing the problem of foreign exchange scarcity. As this problem is prevalent in most parts of the developing world, a number of CPAs have been set up involving developing countries.

The CPAs are usually part of more comprehensive economic cooperation schemes among groups of developing countries. Thus CPAs' role is complementary to other instruments for promoting intra-regional trade. The CPAs, in conjunction with provision of credit facilities to refinance net debit balances of some of the members of the CPA, could be more effective measures of intra-regional trade expansion.

The CPAs in general served as useful instruments for promoting monetary and financial cooperation and integration and helped support the developing countries' economic and trade cooperation. Only after the international debt crisis and the resultant liquidity problems and financial squeeze, that the arrangements have faced serious difficulties. The experience of the multilateral payments and clearing arrangements in various parts of the world shows that favourable domestic and external economic environment is a necessary condition for the smooth running of regional integration efforts.

The CPAs are an initial step in the goal towards higher forms of monetary cooperation and integration in regional groupings. The further forms that monetary cooperation/integration could take include: Swap arrangements, other credit arrangements including a reserve fund, and monetary union. The existence of a CPA could itself lead to other areas of monetary and financial cooperation in a region, e.g., the participating commercial banks could be useful sources of information regarding opportunities for trade and investments in the participating countries.

The membership of the existing clearing and payments arrangements needs to be expanded and links developed among them with appropriate guidelines chalked out for their operation. For example, attempts could be made to link the Asian Clearing Union (ACU) with the financial cooperation schemes in the ASEAN.

**Foreign Banks**

As part of relaxation of entry barriers, the role of foreign banks in the financial sector of individual countries has increased. The possible advantages from foreign competition are increased efficiency, modernisation and computerisation and greater use of information technology by the domestic banks. However, some countries may find it difficult to set up a level-playing field which is satisfactory to both domestic and the foreign banks.

The presence of foreign banks differs in terms of the number of banks and branches, capital requirements, priority-sector lending norms, shareholding percentage, etc.

The Philippines allows only four foreign banks and limits them to three branches each. It was proposed allowing upto eight foreign banks to open branches over a five-year period, but with stricter capital requirements. Opening six branches would cost a foreign bank US $ 16 million. Upto US $ 32.7 million will be required for 60 per cent equity in a locally incorporated bank.

Malaysia requires foreign banks to have capital equal to 10 per cent of risk-weighted assets, while Thailand requires 6.25 per cent but not lower than US $ 5 million. No new full-service branches are allowed, but foreign holdings upto 20 per cent in local banks is permitted. The capital requirement for foreign banks in Indonesia is US $ 50 million or 8 per cent of risk-assets, whichever is higher. Since 1969, no full services branches have been allowed, but 49 per cent holdings of listed shares in local banks and 85 per cent in joint venture banks are allowed.

India and the ASEAN countries could gain by organising a comparative study of their experience, vis-a-vis foreign banks' operations in their respective countries and how best they could utilise the presence of foreign banks in those countries.

**Stock Markets**

Stock markets are a source of long-term funds in the process of privatization of public sector corporations, build-own-operate (BOO) and build-operate-transfer (BOT) schemes, etc.

The emerging stock markets in several Asian countries have established dynamism in recent years. In terms of capitalization, stock market growth and returns, they have become attractive for funds from the industrialized countries.

However, according to a recent study [8]some salient features of the stock markets in some Asian developing countries are :

- lack of adequate financial information about listed firms;
- inadequacy of accounting and auditing of financial reports;
- inadequate monitoring and supervision of the market to protect investors against market manipulation and other forms of excesses.

Initiatives are required, where necessary, to establish credit rating agencies in the developing Asian countries; to impart skills and training of personnel to specialize in activities in the capital market; to introduce new technology; and to establish formal government bodies for effective regulation and supervision of securities operations.

The Asia-Pacific Forum on Securities Market Regulation and Supervision has been established which discusses issues regarding the regulation and supervision of emerging securities markets. The Forum, in its meeting in July 1994, attended by participants from 39 countries, considered the findings and recommendations of the above-mentioned ADB study and identified specific areas where ADB assistance will be required and can be most effective. The Forum also discussed the ways to encourage regional cooperation in dealing with the regulatory and supervisory aspects of securities markets operation.

The economic and political conditions in individual countries determine the movements in the stock prices. An analysis of the inter-relationship between the trend of the prices over a period, the medium-term fluctuations over the trend and large spurts or falls in the stock prices triggered by sudden developments is important for policy-makers. The magnitude of impact of the last factor on stock prices depends on the trend/volatility of stock prices prior to the steep fall. Analysis of this facilitates the policy-makers to take appropriate measures to stabilise the stock market and ensure orderly growth. High volatility of stock prices undermines the financial system as a whole. The stock markets of developing countries exhibit much greater volatility than those of industrialized countries. The reasons for this could be ascribed to various imperfections and segmentations of the capital market, lack of adequate information on corporate performance available to the public, etc.[9]

In the economic and political management of countries, governments do well in some areas and badly in others. If the positive ones predominate or appear to predominate over the negative ones, the governments could ride an economic/political credibility wave depending on the intensity or longevity of the net positive perception. This, aided by stock market 'gurus', institutional investors, speculators and the psychology of investors, determines the trend of the stock market, say over a 3 to 5 year period (as e.g. the bull-phase of 1982-87 in the USA). Variations in the above factors lead to fluctuations of stock prices over the trend. If the trend is steep, especially due to appearance, rather than reality, of good economic management, and/or if the volatility is high, sudden crashes in the stock markets will result following bad news. The movements in individual stock prices depend on the movement of the stock markets as a whole, dividends, yields, P/E ratios, etc.[10]

Stabilizing the stock markets in the developing countries may be attempted by measures such as the following: introduction/strengthening of institutional mechanisms to increase transparency in information about corporations and their performance, and to take quick remedial steps in case of excess volatility or unusually sharp rise in stock prices; and developing orderly competition between commercial banks, merchant banks, and other financial institutions (both domestic and international) for achieving the industrial policy objectives.

India and the ASEAN countries as emerging markets have

witnessed rapid changes in their stock markets. They could learn from each other's experience.

**Concluding Observations**

Developing countries like India and the ASEAN member countries have been undertaking reform and liberalization of their financial sectors as part of their economic liberalization process. One major lesson that emerges from the experience of several countries with financial liberalization that too rapid and indiscriminate liberalization could lead to recession in industry, speculative activities and instability in the financial system.

What is essential is that the reform process should aim at increasing efficiency and range of financial services in the financial instruments and institutions.

In other words, liberalization and reform should not be treated as objectives among themselves, but as means to achieve other set objectives, e.g. improving rural finance, export growth, inflation control, and balance of payments management.

The experience of India and select ASEAN countries shows that they have been exercising prudential control on interest rates, directed-credit allocation, entry of foreign banks, etc., at the same time as encouraging deregulation of their financial service sectors. An analysis of the experience of individual countries would be of interest to other countries and help fostering cooperation in the financial service sectors.

The various possible areas of cooperation in financial services between India and the ASEAN include: setting up of joint venture banks and venture capital funds; exchange of information; training of personnel in specialized fields; gaining expertise in handling financial derivatives; and participating in an effective way in international trade in financial services in the wake of the WTO.

## NOTES

1. See Rao and Das 1993 for a discussion on the issues and suggestions for furthering the partnership.
2. See Chowdhury and Garcia (1993).
3. *Asian Age*, 22 March 1995, p. 7.

4. Chowdhury and Garcia (1993).
5. See Rao (1993 b) for a fuller discussion on cooperation in financial services.
6. See Rao (1991) for a detailed discussion on the operations of Indian banks abroad.
7. See OECD (1994)
8. Conducted by the Asian Development Bank (ADB) of its 13 developing member countries on the securities market regulation and supervision. The countries are: Bangladesh, China, Hong Kong, India, Indonesia, Malaysia, Pakistan, the Philippines, Republic of Korea, Singapore, Sri Lanka, Taiwan Province of China and Thailand.
9. See Singh (1993).
10. See Rao (1993 a) for a detailed discussion.

# V

# CHINA, ASEAN, APEC AND INDIA

# 10

# China-ASEAN: Economic Relations

SHRI PRAKASH

The ongoing process of the growth of an interdependent global economy is taking place in many instances through an increase in regional integration. With the end of the Cold War many of the major political obstacles to the development of economic relations have not only been dismantled, the governments and particularly the business leaders are more willing than before to sidestep or even simply ignore political differences between various countries while undertaking trade with and investments in them provided their safety and profitability are ensured by law and economic opportunities. In this context, there has been the emergence of several regional economic organizations like the ASEAN and the Asia-Pacific Economic Council. The ASEAN countries infact have already set in motion the process of creating an ASEAN Free Trade Area (AFTA) and are discussing the possibility of starting an ASEAN common market. The SAARC countries have recently stepped up their efforts to formally initiate the South Asian Preferential Trade Area (SAPTA). Alongside these established or emerging liberal economic regional institutional frameworks in Asia, there is a proposal to organize an East Asia Economic Caucus or Community to bring together countries including Japan, South Korea, China, Vietnam and the ASEAN countries on a common regional economic platform. The proposal put forward first by the Prime Minister Mahathir of Malaysia is being officially supported by China, i.e., People's Republic of China (P.R.C.). While there is common ground on some issues between the countries of East Asia, it remains to be examined whether there are enough or the right kind of common economics interests between them to form an ASEAN type of grouping or plan to create an European Common Market or European Union kind of framework in the future.

The present study seeks to answer several questions relating to the prospects of better economic relations between China and the ASEAN countries in the post Cold War period, since this aspect is important for assessing the practicality of the proposal to from an East Asia Economic Caucus or Community. Are there complementarities between the economies and trade of China and the ASEAN countries? If there were greater complementarities in the past, have these changed recently? Alternatively is there a greater degree of competition today between China and the ASEAN countries, because of a growing similarity in the nature of the production structure and commerce of these two regions? What is the real direction of trade of China and the ASEAN countries? Can we say that the commerce of these two regions as it has been evolving in the recent decade is of a multipolar and balanced nature enabling the dynamic economies of the East Asian Region to be linked with both the Developed Market Economies of North America and Europe, as well as the Developing Economies of West, South and Central Asia, the last named having recently acquired independence from the centralized economic autarchy of the former Soviet Union?

## PROMINENT EXISTING VIEWS

Political developments not only in the past few years, but also in the preceding twenty years have made many experts and officials especially in China to expect a large scale integration and economic interaction between the ASEAN countries and China. Between 1972 and 1992, it was the fact that China, the USA and the ASEAN countries were opposed to the Soviet Union and hence on the same side of the Cold War which was expected to enhance their trade and other economic relations. Since, the ending of the Cold War and the political demise of the Soviet Union, it is the re-establishment of diplomatic relations between China and some of the leading ASEAN countries as well as the conclusion of new commercial treaties between them and China's indirect participation in various ASEAN forums, which has fuelled fresh hopes of a big renewal of trade and investment ties between South East Asia and China, (i.e. the P.R.C.). Traditionally, also some Chinese nationalists have viewed the South East Asian Region as a part of an indirect "sphere of influence" of China, since in the centuries gone by some of the kingdoms in South East Asia used to send tributes to the ruling dynasties of Beijing. This image has been partly reinforced by the presence of substantial Chinese Settler-communities in Indonesia, Malaysia, Singapore and Vietnam.

A prominent example of such perceptions can be found in an article written and published by Dr. Yu Zhida, a professor at the Tianjin Foreign Trade Institute, an official organization in China. Dr. Yu Zhida's article entitled "Optimistic Prospects for China-Indonesia Trade" has been published in April 1991 issue of the economic journal *Intertrade*. According to him, in "Indonesia about 4 million of its population are people of Chinese origin and overseas Chinese, 2 per cent of the total. These people use the same language, are of the same race and have the same customs and consumption habits as their brethren in China. They, therefore, show great interest in traditional Chinese commodities. Most of Indonesia's 12 largest private enterprise groups such as the Lin Shaoling Group, the Xie Jianlong Group are in the flour, cement, edible oil, timber processing, finance and automobiles as well as other industries having close ties with the Indonesian government. Such being the case, close relationships established with these Chinese *consortia* will surely help expand economic and trade ties with Indonesia." (I)

Secondly, according to Dr. Yu Zhida, "Viewed from the commodity mix, the Chinese and Indonesian economies, complement each other though trade. Over the past few years oil, natural gas, rubber, chemical fertilizers and timber were all needed in China and could be supplied by Indonesia. Likewise, foodstuffs, medicine, tonics, grain and oil products, complete sets of small equipment, chemical products and mineral fuels could be exported by China to Indonesia where they are needed. Also helping Indonesia to turn to China away from its traditional suppliers is the revaluation of the Japanese Yen and Taiwan currency in recent years."

The third reason cited by Dr. Yu Zhida for his great optimism about the prospects of an increase in trade between Indonesia and China is the fact that "The Indonesian government has relaxed its restrictive trade policies in the past few years, lifted quota limitations and import monopolies on 165 kinds of commodities and cancelled the licence system for the import of commodities such as some textiles. At present, among Indonesia's import commodities only 15 per cent are subject to non-tariff restrictions, while machinery, clothing, clocks and watches, toys, pearls and jewels all can be freely imported. Among these commodities, Chinese products, because they are good and cheap and suited to the Indonesian market have great potential for development."[1]

A similar view to that of Dr. Yu Zhida has been expressed by Professor Fa Zhengluo of the International Trade Research Institute of the Ministry of Foreign Economic Relations and Trade (MOFERT).[2] According to Professor Zhengluo "Judging from the structure of commodities traded between the two nations, the Sino-Indonesian trade is to a large measure, mutually supplementary. Take their trade in industrial raw materials for example. Although both nations are among the world's major producers and exporters of a number of important industrial raw materials, neither is able to provide all the raw materials it needs. With the development of its home economy, China imports considerable amounts of such Indonesian industrial raw materials as raw rubber and timber. Likewise, Indonesia can count on China for the supply of many materials such as soyabeans, cotton, coal and pig iron. In the field of manufactured goods, China has just launched its export of machinery and transport equipment. By contrast commodities exported by Indonesia as a ASEAN member nation are closely associated with its abundant natural resources, timber in particular. Thus more than half of Indonesian exports are resource intensive goods, neatly complementing the labour intensive export goods in which China enjoys a competitive edge." In addition, the resumption of Sino-Indonesian diplomatic relations in 1990 and the trade agreement signed by them also in 1990, granting each other the Most Favoured Nation Status were expected to act as major factors in enhancing the scope of trade between Indonesia and China.[3]

Similarly, the resumption of full diplomatic relations between Singapore and China in 1990 was expected to lead to a spurt in bilateral trade and investments.[4] According to Dr. Cao Yunhua of the Institute of Southeast Asia Studies, Ji Nan University "Singapore enjoys unique advantages in developing economic relations with China. Singaporean business people generally understand both English and Mandarin and therefore are not hindered by the language barrier when they do business with China. Singapore has rich experience and human resources in developing infrastructure, urban construction and service trades, areas where China is relatively inexperienced."[5]

The above mentioned expectations have also been aroused because of the more friendly international political environment in the post Cold War period. Today, China has a guest status at ASEAN meetings. It is also a guest observer alongwith Russia, Vietnam and Laos at the recently formed ASEAN Regional Forum (ARF) meant to try and think about as well as coordinate a new post Cold War security structure for Asia.[6] There has been a resumption of a dialogue and diplomatic relations between China and Vietnam who until a few years ago were considered as rivals in South East Asia. Alongwith the ASEAN countries, China is a full member of the emerging Asia-Pacific Economic Council (APEC) and as pointed out in the Preface to the present study, supports the idea put forward by the Malaysian Prime Minister Mr. Mahathir for the formation of an East Asia Economic Community or Council (EAEC). The point to be discussed below is how far are these optimistic expectations about the emergence of the EAEC justified by actual economic facts and current trends in trade with this part of Asia? This study does not address itself to any of the territorial disputes or security problems between China and the other East/South East Asian countries.

## CHINA-ASEAN TRADE

Only a close analysis of the ongoing commercial trends can provide an accurate basis for making any predictions about the likely future course of trade and investment ties between China and the ASEAN countries. Three major sources of data have been used for the statistical analysis presented in this Section: the Direction of Trade Statistics data published by the International Monetary Fund from Washington D.C., the statistics included in the Almanac of China's Foreign Economic Relations and Trade published by the Ministry of Foreign Economic Relations and Trade [MOFERT], from Beijing and the data provided by the China Customs Statistics Year Book 1993 also published by the

Chinese Government from Beijing. An additional source of information used is the International Trade Statistics Yearbook published by the United Nations. Some of these data are being cited in the text itself. The greater number of the statistical tables are cited after the footnotes.

As shown in Table A, the analysis done by Fred Herschede of the direction of ASEAN Trade provided a prognostication of the hypothesis argued for in my present study. According to Herschede's analysis China accounted for 5.1 per cent of the total value of ASEAN imports in 1985 but only 3.1 per cent in 1989. When the 1991 IMF data was taken into account, China's share of ASEAN imports had further declined to 2.85 per cent [cf. Table B]. In the case of exports from ASEAN countries, China's share of value rose initially from 1.3 per cent in 1985 to 2.5 per cent in 1988 but progressively declined to just 2 per cent in 1991. [cf. Tables A and B]. When the exports and imports are considered together then China's share of the ASEAN trade of 135658 million in 1985 was 43202 million dollars or 3.1 per cent. By 1991 of the total value of ASEAN trade of 342851 million US dollars China's share was 8409 million dollars or just 2.45 per cent [Table B].

A further analysis of the available data allows us to compare the aggregate value of China's trade with the ASEAN countries and see how the trade of these two regions with other parts of the world has been increasing much faster than with themselves.

In simple aggregate terms, the value of ASEAN's trade with China increased from 830 million dollars in 1975 to 1773 million dollars in 1980 to 3365 million dollars in 1985; 6704 million dollars in 1989 and 8409 million dollars in 1991 [Table C]. What is noticeable is that after 1989 the rate of increase in the value of China's trade with ASEAN countries has been lower than the growth of its global trade and so also for the value of ASEAN's trade with China. In 1980, it was 114 per cent more than in 1975; in 1985, it was 90 per cent more than in 1980; in 1989 it was only 99 per cent more than in 1985 and in 1991 it was just 25 per cent more than in 1989. During the same successive periods, the value of ASEAN's global trade however mostly increased by a much greater margin than its trade with China [Table C]. This fact explains why there was a secular decline in China's share of ASEAN trade between 1975 and 1991 [Table A and B].

How does this picture look when one considers ASEAN's share

**Table A**
**Direction of ASEAN Trade**

*(Percentage Distribution)*

| Year | $ 1000,000 Grand Total Total* | Industrial Countries Total | USA | Japan | Europe | **Intra Asean | China | All Other Countries |
|---|---|---|---|---|---|---|---|---|
| Imports | | | | | | | | |
| 1975 | 23494 | 56.9% | 15.4% | 23.8% | 17.7% | 12.7% | 3.0% | 27.4% |
| 1980 | 63170 | 53.0% | 15.4% | 21.8% | 14.8% | 17.6% | 2.7% | 27.7% |
| 1985 | 64153 | 52.0% | 15.7% | 20.1% | 15.6% | 19.7% | 5.1% | 23.2% |
| 1986 | 62289 | 54.6% | 16.1% | 22.2% | 16.3% | 17.5% | 3.9% | 24.0% |
| 1887 | 76898 | 54.6% | 14.8% | 22.6% | 17.2% | 17.4% | 3.6% | 24.4% |
| 1988 | 103923 | 54.9% | 15.5% | 23.0% | 16.4% | 17.3% | 3.4% | 24.4% |
| 1989 | 126386 | 55.3% | 15.5% | 23.7% | 16.1% | 16.3% | 3.1% | 25.3% |
| Exports | | | | | | | | |
| 1975 | 20811 | 61.0% | 19.8% | 27.0% | 14.2% | 17.3% | 0.6% | 21.1% |
| 1980 | 66490 | 57.6% | 16.9% | 26.8% | 13.9% | 18.1% | 1.0% | 23.3% |
| 1985 | 71505 | 56.4% | 19.7% | 25.4% | 11.3% | 19.4% | 1.3% | 22.9% |
| 1986 | 66558 | 52.5% | 20.0% | 19.6% | 12.9% | 17.7% | 1.8% | 28.0% |
| 1987 | 82351 | 56.3% | 21.3% | 20.7% | 14.3% | 17.6% | 2.3% | 23.8% |
| 1988 | 104592 | 55.5% | 20.9% | 19.2% | 15.4% | 18.3% | 2.5% | 23.7% |
| 1989 | 121407 | 55.7% | 21.3% | 18.9% | 15.5% | 18.7% | 2.3% | 23.3% |

*N.B.* 1993 Brunei included after 1983.

** The International Monetary Fund (IMF) defines industrial Europe to include : Austria, Belgium, Denmark, Finland, France, Germany, Iceland, Ireland, Italy, Netherlands, Norway, Spain, Sweden, Switzerland and the United Kingdom.

*Source :* 1975-89, International Monetary Fund, Direction of Trade Statistics Yearbook, (IMF :Washington, D.C. *various issues*).
Cited in Fred Herschede, trade between China and ASEAN : The Impact of the Pacific Rim Era; Published in Pacific Affairs Vol. 64, No. 2 (from Univ. of British Columbia, Vancouver, Canada) Summer 1991, p. 182.

in the total value of China's trade in recent years? The same trends are to be seen in the case of China as well—its trade is getting more diversified in terms of direction and destinations. When the share of the USA, Japan, Europe and the six ASEAN countries is excluded the share of other countries in the value of China's trade rose from 51.8 per cent in 1980 to 60 per cent in 1993. During the same period the USA's share in China's trade rose from 13.4 per cent to 14.1 per cent while that of Japan declined from 25 per cent to 20 per cent. ASEAN's share of China's trade too declined from 6.1 per cent to 5.46 per cent (cf. Table I in the Appendices]. New destinations like South Korea and Taiwan were gainers from China's growing trade as was India. This point may be seen when we analyze the data in Table II concerning the trade of individual ASEAN countries with their major trading partners.

## CHINA-ASEAN TRADE: STATISTICAL ANALYSIS

The data and its analysis for assessing the current trends in China's trade with individual ASEAN countries are contained in Tables II (a) to (i); Table III; and Tables IV(a) to IV(h). While these confirm the general trends observed and discussed in the preceding sections, the statistical analysis in this section allows us to see the variations in the economic relationship between China and the various ASEAN countries in the post Cold War period between 1988 and 1992.

The first point to be observed is from Table III and it relates to the fact that the value of the global trade of the ASEAN countries has been increasing much faster than that of their trade with China. Whereas the value of the trade of five ASEAN countries, viz., Indonesia, Singapore, Malaysia, Thailand and Philippines was in 1992, 194 per cent more than the value in 1988, the corresponding increase in the value of these countries' trade with China was only 58 per cent. In other words, the post Cold War period has seen a substantial relative decline in the rate of growth of Sino-ASEAN trade when official expectations especially in China were to the contrary [cf. Table III]. A countrywise breakdown of ASEAN trade with China as also provided in Table III shows that with the exception of Indonesia and Malaysia in every other case, the difference in the margin by which total trade and trade with China increased was substantial. Whereas

**Table B**
**Direction of ASEAN trade in 1991**

| | *Total Global Value of Mis of US Dollars* | *% share of USA* | *% share of Japan* | *% share of Europe* | *% share of China* |
|---|---|---|---|---|---|
| Exports to | 161734 | 30189 [18.7%] | 29531 [18.3%] | 1394.4 [0.86%] | 3240 [2.0%] |
| Imports From | 181116 | 26309 [14.5%] | 43486 [24.0%] | 1009 [0.56%] | 5169 [2.85%] |
| Exports + Imports | 342850 | 56498 [16.5%] | 73016 [21.3%] | 2403 [0.7%] | 8409 [2.45%] |

*Source :* Direction of Trade Statistics, IMF, Washington D.C.

**Table C**
**Comparative analysis of Sino-ASEAN trade 1975-91**

| *Year* | *Value of Total ASEAN Trade in $ Million* | *% increase over preceding year* | *Value of ASEAN Trade with China in $ Million* | | | |
|---|---|---|---|---|---|---|
| | | | *Imports From China* | *Exports To China* | *Total Value* | *% + or – Total Value of ASEAN Trade with China* |
| 1975 | 44305 | | 705 | 125 | 830 | |
| 1980 | 129660 | + 193% over 1975 | 1706 | 67 | 1773 | + 114% over 1975 |
| 1985 | 135658 | + 5% over 1980 | 3272 | 93 | 3365 | + 90% over 1980 |
| 1989 | 247793 | + 83% over 1985 | 3912 | 2792 | 6704 | + 99% over 1985 |
| 1991 | 342850 | + 38% over 1989 | 5169 | 3240 | 8409 | + 25% over 1989 |

*Source :* IMF data cited above in Tables A and B.

between 1988 and 1992 the value of Indonesia's global trade increased by 90 per cent its trade with China grew by 130 per cent. However, Malaysia's trade with China increased 120 per cent compared to the 128 per cent increase in its total trade. In Singapore's case, the increase in total trade was by 63 per cent whereas with China its trade increased only by 18 per cent. For Thailand again, the increase in total trade was by 90 per cent but with China only by 29 per cent. In the case of Philippines its total trade value between 1988 and 1992 grew by 60 per cent but the value of its trade with China declined in 1992 by 6 per cent compared to its 1988 value, [cf. Table III].

**Table D**
**Value of imports from China (in million US Dollars)**

| | *1988 Value* | *% of Total Value of Global Imports (1988)* | *1992 Value* | *% of Total Value of Global Imports (1992)* |
|---|---|---|---|---|
| Indonesia | 439 | 3.3% | 752 | 2.75% |
| Singapore | 1683 | 3.8% | 2252 | 3.1% |
| Malaysia | 376 | 3.0% | 803 | 2.3% |
| Thailand | 630 | 3.4% | 1149 | 2.8% |
| Philippines | 268 | 3.0% | 201 | 1.3% |
| Brunei | 12 | 2.0% | 20 | 2.3% |
| Total of ASEAN Countries Trade with China | 3458 | 3.1% | 5177 | 2.4% |

Table II and IV provide a countrywise breakdown of increases in the values of each country's imports and exports with China particularly for the ASEAN countries. With reference to the ASEAN countries, the value of imports is given in Table D (from Table II).

With the exception of Brunei, China's share in the value of global imports of all other ASEAN countries had declined in the post Cold War period. In other words, while China has been selling more to the world especially to Japan, USA, Hong Kong and now South Korea, by comparison it has witnessed a relative decline in its exports to the ASEAN countries. This fact may be

confirmed further from the country table on China (Table IId). The value of China's exports to the five ASEAN economies—Singapore, Malaysia, Indonesia, Philippines and Thailand—in 1988 was 5.76 per cent of its total exports. In 1992 this ratio had declined to 5.62 per cent. China's exports to South Korea in the same period of 1988-92 increased from 87.8 million dollars or 0.18 per cent of its exports to 2405 million dollars or 2.83 per cent of its total exports. In the case of USA, China's exports in 1988 were 3358 million dollars or 7 per cent of total export value. In 1992, China's exports to USA were valued at 8599 million dollars which was 10 per cent of China's total export value in that year. Similarly the value of Indonesia's imports from USA increased from 13 per cent to 14 per cent of its total value; from South Korea the value of Indonesian imports jumped from 2.84 per cent to 7 per cent of total import value between 1988 and 1992, for Australia from 4.4 per cent to 5.12 per cent; for India from 0.27 per cent to 3.59 per cent [cf. Table I (c)].

In the case of Singapore , the share of the value of imports from USA increased form 15.6 per cent to 16.5 per cent, from South Korea from 2.3 per cent to 3.3 per cent, from Saudi Arabia from 4.4 per cent to 5.13 per cent, from Thailand from 2.71 per cent to 3.71 per cent and from India from 0.61 per cent to 0.94 per cent [cf. Table I(d)] . In the case of Malaysia, it was its imports from Japan which increased their share from 21.8 per cent in 1988 to 27.1 per cent in 1992 as also from South Korea from 2.65 per cent to 2.8 per cent and from Hong Kong from 0.78 per cent to 1.93 per cent. USA's share in Malaysian imports declined from 18.7 per cent to 15.9 per cent and Singapore's share from 14.5 per cent to 11.6 per cent. India's hare remained steady at a nominal 0.8 per cent [Table I(f)]. In Thailand's case the increase in the share of import value was from South Korea from 2.8 per cent to 4.4 per cent, Malaysia from 2.1 per cent to 3.9 per cent, from Australia from 1.69 per cent to 1.95 per cent and from Saudi Arabia from one per cent to 1.3 per cent [Table I(g)]. The share of Japan in the value of Thailand's imports remained steady at 29 per cent while that of USA declined from 13.6 per cent to 11.8 per cent. In the case of Philippines the shares in its import value increased for Germany from 3.9 per cent to 4.5 per cent, for Hong Kong from 4.5 per cent to 4.8 per cent, for Indonesia from 1.05 per cent to 1.27 per cent, for Canada from 1.04 per cent to 1.41 per cent, and for India from 0.33 per cent to 0.61 per cent [cf. Table I (h)]. In the case of Japan, the share of its value in Philippines imports declined from 17.4 per cent in 1988 to 17.3 per cent in 1992 and for USA from 21.2 per cent to 18.2 per cent. The two largest increases in the case of the value of imports into Brunei were for USA from 5.3 per cent, in 1988 to 10.9 per cent in 1992 and for Singapore from 24.5 per cent to 27 per cent while a significant decline was there for Japan from 19.9 per cent to 14.8 per cent [Table I(i)]. In the case of Indonesia, it should be noted that Japan's share of import value declined from 25.6 per cent in 1988 to 22 per cent in 1992.

Thus we can conclude that the pattern of imports of the ASEAN countries far from increasingly centering on China actually diversified to enhance its share of imports from South Korea, USA, Australia, Canada, Saudi Arabia and India to name a few of the prominent gainers. It might also be noted here that even when the values of ASEAN's trade with Hong Kong are included in Sino-ASEAN trade, the share of China in ASEAN's Total Trade Value after 1989 shows a decline. This exercise has been done in another Research Paper written by the author.

As far as the structure of the value of exports from the ASEAN countries is concerned it must first of all be noted that between them Japan and USA occupy by far the major share:

Between 1988 and 1992 the share of ASEAN exports going to Japan and USA have declined for Indonesia from 58.7 per cent to 45 per cent for Singapore from 33 per cent to 29 per cent, for Malaysia from 36.1 per cent to 33 per cent, for Philippines from 55.7 per cent to 56 per cent. In the case of Thailand the share of exports going to USA and Japan has increased from 35.6 per cent to 39 per cent, for Brunei however it has again declined from 68.3 per cent to 63 per cent. Even with this relative decline USA and Japan remain the biggest destination for ASEAN exports. The relative decline in their share as also that of China shows a growing and greater diversification of the direction of ASEAN exports when compared to imports or overall trade values.

Whereas between 1988 and 1992 the value of imports from China declined from 3.1 per cent of the total value of imports coming into ASEAN countries in 1988 to 2.4 per cent in 1992, China's share in ASEAN exports declined from an even lower level of 1.86 per cent in 1988 to 1.75 per cent in 1992.

**Table E**

**Value and share of exports going to USA and Japan in 1988 and 1992**

*(in million US dollars)*

| *Country* | 1988 | | | | | 1992 | | | | |
|---|---|---|---|---|---|---|---|---|---|---|
| | *Value to USA* | *% of Total Value* | *Value of Exports to Japan* | *% of Total Value* | *Total %age* | *Value to USA* | *% of Total Value* | *Value of Exports to Japan* | *% of Total Value* | *Total %age* |
| Indonesia | 3074 | 16.3% | 8018 | 42.4% | 58.7% | 4419 | 13.0% | 10753 | 32.0% | 45% |
| Singapore | 9369 | 23.4% | 3364 | 8.6% | 33.0% | 13391 | 21.2% | 4825 | 7.6% | 29% |
| Malaysia | 2969 | 16.6% | 3504 | 19.5% | 36.1% | 5802 | 17.0% | 5388 | 15.7% | 33% |
| Thailand | 3200 | 20.0% | 2546 | 15.6% | 35.6% | 6062 | 21.3% | 5133 | 18.0% | 39% |
| Philippines | 2522 | 35.6% | 1424 | 20.1% | 55.7% | 3843 | 39.2% | 1745 | 17.8% | 56% |
| Brunei | 218 (1985) | 7.33% | 1820 | 61.2% | 68.3% | 93 (1989) | 4.9% | 1095 | 58.2% | 63% |

Based on Data in Table II (a) to (i).

**Table F**
**Value of exports to China**

*[in Million US Dollars]*

| *Country* | *1988* | *% of Total Global Value of each Country's Exports* | *1992* | *% of Total Value of Global Exports of each country* |
|---|---|---|---|---|
| Indonesia | 492 | 2.6% | 1397 | 4.1% |
| Singapore | 1178 | 3.0% | 1112 | 1.75% |
| Malaysia | 279 | 1.6% | 639 | 1.9% |
| Thailand | 475 | 3.0% | 335 | 1.18% |
| Philippines | 67 | 0.94% | 113 | 1.16% |
| Brunei | 22 | 0.0007% | 77 | 0.41% |
| Average for six ASEAN countries | | 1.86% | | 1.75% |

*N.B.* : Based on Data in Tables II (a) to II (i).

An additional test was devised for the hypothesis that China's trade with the ASEAN countries has seen a relative decline in the post Cold War period between 1988 and 1992. This was to rank China by share of value of imports to and exports from the ASEAN countries and compare the results for 1988 and 1992, which are being summarized below:

**Table G**
**China's rank among ASEAN countries by share of total trade value**

| *Country* | *% Share of Imports From* | | *% Share of Exports to* | |
|---|---|---|---|---|
| | *1988 Rank* | *1992 Rank* | *1988 Rank* | *1992 Rank* |
| Indonesia | 7 | 6 | 6 | 4 |
| Singapore | 5 | 8 | 8 | 9 |
| Malaysia | 8 | 9 | 12 | 9 |
| Thailand | 5 | 7 | 7 | 12 |
| Philippines | 7 | 9 | 10 | 8 |

Based on Data and Calculations in Table II (a) to (h).

On the imports front China's share has declined in four out of five cases. In the matter of exports China's rank has declined in three out of the five cases. It is worthwhile noticing the countries to whom Indonesia is exporting more in the post Cold War period. Apart from China whose rank has gone up from 6 to 4 in the list of countries to whom Indonesia is exporting, there is Saudi Arabia whose rank has gone up from 10 to 7; Germany whose rank has increased from 7 to 5, Malaysia from 9 to 8; Thailand from 11 to 7 and Australia from 8 to 6. In the case of Singapore, its rank in the list of countries to whom Indonesia is exporting has declined from 3 to 10. The ranking for countries to whom Singapore is exporting has remained stable. In the case of Malaysian exports, Singapore's rank has increased from 2 to 1, UK from 6 to 5, Indonesia from 14 to 11 and China from 12 to 9. For Thailand in the list of its export destinations the ranking of France has gone up from 9 to 7, of Australia from 11 to 9, South Korea from 12 to 10. In the case of Philippines, exports the rank of France has gone up from 9 to 7, of Australia from 11 to 9, South Korea from 12 to 10 and of Indonesia from 15 to 13 while the rank of China has declined from 7 to 12. [cf. Table IV(a) to IV (g)]. The emerging pattern of exports of the ASEAN countries shows the emergence of a complex and more widespread network of trading relationships largely concentrated in the Asia-Pacific region but with many linkages reaching out to the European economies as well. The potential for the creation of such a network or a new trade grid had existed earlier but it is the post Cold War situation which has allowed economic relations to move along its own logic and axis and not to be bogged down by a politics based on a highly competitive arms race and strategies of power projection and construction of spheres of influence by Big Powers. The fact that the future movement of ASEAN trade is not going to center only or even mainly on China but have a varied and more international character puts another nail in the coffin of the Cold War politics and promotes the emergence of a more multi-polar international system.

## COMMERCIAL AGREEMENTS AND TRADE COMPOSITION: CHINA-ASEAN

One needs an explanation for why — China's trade with the ASEAN countries grew during the latter half of the 1970s and the first half of the 1980s but has showed a relative decline after 1985. The answer lies partly in the fact that China signed many trade treaties with the ASEAN countries after it decided to "open up" its economy in 1978 even though it did not have formal diplomatic relations with Singapore and Indonesia until 1990. With Thailand, Malaysia and Philippines formal diplomatic relations were established in 1975. The following commercial agreements were signed between China and the ASEAN countries.

| | *Country* | | *Nature of Commercial Agreements Signed between ASEAN Countries and China* | | |
|---|---|---|---|---|---|
| I. | Singapore | 1. | 1979 and 1980 | | Bilateral Trade Agreements Signed |
| | | 2. | 1981 | : | Trade Representatives Exchanged |
| | | 3. | 1986 | : | Tourism Promotion Treaty |
| | | 4. | 1986 | : | Investment Protection Treaty |
| | | 5. | 1989 | : | Advance of Double Taxation Treaty |
| II. | Thailand | 1. | 1985 | : | Investment Protection Treaty |
| | | 2. | 1986 | : | Double Taxation Treaty |
| | | 3. | 1986 | : | Untie the Present Annual Trade Protocols |
| III. | Malaysia | 1. | 1985 | : | Memorandum of Understanding on Direct Trade; Avoidance of Double Taxation Treaty. |
| | | 2. | 1989 | : | Trade Agreement, Investment Protection Treaty, Joint Economic and Trade Committee Established. |

**Commercial agreements Signed with China**

| | | | | |
|---|---|---|---|---|
| Indonesia | 1. | 1985 | : | Direct Trade Agreement. |
| Philippines | 1. | 1975, 1986, 1989 | : | Trade Agreements. |

*Source* : The China Business Review, May-June 1990, p. 34.

It should be noted that some of these commercial agreements were signed when the process of relative decline of trade had become visible after 1985. If they were meant to stop the relative decline of trade between China and the ASEAN countries, then they have failed so far to have any significant positive impact.

Another important reason why in the 1970s and the 1980s trade grew at a fast pace between the ASEAN countries and China was the greater complementarities between their exports and imports in that period. This point can be better understood if we analyze the commodity composition of the Sino-ASEAN Trade between 1975 and 1985.

**Commodity composition of Sino-ASEAN trade in the 1970s and the early 1980s**

| *Country* | *China's Major Imports From* | *China's Major Exports To* |
|---|---|---|
| Indonesia | Industrial Machinery, Transport and Electrical Equipment, Rubber Products and Processed Wood | Petroleum, Foodstuffs, Chemicals, Textiles, Iron and Steel |
| Thailand | Rice, Corn Sugar, Rubber, Tobacco, Steel, Synthetic Fibre | Crude and Diesel Oil, Chemicals Produce, Pharmaceuticals and Machinery. |
| Malaysia | Rubber, Palm Oil, Timber, Logs, Cocoa, Beans | Textiles, Cereals, Oils, Produce light industrial goods, and Machinery |
| Indonesia | Plywood, Rubber, Rattan, Cement, Pepper, Coffee | Coal, Cotton, Machinery, Electrical appliances, Light industrial and agricultural equipments. |
| Philippines | Fertilizers, Coconut Oil, Bananas, Copper concentrates and Cathodes | Crude Oil, Machinery, Electrical Goods, Coal, Textiles, Foodstuffs. |
| Brunei | Crude Oil | Light Industrial Products, Steel, Machinery, Foodstuffs. |

*Source:* The China Business Review, May-June 1990, p. 34.

Two main items of export from China to the ASEAN countries were oil and textiles in the 1970s and the early 1980s. China has decreased its exports of oil to a large extent in order to meet increase in domestic demand and conserve existing reserves for the future, since no new sources of oil have been discovered. This has made ASEAN countries increase their imports of oil from Saudi Arabia and Brunei. On the other hand, increasing production and exports of textiles in and from the ASEAN countries have again curtailed China's exports to these countries. The growing proportion of similar commodities being imported and exported by China and the ASEAN countries to similar destinations makes them less likely to increase their mutual trade substantially and more likely to compete in major markets like Japan, USA, South Korea, Taiwan and the South East Asian and South Asian region as well.

An analysis of data of imports and exports reveals that whereas earlier in 1987 the similarity in the structure of trade between China and the ASEAN countries was limited to imports, by 1992 in the post Cold War period due especially to the growing presence and penetration of Foreign Direct Investments (FDI) the nature of exports has also become similar with the share of manufactured exports growing at a fast pace. The import data show that all the six ASEAN nations and China in 1987 had similar shares of manufactured imports, for example, lumping together SITC import classifications 5, 6, 7 and 8 (chemicals, basic manufacturing, machines, transport equipment and miscellaneous manufactures) the respective shares are : Brunei, 74 per cent; Indonesia, 80 per cent, Malaysia, 75 per cent; Philippines, 45 per cent; Singapore, 69 per cent; Thailand, 68 per cent; and China, 72 per cent. In 1987, on the export side there were differences in the pattern of trade of various ASEAN countries. Brunei and Indonesia's exports were concentrated in petroleum and so also Malaysia to a much less extent. Thailand was heavily dependent on food exports. The bulk of Malaysia's exports too were resource based, i.e., they included products in SITC categories 0-4, (food, beverages, crude materials, mineral fuels and vegetable oils) as well as category 68, non-ferrous metals. Singapore, the most industrialized of the group, earned most of her export earnings from processed mineral fuels and machinery. China had about one-third of her exports in the resource based category and nearly one-half in manufactured goods (20 per cent of exports were "not classified"). Export data for the Philippines too had a large "not classified" component. This pattern may be seen from the SITC data presented below:

**Table H**
**Exports of resource based commodities**

*(Percentage of Total Exports)*

| *Country* | *1975* | *1980* | *1985* | *1986* | *1987* |
|---|---|---|---|---|---|
| Indonesia | 100% | 97% | 89% | 82% | NA |
| Malaysia | 81% | 81% | 73% | 63% | NA |
| Philippines | 83% | 63% | 45% | 38% | NA |
| Singapore | 56% | 48% | 41% | 42% | 29% |
| Thailand | 81% | 70% | 60% | 55% | NA |
| China | — | — | — | 52% | 35% |

*Source :* United Nations, 1987 Yearbook of International Trade Statistics (UN : New York, 1989) also cited by Fred Herschede, *op. cit.*

As Table V(a) and V(b) compiled by me show (attached at the end of this study) the picture had substantially changed by 1992. The bulk of ASEAN's exports as well as that of China now consist of manufactured exports the ratios being 87 per cent for China; 81 per cent for Thailand; 88 per cent for Philippines; 76 per cent for Malaysia and 58 per cent for Indonesia, the average for these five countries then being 78 per cent. Of these the bulk consisted of textiles, metal manufacturers and chemicals. On the import side capital equipment, with parts and processed fuels accounted for 72 per cent of China's imports; 64 per cent of Thailand's imports; 39 per cent of Philippines' imports with combustible fuels for another 14 per cent, 71 per cent of Malaysia's imports and 72 per cent of Indonesia's imports [cf Tables V(a) and (b)]. Given this similarity in the commodity composition of the trade of China and the ASEAN countries, it is clear why the trade between them has not increased as fast as their trade with other countries thus showing a relative decline since the two sets of countries, i.e., the ASEAN countries and China are selling and buying similar commodities mainly to/from Japan, USA, South Korea, EEC countries and Australia they are more of competitors in these markets and cannot also hope for any dramatic increase in their own bilateral trade in spite of the fact that Singapore based entrepreneurs have recently emerged as not insignificant investors in China.

The commodity composition of the trade between China and the ASEAN countries has been depicted in detail in Tables VI A and B for 1984 and Tables VIIA and B for the year 1993. These tables are based on data collected and published by the Chinese Government. The two Reference Sources on which Tables VI and VII are based upon the Almance of China's Foreign Economic Relations and Trade, 1985 as well as the China Customs Statistics Yearbook, 1993-94.

Table VIA shows the principal items of exports from China to the ASEAN countries in 1984. It is clear from Table VIA that even in 1984 the ASEAN countries did not figure as a significant destination point for China's exports. According to the Chinese Government classification in 1984, of the total value of China's exports only 0.79 per cent went to Malaysia; 0.28 per cent to Indonesia; 4.89 per cent to Singapore; 0.94 per cent to Philippines; one per cent to Thailand and 0.12 per cent to Brunei or a total of 8.02 per cent. The prominent exports from China to the ASEAN countries in 1984 were cereals; cotton piece goods; readymade garments; shoes; embroidered articles; pottery and porcelain; petroleum products and pharmaceuticals. When one turns to Table VIIA for a comparison with 1993 the first point to notice is that Chinese Government data show a greater fall in the share of the ASEAN countries in the value of China's exports than that shown by the IMF data. Thus by 1993 Malaysia's share in the value of China's exports has gone down to 0.77 per cent; that of Indonesia to 0.75 per cent; of Singapore to 2.4 per cent, of Philippines to 0.31 per cent; of Thailand to 0.81 per cent and of Brunei to 0.01 per cent. Compared to the 8.02 per cent ASEAN share in the value of China's exports in 1984, according to the official Chinese data this had declined to 5.14 per cent in 1993. Although the commodity composition of China's exports globally had changed dramatically to the ASEAN countries it was still mainly exporting cereals; mineral products including some fuel; textiles and textile articles; footwear and some transport equipment plus machinery and consumer electronics like television and tape recorders. The share of the last two categories was minimal. 6.88 per cent of China's exports of transport equipment went to the ASEAN countries, i.e., the actual value being 132.5 million dollars in 1993. Similarly just 6.07 per cent of the value of China's exports of machinery, televisions and tape recorders went to the ASEAN countries, i.e., worth 931.7 million dollars. Taken together these two categories were 1064.2 million dollars which was only 22.6 per cent of the total value of China's exports to the ASEAN countries valued at 4715.6 million US dollars [cf. Table VIIA]. If we add the exports from China to the ASEAN countries of the products of the chemical and allied industry [9.54 per cent worth 419.5 million US dollars]; of prepared foodstuffs [9.57 per cent worth 345.6 million US dollars] and of textile articles [2.78 per cent worth 724.5 million US dollars], then also we get a ratio of 54 per cent of China's exports. Compared to the average of 87 per cent of China's exports being those of manufactured items a ratio 54 per cent for the ASEAN countries in 1993 is 33 per cent below average. This shows that the potential for the growth of manufactured goods from China to the ASEAN countries is low.

When one analyzes the commodity composition of the imports from the ASEAN countries to China the fact is again underlined that these two regions are not trading much in manufactured products and even less in high value added manufactured articles. In 1984 Malaysia accounted for 0.75 per cent of the value of China's imports; Indonesia for 0.03 per cent; Singapore for 0.22 per cent; Philippines for 0.009 per cent and Thailand for 0.32 per cent or the ASEAN countries together for 1.12 per cent worth 364.9 million US dollars. Of these about 22 per cent consisted of aluminium ingots; 44 per cent of natural rubber; 12 per cent of timber; and 1.5 per cent of sugar accounting for almost 80 per cent of the total imports from ASEAN into China. By 1993 as opposed to the share of China's exports going to the ASEAN countries which had declined the proportion of China's imports from the ASEAN countries had increased to 5.76 per cent worth 5988.1 million US dollars. Of the imports from ASEAN into China, in 1993 vegetable products including rubber was worth 93.7 million US dollars accounting for 7.34 per cent of total imports in this category; cereals were worth 34.9 million US dollars or 3.5 per cent of imports of all cereals; minerals were worth 1961.8 million US dollars or 27.41 per cent of imports in this category; fuels were worth 2496.3 million US dollars or 42.9 per cent of fuel imports into China; raw hides and skins were worth 204.3 million US dollars or 11.09 per cent of imports in this category; cotton was worth 12.12 million US dollars are 0.98 per cent; and semi-processed base metals worth 297.7 million US dollars or 1.8 per cent of imports of this commodity into China. The non-manufactured imports from ASEAN into China accounted for about 5100 million US dollars or 85 per cent of total imports from ASEAN into China in 1993. The manufactured imports from ASEAN into China in the same year were about 13.5 per cent of total imports from ASEAN and consisted mainly of textile and paper products; goods produced by the chemical and allied industries; some transport equipment, machinery and television sets. Once again the share of manufactured goods in ASEAN imports into China even in 1993 was much below the average of 78 per cent for overall exports from ASEAN. Thus the basis for any significant increase of trade between ASEAN and China is weak, as also for any efforts at forming a common market or preferential trade bloc like the proposed EAEF.

## FDI IN CHINA AND THE ASEAN

The principal reason for the increasing lack of complementarity between China and the ASEAN countries is to be found in the fact that their growth of exports is fuelled by similar injections of Foreign Direct Investments often from the same sources. For a variety of reasons, ASEAN and China have emerged as the leading areas for FDI and because they have been making many incremental policy changes and providing an increasing number of incentives to attract foreign investments, they have also provided alternative avenues for investors functioning, therefore as competitors in the international capital markets.

Table VIII at the end of this study presents data regarding the inflow of FDI into China and the ASEAN countries. Between 1987 and 1993 the People's Republic of China received 53910 million US dollars worth of FDI. By comparison Singapore got 33400 million US dollars worth of FDI in the same period; Malaysia got 17960 million US dollars FDI; Indonesia 7999 million US dollars; Philippines 3871 and Thailand 11427 million US dollars FDI. Hence, as a region the ASEAN countries between 1987 and 1993 got 74657 million US dollars FDI which is 38 per cent more than what China got. It is worthwhile to try and understand the reasons behind this phenomenon.

In the 1980s, the trade policies of the developed countries especially the United States, also encouraged the inflow of FDI into the ASEAN region. US actions included the removal in 1988 of General System of Preferences (GSP) tariff rates for the Newly Industrializing Countries (NICs), mounting pressures for currency appreciation, and stepped up investigations of dumping and countervailing duty complaints, all of which helped turn Japan and the NICs toward the South East Asian countries as a base for economic activities. In addition, Taiwan and South Korea experienced rapid wage increases in the 1980s, in Taiwan, for example, the wages increased by 35 per cent in 1987 and an additional 12 per cent in 1988, making Taiwan's wage rate about three times greater than comparable rates in Indonesia and five times more than those in Thailand and Malaysia. The rapid rise in labour costs has encouraged North East Asian investors to relocate their labour intensive industries to South East Asia. Major adjustments of individual currency rates is another key factor in promoting FDI into the ASEAN countries. The currencies of Korea and Taiwan followed later by that of Japan have appreciated significantly during the 1980s. Since 1985, the South Korean won has risen almost 30 per cent against the dollar, while the New Taiwan dollar has risen by over 40 per cent. Since the currencies of Malaysia, Thailand, Indonesia and Philippines did not appreciate significantly, they could attract new foreign investors eager to capitalize on the cheaper currency rates.[7] In all these respects for sometime China provided keen competition during the 1980s attracting large amounts of FDI especially into its special Economic Zones (SEZs). Partly, as a response to China's economic liberalization programme and to counter the negative impact of an increase in real wages in its own economies, the ASEAN countries launched the ASEAN Free Trade Area (AFTA), an economic liberalization programme which aims at reducing internal tariffs to a maximum of 5 per cent in 15 years (i.e. by 2000 A.D.). The ASEAN governments and entrepreneurs also identified three major growth areas within their region, encompassing southern Thailand, Indonesia's Sumatra and Northern Malaysia; Southern Malaysia, Singapore and Indonesia; and the Southern Philippines, Indonesia's Sulawesi Island and Malaysia Sabah.[8]

The steps taken by ASEAN countries to further their economic liberalization process has had a positive impact on the amount of Foreign Direct Investments they received in 1994 :

**Table I**
**Authorized foreign investment in ASEAN in 1994**

*(in Billions of US dollars)*

| *Country* | *Amount (in $ Bi)* | *% Year on Year Growth* |
|---|---|---|
| Indonesia | 23.7 | 191.3% |
| Malaysia | 4.3 | 78.5% |
| Philippines | 2.3 | 328.5% |
| Singapore | 2.8 | 36.2% |
| Thailand | 4.3 | 48.2% |

*Source :* Report on Foreign Capital buoys ASEAN's health, *The Nikkei Weekly*, an economic newspaper published in Tokyo, 13.2.1995, p. 18.

In contrast to the ASEAN areas, China's overall contracted foreign investment slumped a year on year 44 per cent to US dollar 32 billion in the first five months of 1994, according to the official newspaper, *China Daily*.[9] The pattern of decline was interesting to analyze. Foreign investment in Guangdong province plunged a year, on year 33 per cent during the first five months of 1994. Western investment was up by nearly 50 per cent, but Taiwanese and Hong Kong investors retreated before an onslaught of tax, trade and land use reforms according to the Guangdong Vice-Governor Lu Ruihua.[10]

At the macro level the relative drop in investment into China was ascribed to tighter regulation, recessionary macro-economic policies and stiffer competition from other Asian investment havens.[11] It's obvious that AFTA will provide long term competition to China and other investment destinations in Asia trying to attract an inflow of foreign investments.

It is interesting to note how Taiwanese investors in particular are no longer investing only or mainly in China but diversifying their regional portfolio by sending much larger amounts to the ASEAN countries. In Malaysia, the outstanding feature of the Malaysian dollar 11.2 billion pumped into its manufacturing sector last year was the high profile of Taiwanese businesses. Investment from Taiwan nearly tripled making it the largest single investor, while investment from Japan only grew by 6.3 per cent the cumulative total still remained at a high level. In Singapore, it was the investment by the US companies which soared 69 per cent centering on the personal computers field. In Indonesia, the amount of authorized investments nearly doubled over 1993's total as the government relaxed some restrictions on foreign businesses. Investment in manufacturing industries, such as petrochemical and electrical machinery stood at 5.5 times the figure for 1993. The amount of approved investment in Indonesia from Japan grew by 87 per cent year on year. Particularly, noticeable was the surge in investment from the UK and Hong Kong. A phalanx of Honk Kong companies won orders for large infrastructure projects leading to a 16 fold increase in approved investments from Hong Kong. In Philippines, investment from the US swelled by 6.4 times and accounted for nearly 30 per cent of the total investment, which was up 400 per cent on the year before. However, investment form Japan, which has been lagging fell 10 per cent year on year.[12]

Another report has pointed out the reasons for the relative decline of Taiwanese and Hong Kong investments in China. In recent years investment from Hong Kong and Taiwanese investment had accounted for 12 per cent and 15 per cent respectively of FDI into China. But the climate is changing as land and labour costs rise. With the Central Government trying to rein in inflation by restricting credit, it has become difficult for mainland enterprises and foreign joint ventures alike to collect on debts. Meanwhile the mainland fever that pushed Taiwanese investment in China to about $ 20 billion in recent years has cooled as investors from the island across the Formosa straits begin to respond to Taipei's "Go South" policy. Worried about mainland China commanding so much of Taiwan's financial resources, Taipei has urged companies to diversity their oversea investments elsewhere in Asia. Consequently, although as a result of prior commitments made, during the first ten months of 1994, China absorbed 25.2 billion US dollars worth of investments, a 44 per cent increase over the same period the last year, the number of new ventures dropped by 46 per cent through the end of September and investment pledges fell 32 per cent to $ 57 billion. Business experts say a part of the foreign investor's growing wariness is their apparent lack of legal protection in China.[13]

A final factor which would prevent the growth of any grand axis of trade between China and ASEAN is the growth of bilateral aid by Japan and Taiwan to ASEAN countries which together figure among the top ten recipients of aid from these two major aid givers especially Japan, now the world's largest aid giver.[14] [cf. Report on Japan's ODA 1992, Tokyo, Chapter I]. By comparison China provides very little in terms of aid to the ASEAN countries and is not likely to do so in the future since its total debt is expected to increase from 67040 million US dollars in 1993 to 99713 million US dollars in 2000 A.D.[15] [World Bank Report, No. 10199, 1992].

Thus, it is fairly clear that the ASEAN economies will see not a China centered growth but a more internationalized system of trade and economic interaction in the post Cold War period in the 1990s and beyond. This provides a practical basis for building better economic relations between the leading Asian economies in the immediate future and also for the ASEAN countries to secure the cooperation of other countries in ensuring their own security and progressing with their own development.

## NOTES

1. Yu Zhida, Optimistic Prospects for China-Indonesia Trade, *Intertrade*, April 1991, pp. 66-67.
2. Fu Zhengluo, Sino-Indonesian Trade : Today and Tomorrow, *Intertrade*, February 1991.
3. *Ibid.*
4. Cao Yunhua, Sino-Singapore Economic Relations and Trade, *Intertrade*, February 1991, p. 7.
5. *Ibid.*
6. Report on, ASEAN, Preventive Measure in *Far Eastern Economic Review*, 4.8.1994, p. 14.

7. Linda Y.C. Lim and Clyde D. Stoltenberg, Becoming a Region, *The China Business Review*, May-June 1990, pp. 24-29.

8. Report on ASEAN, Growing Pains, *Far Eastern Economic Review*, 28.7.1994, pp. 22-23.

9. Business Briefing, *Fear Eastern Economic Review*, 7.7.1994, p. 71.

10. *Ibid.*, 23.6.1994, p. 63.

11. *Ibid.*, 7.7.1994.

12. Report on Foreign Capital Buoys ASEAN Health, *The Nikkei Weekly*, 13.2.95, Tokyo, p. 18.

13. Report on Taiwan Investors Rethinking China Strategy, *The Daily Yomiuri*, 28.1.1995, Tokyo, p. 15.

14. Report on Japan's ODA, Tokyo, Ministry of Foreign Affairs, 1992, Chapter I.

15. World Bank Report, No. 10199, 1992.

TABLE I
**Direction of China's trade (1975-93)**

*(in Millions of US dollars)*

| *Year* | *Total value one million $* | *Value and % share of* | | *Japan* | | *Europe* | | *Six ASEAN countries** | | *Rest of the countries* | |
|---|---|---|---|---|---|---|---|---|---|---|---|
| Exports To | | | | | | | | | | | |
| 1980 | 17087 | 1059 | (6.2%) | 3951 | (23.1%) | 773 | (4.5%) | 1571 | (9.2%) | 9733 | (57.0%) |
| 1985 | 27327 | 2336 | (8.5%) | 6091 | (22.2%) | 955 | (63.5%) | 2806 | (10.3%) | 15139 | (55.3%) |
| 1986 | 31367 | 2633 | (8.4%) | 5079 | (16.2%) | 1247 | (4.0%) | 1882 | (5.9%) | 20526 | (65.4%) |
| 1987 | 39464 | 2363 | (6.0%) | 6392 | (16.2%) | 1400 | (3.6%) | 2316 | (5.8%) | 26993 | (68.3%) |
| 1988 | 47663 | 3399 | (7.1%) | 8046 | (16.9%) | 1381 | (2.9%) | -2822 | (5.9%) | 32015 | (67.2%) |
| 1989 | 52914 | 4414 | (8.3%) | 8395 | (15.9%) | 1256 | (2.4%) | 3110 | (5.8%) | 35739 | (67.5%) |
| 1991 | 71986 | 6192 | (8.6%) | 10265 | (14.2%) | 345 | (0.48%) | 4132 | (5.7%) | 51052 | (70.9%) |
| 1993 | 91744 | 16965 | (18.5%) | 15777 | (17.2%) | 352 | (0.38%) | 4683 | (5.1%) | 53967 | (58.8%) |
| Imports From | | | | | | | | | | | |
| 1980 | 19505 | 3830 | (19.6%) | 5169 | (26.5%) | 629 | (3.2%) | 654 | (3.4%) | 9223 | (47.2%) |
| 1985 | 42534 | 5199 | (12.2%) | 15178 | (35.7%) | 3009 | (7.1%) | 1129 | (2.7%) | 18019 | (42.3%) |
| 1986 | 43247 | 4718 | (10.9%) | 12463 | (28.8%) | 1886 | (4.4%) | 1480 | (3.4%) | 22700 | (52.4%) |
| 1987 | 43222 | 4836 | (11.1%) | 10087 | (23.3%) | 1662 | (3.8%) | 2057 | (4.8%) | 24580 | (56.7%) |

*(Contd.)*

| Year | Total value one million $ | Value and % share of | | Japan | | Europe | | Six ASEAN countries* | | Rest of the countries | |
|---|---|---|---|---|---|---|---|---|---|---|---|
| 1988 | 55352 | 6633 | (12.0%) | 11062 | (19.2%) | 1951 | (3.52%) | -2043 | (3.7%) | 33663 | (61.0%) |
| 1989 | 59140 | 7864 | (13.3%) | 10534 | (17.8%) | 1817 | (3.1%) | 3620 | (6.1%) | 35305 | (60.0%) |
| 1991 | 63957 | 8003 | (12.5%) | 10079 | (15.8%) | 966 | (1.5%) | 3820 | (6.0%) | 41089 | (4.2%) |
| 1993 | 103958 | 10687 | (10.3%) | 23289 | (22.4%) | 981 | (0.94%) | 6012 | (5.8%) | 62989 | |
| Total value of Trade | | | | | | | | | | | |
| 1980 | 36592 | 4889 | (13.4%) | 9120 | (25.0%) | 1402 | (3.8%) | 2225 | (6.1%) | 18956 | (51.8%) |
| 1985 | 69861 | 7535 | (10.8%) | 21269 | (30.4%) | 3964 | (5.7%) | 3935 | (5.6%) | 33158 | (47.5%) |
| 1986 | 74614 | 7351 | (9.9%) | 17542 | (23.5%) | 3133 | (4.2%) | 3362 | (4.5%) | 43226 | (57.9%) |
| 1987 | 82686 | 7199 | (8.7%) | 16479 | (19.9%) | 3062 | (3.7%) | 4373 | (5.3%) | 51573 | (62.3%) |
| 1988 | 103015 | 10032 | (9.7%) | 18133 | (17.6%) | 3332 | (3.2%) | 4865 | (4.7%) | 66653 | (64.7%) |
| 1989 | 112054 | 12278 | (11.0%) | 18929 | (16.9%) | 3073 | (2.7%) | 6730 | (6.0%) | 71044 | (63.4%) |
| 1991 | 135943 | 14195 | (10.4%) | 20344 | (15.0%) | 1311 | (0.96%) | 7952 | (5.85%) | 92141 | (67.8%) |
| 1993 | 195702 | 27652 | (14.12%) | 39066 | (20.0%) | 1333 | (0.68%) | 10695 | (5.46%) | 116956 | (60.0%) |

*Source* : (a) Direction of Trade Statistics, IMF, Washington D.C., Relevant Issues

(b) China Customs Statistics, Yearbook—1993-94

* The Six ASEAN countries are: Indonesia, Malaysia, Philippines, Thailand, Singapore and Brunei.

## TABLE II
## Direction of trade of Japan, China, India and the leading South East Asian countries

**Table II(a) JAPAN**

*(Value in Million US dollars)*

| *With/To* | *Value of Imports from* | | | | *Value of Exports to* | | | |
|---|---|---|---|---|---|---|---|---|
| | *1988 Value* | *% of Total* | *1992 Value* | *% of Total* | *1988 Value* | *% of Total* | *1992 Value* | *% of Total* |
| World | 183252 | 100.0% | 230975 | 100.0% | 264772 | 100.0% | 339492 | 100.0% |
| USA | 42190 | 23.0% | 52607 | 22.7% | 90238 | 34.0% | 96486 | 28.4% |
| China | 9859 | 5.4% | 16923 | 7.3% | 9475 | 3.6% | 11926 | 3.5% |
| South Korea | 11771 | 6.4% | 11568 | 5.0% | 15430 | 5.8% | 17786 | 5.2% |
| United Kingdom | 3745 | 2.04% | 4565 | 1.98% | 10632 | 4.01% | 12304 | 3.62% |
| Indonesia | 9497 | 5.1% | 12219 | 5.3% | 3054 | 1.2% | 5576 | 1.64% |
| Australia | 9666 | 5.3% | 11836 | 5.1% | 6680 | 2.52% | 7044 | 2.07% |
| Germany | 8097 | 4.4% | 10750 | 4.7% | 15792 | 6.0% | 20337 | 6.0% |
| Canada | 7783 | 4.25% | 7626 | 3.3% | 6424 | 2.43% | 7089 | 2.01% |
| France | 4268 | 2.33% | 5395 | 2.3% | 4989 | 1.89% | 6325 | 1.86% |
| Malaysia | 4710 | 2.6% | 6572 | 2.8% | 3060 | 1.2% | 8113 | 2.4% |
| Thailand | 2751 | 1.5% | 5945 | 2.6% | 5158 | 1.95% | 10352 | 3.0% |
| Singapore | 2308 | 1.3% | 3075 | 1.3% | 8235 | 3.1% | 12885 | 3.8% |
| Philippines | 1914 | 1.0% | 2337 | 1.01% | 1740 | 0.65% | 3512 | 1.03% |
| Hong Kong | 2109 | 1.16% | 2041 | 0.88% | 11697 | 4.4% | 20702 | 6.1% |
| India | 1804 | 0.98% | 2043 | 0.89% | 2081 | 0.79% | 1486 | 0.43% |
| Brunei | 1117 | 0.61% | 1360 | 0.59% | N.A. | — | N.A. | — |
| Pakistan | 552 | 0.31% | 530 | 0.23% | 1126 | 0.43% | 1295 | 0.38% |
| Vietnam | 196 | 0.1% | 868 | | N.A. | — | N.A. | — |

*Source :* International Trade Statistics, Trade by Country Yearbook UN, Vol. I, 1992, pp. 488-89.

**Table II (b) INDIA**

*[Value in million US dollars]*

| *With/To* | *Value of Imports from* | | | | *Value of Exports to* | | | |
|---|---|---|---|---|---|---|---|---|
| | *1988 Value* | *% of Total* | *1992 Value* | *% of Total* | *1988 Value* | *% of Total* | *1992 Value* | *% of Total* |
| World | 17154 | | 19509 | | 12088 | | 17900 | |
| USA | 1538 | 9.0% | 1891 | 9.7% | 2252 | 18.7% | 2927 | 16.3% |
| Germany | 1661 | 9.7% | 1551 | 7.8% | 817 | 6.8% | 1272 | 7.1% |
| Japan | 1636 | 9.5% | 1364 | 7.0% | 1244 | 10.3% | 1655 | 9.2% |
| United Kingdom | 1406 | 8.2% | 1186 | 6.07% | 783 | 6.48% | 1141 | 6.37% |
| France | 614 | 3.59% | 580 | 2.97% | 292 | 2.4% | 426 | 2.39% |
| Australia | 381 | 2.22% | 561 | 2.9% | 1387 | 1.15% | 203 | 1.13% |
| Malaysia | 649 | 3.78% | 391 | 2.0% | 696 | 0.58% | 203 | 1.13% |
| Singapore | 266 | 1.5% | 311 | 1.6% | 210 | 1.74% | 390 | 2.2% |
| South Korea | 260 | 1.49% | 314 | 1.6% | 112 | 0.93% | 242 | 1.35% |
| Hong Kong | 926 | 0.54% | 107 | 0.55% | 344 | 2.84% | 616 | 3.44% |
| Thailand | 500 | 0.29% | 487 | 0.25% | 632 | 0.92% | 199 | 1.11% |
| China | 113 | 0.66% | 21 | 0.11% | 15 | 0.12% | 48 | 0.27% |
| Indonesia | 530 | 0.31% | 673 | 0.34% | 207 | 0.17% | 147 | 0.82% |
| Philippines | — | — | Nil | — | 16 | 0.13% | 64 | 0.36% |
| ASEAN XVI, XIV, X, XI | | 5.88% | | 4.19% | | 3.41% | | 5.26% |

*Source :* International Trade Statistics Yearbook Vol. I, Trade By Country, 1992, pp. 440-41.

**Table II (c) INDONESIA** *[Value in million US dollars]*

| *With/To* | *Value of Imports from* | | | | *Value of Exports to* | | | |
|---|---|---|---|---|---|---|---|---|
| | *1988 Value* | *% of Total* | *1992 Value* | *% of Total* | *1988 Value* | *% of Total* | *1992 Value* | *% of Total* |
| World | 13249 | | 27280 | | 18901 | | 33815 | |
| Japan | 3386 | 25.6% | 6014 | 22.0% | 8018 | 42.4% | 10753 | 32.0% |
| USA | 1736 | 13.1% | 3823 | 14.0% | 3074 | 16.3% | 4420 | 13.0% |
| China | 439 | 3.3% | 752 | 2.75% | 492 | 2.6% | 1397 | 4.1% |
| Saudi Arabia | 565 | 4.3% | 852 | 3.12% | 170 | 0.90% | 583 | 1.72% |
| Singapore | 895 | 6.76% | 1671 | 6.12% | 1336 | 7.2% | 3194 | 9.4% |
| Germany | 886 | 6.7% | 2141 | 7.8% | 455 | 2.4% | 978 | 2.9% |
| South Korea | 376 | 2.84% | 1894 | 7.0% | 840 | 4.44% | 2083 | 6.16% |
| United Kingdom | 390 | 2.6% | 719 | 2.63% | 349 | 1.9% | 844 | 2.5% |
| Australia | 578 | 4.4% | 1413 | 5.12% | 293 | 1.56% | 746 | 2.2% |
| Hong Kong | 1332 | 1.01% | 229 | 0.39% | 554 | 2.9% | 856 | 2.5% |
| Malaysia | 276 | 2.1% | 525 | 1.9% | 184 | 0.97% | 488 | 1.45% |
| Thailand | 96 | 0.72% | 345 | 1.26% | 151 | 0.80% | 353 | 1.04% |
| Philippines | 36 | 0.28% | 52 | 0.19% | 86 | 0.46 | 181 | 0.54% |
| India | 36 | 0.27% | 216 | 3.59% | 67 | 0.35% | 70 | 0.2% |
| Pakistan | 55 | 0.42% | 100 | 0.37% | 38 | 0.21% | 81 | 0.24% |
| Vietnam | 7.4 | 0.06% | 33 | 0.12% | 23 | 0.12% | 19 | 0.56% |

*Source :* As in Table II(a), p. 449.

Table II (d) CHINA

[Value in million US dollars]

| With/To | Value of Imports from | | | | Value of Exports to | | | |
|---|---|---|---|---|---|---|---|---|
| | 1988 Value | % of Total | 1992 Value | % of Total | 1988 Value | % of Total | 1992 Value | % of Total |
| World | 55268 | | 80585 | | 47516 | | 84940 | |
| Japan | 11035 | 20.0% | 13682 | 17.0% | 7902 | 17.0% | 11679 | 14.0% |
| USA | 6649 | 12.0% | 8901 | 7.0% | 8600 | 7.0% | 8600 | 10.0% |
| Hong Kong | 11889 | 22.0% | 20534 | 25.4% | 18263 | 38.4% | 37512 | 44.2% |
| Germany | 3431 | 6.2% | 4015 | 0.5% | 1484 | 3.12% | 2448 | 2.89% |
| Canada | 1848 | 4.98% | 1638 | 2.03% | 389 | 0.82% | 653 | 0.77% |
| Singapore | 1018 | 1.8% | 1236 | 1.53% | 1482 | 3.11% | 2031 | 3.0% |
| Indonesia | 682 | 1.23% | 1554 | 1.93% | 236 | 0.5% | 471 | 0.56% |
| South Korea | 197 | 0.36% | 2623 | 3.25% | 88 | 0.18% | 2405 | 2.83% |
| Malaysia | 569 | 1.03% | 830 | 1.03% | 308 | 0.65% | 645 | 0.76% |
| Thailand | 633 | 1.15% | 425 | 0.53% | 443 | 0.93% | 895 | 1.05% |
| India | 98 | 0.18% | 181 | 0.23% | 149 | 0.31% | 158 | 0.19% |
| Pakistan | 55 | 0.10% | 91 | 0.11% | 282 | 0.59% | 551 | 0.65% |
| Philippines | 135 | 0.25% | 155 | 0.19% | 270 | 0.57% | 210 | 0.24% |
| Singapore, Malaysia, Indonesia, Philippines, Thailand, South East Asian countries | | 5.53% | | 5.21% | | 5.76% | | 5.62% |

*Source :* As in Table II (a), p. 174.

**Table II(e) SINGAPORE** *[Value in million US dollars]*

| *With/To* | *Value of Imports from* | | | | *Value of Exports to* | | | |
|---|---|---|---|---|---|---|---|---|
| | *1988 Value* | *% of Total* | *1992 Value* | *% of Total* | *1988 Value* | *% of Total* | *1992 Value* | *% of Total* |
| World | 43765 | 100.0% | 72067 | 100.0% | 39205 | 100.0% | 63386 | 100.0% |
| Japan | 9554 | 21.2% | 15122 | 21.0% | 3364 | 8.6% | 4825 | 7.6% |
| USA | 6808 | 15.6% | 11879 | 16.5% | 9370 | 23.4% | 13391 | 21.2% |
| Malaysia | 6426 | 14.7% | 10613 | 14.7% | 5292 | 13.5% | 7901 | 12.5% |
| Germany | 1619 | 3.7% | 2351 | 3.3% | 1364 | 3.5% | 2689 | 4.2% |
| China | 1683 | 3.8% | 2252 | 3.1% | 1178 | 3.0% | 1112 | 1.75% |
| Thailand | 1186 | 2.71% | 2681 | 3.71% | 2137 | 5.5% | 3947 | 6.3% |
| South Korea | 1264 | 2.3% | 2370 | 3.3% | 769 | 1.97% | 1426 | 2.25% |
| Hong Kong | 1207 | 2.76% | 2202 | 3.05% | 2456 | 6.3% | 4960 | 7.8% |
| United Kingdom | 1273 | 2.9% | 2015 | 2.8% | 1144 | 2.9% | 1845 | 2.9% |
| Australia | 867 | 1.99% | 1226 | 1.7% | 1065 | 2.7% | 1509 | 2.4% |
| Iran | 400 | 0.91% | 507 | 0.70% | 108 | 2.74% | 187 | 0.30% |
| Saudi Arabia | 1926 | 4.4% | 3696 | 5.13% | 276 | 0.7% | 412 | 0.66% |
| India | 266 | 0.61% | 533 | 0.74% | 736 | 1.9% | 932 | 1.47% |
| Pakistan | 44 | 0.10% | 82 | 0.11% | 161 | 0.41% | 264 | 0.42% |
| Bangladesh | 46 | 0.11% | 29 | 0.04% | 282 | 0.72% | 332 | 0.52% |
| Brunei | 112 | 0.26% | 266 | 0.37% | 414 | 1.06% | 663 | 1.05% |
| Philippines | 263 | 0.61% | 317 | 0.44% | 513 | 1.3% | 801 | 1.23% |
| France | 789 | 1.8% | 1797 | 2.49% | 652 | 1.66% | 972 | 1.53% |

*Source :* As in Table II(a), p. 835.

**Table II(f) MALAYSIA** *[Value in million US dollars]*

| *With/To* | *Value of Imports from* | | | | *Value of Exports to* | | | |
|---|---|---|---|---|---|---|---|---|
| | *1988 Value* | *% of Total* | *1992 Value* | *% of Total* | *1988 Value* | *% of Total* | *1992 Value* | *% of Total* |
| World | 12589 | | 35183 | | 17912 | | 34300 | |
| Japan | 2746 | 21.8% | 9541 | 27.1% | 3503 | 19.5% | 5388 | 15.7% |
| USA | 2363 | 18.7% | 5596 | 15.9% | 2969 | 16.6% | 5802 | 17.0% |
| Singapore | 1824 | 14.5% | 4071 | 11.6% | 3252 | 18.2% | 7992 | 23.3% |
| Germany | 538 | 4.27% | 1595 | 4.53% | 612 | 3.4% | 1242 | 3.62% |
| United Kingdom | 517 | 4.1% | 1165 | 3.3% | 569 | 4.1% | 1503 | 4.4% |
| France | 204 | 1.62% | 466 | 1.32% | 239 | 1.33% | 475 | 1.39% |
| Canada | 129 | 1.03% | 288 | 0.82% | 139 | 0.78% | 267 | 0.78% |
| Australia | 526 | 4.2% | 961 | 2.73% | 399 | 2.23% | 586 | 1.7% |
| South Korea | 34 | 2.65% | 989 | 2.8% | 951 | 5.3% | 1514 | 4.4% |
| China | 376 | 3.0% | 803 | 2.3% | 279 | 1.6% | 639 | 1.9% |
| Hong Kong | 276 | 0.78% | 679 | 1.93% | 499 | 2.78% | 1152 | 3.36% |
| Indonesia | 176 | 1.4% | 494 | 1.4% | 146 | 0.82% | 503 | 1.5% |
| Thailand | 443 | 3.36% | 890 | 2.53% | 512 | 2.86% | 1094 | 3.4% |
| India | 100 | 0.8% | 281 | 0.8% | 519 | 2.9% | 317 | 0.93% |
| Pakistan | 16 | 0.12% | 35 | 0.10% | 170 | 0.96% | 352 | 1.03% |
| Philippines | 148 | 1.18% | 164 | 0.47% | 323 | 1.8% | 330 | 0.97% |
| Vietnam | 14 | 0.11% | 63 | 0.18% | Nil | | Nil | |

*N.B.* : Countries not mentioned do not have significant trade with Malaysia.
*Source* : As in Table II(a), p. 569.

**Table II (g) THAILAND** *[Value in million US dollars]*

| *With/To* | *Value of Imports from* | | | | *Value of Exports to* | | | |
|---|---|---|---|---|---|---|---|---|
| | *1988 Value* | *% of Total* | *1992 Value* | *% of Total* | *1988 Value* | *% of Total* | *1992 Value* | *% of Total* |
| World | 20225 | 100.0% | 40467 | 100.0% | 15952 | 100.0% | 28416 | 100.0% |
| Japan | 5880 | 29.0% | 11899 | 29.4% | 25460 | 15.6% | 5133 | 18.0% |
| USA | 2749 | 13.6% | 4774 | 11.8% | 3200 | 20.0% | 6062 | 21.3% |
| Germany | 1084 | 5.4% | 2149 | 5.3% | 735 | 4.6% | 1469 | 5.2% |
| United Kingdom | 582 | 2.9% | 911 | 2.26% | 588 | 3.7% | 1028 | 3.6% |
| France | 491 | 2.43% | 943 | 2.33% | 379 | 2.34% | 699 | 2.47% |
| Australia | 342 | 1.69% | 788 | 1.95% | 296 | 1.86% | 463 | 1.63% |
| China | 679 | 3.4% | 1149 | 2.8% | 475 | 3.0% | 335 | 1.18% |
| South Korea | 563 | 2.8% | 1786 | 4.4% | 254 | 1.6% | 459 | 1.6% |
| Singapore | 1503 | 7.4% | 2950 | 7.3% | 1225 | 7.7% | 2335 | 8.2% |
| Hong Kong | 250 | 1.23% | 492 | 1.22% | 710 | 4.5% | 1348 | 4.74% |
| Malaysia | 425 | 2.1% | 1596 | 3.9% | 472 | 3.0% | 684 | 2.4% |
| Indonesia | 174 | 0.85% | 291 | 0.7% | 85 | 0.5% | 214 | 0.8% |
| Philippines | 190 | 0.94% | 121 | 0.3% | 59 | 0.37% | 105 | 0.37% |
| India | 171 | 0.84% | 335 | 0.83% | 221 | 1.4% | 64 | 0.22% |
| Saudi Arabia | 203 | 1.0% | 519 | 1.3% | 356 | 2.2% | 445 | 1.6% |

*Source :* As in Table XI(a), p. 909.

**Table II (h) PHILIPPINES** *[Value in million US dollars]*

| *With/To* | *Value of Imports from* | | | | *Value of Exports to* | | | |
|---|---|---|---|---|---|---|---|---|
| | *1988 Value* | *% of Total* | *1992 Value* | *% of Total* | *1988 Value* | *% of Total* | *1992 Value* | *% of Total* |
| World | 8729 | | 15465 | | 7074 | | 9790 | |
| USA | 1850 | 21.2% | 2821 | 18.2% | 2522 | 35.6% | 3843 | 39.2% |
| Japan | 1519 | 17.4% | 3282 | 17.3% | 1424 | 20.1% | 1745 | 17.8% |
| Germany | 342 | 3.9% | 699 | 4.5% | 298 | 4.2% | 521 | 5.3% |
| United Kingdom | 171 | 1.96% | 314 | 2.0% | 328 | 4.6% | 436 | 4.46% |
| France | 129 | 1.48% | 225 | 1.5% | 165 | 2.34% | 179 | 1.83% |
| Canada | 91 | 1.04% | 218 | 1.41% | 108 | 1.52% | 160 | 1.63% |
| Australia | 314 | 3.6% | 458 | 3.0% | 111 | 1.6% | 113 | 1.16% |
| China | 268 | 3.0% | 201 | 1.33% | 67 | 0.94% | 114 | 1.16% |
| Hong Kong | 388 | 4.5% | 745 | 4.8% | 346 | 4.9% | 463 | 4.72% |
| Singapore | 352 | 4.0% | 573 | 3.7% | 224 | 3.16% | 252 | 2.58% |
| Malaysia | 258 | 3.0% | 410 | 2.65% | 117 | 1.65% | 128 | 1.3% |
| Indonesia | 91 | 1.05% | 196 | 1.27% | 28 | 0.38% | 40 | 0.41% |
| India | 29 | 0.33% | 95 | 0.61% | 71 | 1.0% | 8.6 | 0.09% |

*Source* : As in Table II (a), p. 726.

**Table II (i) BRUNEI** *[Value in million US dollars]*

| *With/To* | *Value of Imports from* | | | | *Value of Exports to* | | | |
|---|---|---|---|---|---|---|---|---|
| | *1984 Value* | *% of Total* | *1989 Value* | *% of Total* | *1984 Value* | *% of Total* | *1989 Value* | *% of Total* |
| World | 610 | | 856 | | 2972 | | 1883 | |
| USA | 96 | 5.3% | 94 | 10.9% | 218 | 7.33% | 93 | 4.9% |
| Japan | 122 | 19.9% | 123 | 14.8% | 1820 | 61.2% | 1095 | 58.2% |
| Singapore | 150 | 24.5% | 231 | 27.0% | 259 | 8.7% | 90 | 4.79% |
| United Kingdom | 53 | 8.62% | 73 | 8.53% | 1.2 | 0.04% | 9.5 | 0.05% |
| China | 12 | 2.0% | 20 | 2.3% | 22 | 0.0007% | 7.7 | 0.41% |
| Hong Kong | 9.1 | 1.49% | 10 | 1.16% | 1.4 | 0.005% | 2.4 | 0.013% |
| South Korea | 6.3 | 1.02% | 8.8 | 1.03% | 209 | 7.02% | 177 | 9.4% |
| Thailand | 190 | 3.1% | 33 | 3.84% | 315 | 1.06% | 194 | 10.3% |
| Indonesia | 1.2 | 0.2% | 8.8 | 1.02% | 9.8 | 0.33% | 0.11 | 0.006% |
| Malaysia | 321 | 5.25% | 780 | 9.1% | 1.9 | 0.65% | 22 | 1.17% |

*Source :* As in Table II (a), p. 113.

TABLE III

**Value of total trade (exports and imports) of select Asian countries with China**

*[in million US dollars]*

| | *With China* | | | *With World* | | |
|---|---|---|---|---|---|---|
| | *1988* | *1992* | *% + or –* | *1988* | *1992* | *% + or –* |
| Japan | 19334 | 28852 | +49% | 448024 | 565466 | +26% |
| India | 128 | 169 | +32% | 29242 | 37409 | +28% |
| Indonesia | 931 | 2148 | +130% | 32150 | 61095 | +90% |
| Singapore | 2861 | 3365 | +18% | 82970 | 135453 | +63% |
| Malaysia | 655 | 1443 | +120% | 30499 | 69499 | +128% |
| Thailand | 1154 | 1484 | +29% | 36177 | 68882 | +90% |
| Philippines | 335 | 315 | -6% | 15803 | 25255 | +60% |
| Average for 5 ASEAN countries | | | +58% | | | +194% |

*N.B.* : Based on Data in Table II above.

## TABLE IV

**Aggregate increase in exports and imports of different countries (1988-92)**

**Table IV (a) JAPAN**

*[Value in million US dollars]*

| | *Import from* | | | | | *Export to* | | | | |
|---|---|---|---|---|---|---|---|---|---|---|
| | *1988* | *Rank* | *1992* | *Rank* | *% + or –* | *1988* | *Rank* | *1992* | *Rank* | *% + or –* |
| World | 183253 | | 230975 | | +26% | 264772 | | 339492 | | +28% |
| USA | 42190 | 1 | 52607 | 1 | +25% | 90239 | 1 | 96486 | 1 | +17% |
| China | 9859 | 3 | 16926 | 2 | +72% | 9475 | 3 | 11927 | 3 | +26% |
| Malaysia | 4800 | 5 | 6572 | 4 | +40% | 3060 | 6 | 8113 | 6 | +265% |
| Indonesia | 9497 | 4 | 1222 | 3 | +29% | 3054 | 7 | 5576 | 7 | +83% |
| Philippines | 1914 | 8 | 2337 | 7 | +22% | 1740 | 9 | 3512 | 8 | +102% |
| Thailand | 2751 | 6 | 5945 | 5 | +16% | 5158 | 5 | 10352 | 5 | +101% |
| Singapore | 2308 | 7 | 3075 | 6 | +33% | 8235 | 4 | 12885 | 5 | +56% |
| India | 1804 | 9 | 2043 | 8 | +13% | 2082 | 8 | 1487 | 9 | -29% |
| South Korea | 11771 | 2 | 11568 | 4 | -2% | 15430 | 2 | 17787 | 2 | +15% |

**Table IV (b) INDIA**

*[Value in million US dollars]*

| | *Import from* | | | | | *Export to* | | | | |
|---|---|---|---|---|---|---|---|---|---|---|
| | *1988* | *Rank* | *1992* | *Rank* | *% + or –* | *1988* | *Rank* | *1992* | *Rank* | *% + or –* |
| World | 17154 | | 19510 | | +14% | 12088 | | 17900 | | +48% |
| USA | 1538 | 3 | 1891 | 1 | +23% | 2252 | 1 | 2927 | 1 | +29% |
| Germany | 1661 | 1 | 1551 | 2 | -7% | 817 | 3 | 1272 | 3 | +56% |
| Japan | 1636 | 2 | 1364 | 3 | -16% | 1244 | 2 | 1655 | 2 | +33% |
| UK | 1406 | 4 | 1186 | 4 | -15% | 783 | 4 | 1141 | 4 | +46% |
| France | 614 | 6 | 580 | 5 | -6% | 292 | 6 | 426 | 6 | +46% |
| Malaysia | 648 | 5 | 391 | 6 | -40% | 70 | 9 | 203 | 9 | +91% |
| Singapore | 266 | 7 | 311 | 8 | +17% | 211 | 7 | 390 | 7 | +86% |
| South Korea | 256 | 8 | 314 | 7 | +23% | 112 | 8 | 241 | 8 | +115% |
| China | 113 | 9 | 210 | 9 | -81% | 15 | 10 | 148 | 10 | +331% |
| Hong Kong | 92603 | 10 | 106723 | 10 | +15% | 343967 | 5 | 615490 | 5 | +79% |

**Table IV (c) INDONESIA**

*[Value in million US dollars]*

| | *Import from* | | | | | *Export to* | | | | |
|---|---|---|---|---|---|---|---|---|---|---|
| | *1988* | *Rank* | *1992* | *Rank* | *% + or –* | *1988* | *Rank* | *1992* | *Rank* | *% + or –* |
| World | 13249 | | 27280 | | +106% | 18901 | | 23816 | | +79% |
| Japan | 3386 | 1 | 6014 | 1 | +78% | 8018 | 1 | 10753 | 1 | +34% |
| USA | 1736 | 2 | 3822 | 2 | +120% | 3074 | 2 | 4420 | 2 | +44% |
| China | 439 | 7 | 752 | 6 | +71% | 492 | 6 | 1496 | 4 | +184% |
| Saudi Arabia | 565 | 6 | 852 | 5 | +51% | 170 | 10 | 583 | 7 | +243% |
| Singapore | 869 | 3 | 1671 | 11 | +87% | 1336 | 3 | 3195 | 10 | +140% |
| Germany | 887 | 4 | 2141 | 10 | +141% | 456 | 7 | 978 | 5 | +115% |
| South Korea | 376 | 8 | 1894 | 3 | +403% | 840 | 4 | 2083 | 3 | +148% |
| India | 36 | 9 | 216 | 9 | +504% | 67 | 5 | 70 | 11 | +4% |
| Malaysia | 276 | 10 | 525 | 7 | +90% | 184 | 9 | 488 | 8 | +165% |
| Thailand | 96 | 11 | 345 | 8 | +259% | 151 | 11 | 353 | 7 | +133% |
| Australia | 578 | 5 | 1413 | 4 | +144% | 293 | 8 | 746 | 6 | -75% |

**Table IV (d) CHINA**

*[Value in million US dollars]*

| | Import from | | | | | Export to | | | | |
|---|---|---|---|---|---|---|---|---|---|---|
| | *1988* | *Rank* | *1992* | *Rank* | *% + or –* | *1988* | *Rank* | *1992* | *Rank* | *% + or –* |
| World | 55268 | | 80586 | | +46% | 47516 | | 84940 | | +79% |
| Hong Kong | 11889 | 1 | 20534 | 1 | +73% | 18263 | 1 | 37512 | 1 | +105% |
| Japan | 11035 | 2 | 13683 | 2 | +24% | 7902 | 2 | 11679 | 2 | +48% |
| Singapore | 1018 | 4 | 1236 | 6 | +21% | 1482 | 4 | 2031 | 5 | +37% |
| Indonesia | 682 | 5 | 1554 | 5 | +130% | 236 | 8 | 471 | 8 | +99% |
| South Korea | 198 | 8 | 2623 | 4 | +1228% | 878 | 9 | 2405 | 4 | +274% |
| Malaysia | 569 | 7 | 830 | 7 | +46% | 308 | 6 | 645 | 7 | +109% |
| Thailand | 633 | 6 | 425 | 8 | -33% | 443 | 5 | 895 | 6 | +102% |
| Philippines | 135 | 9 | 155 | 10 | +59% | 270 | 7 | 210 | 9 | +78% |
| India | 98 | 10 | 181 | 9 | +85% | 149 | 10 | 159 | 10 | +7% |
| Germany | 3432 | 3 | 4015 | 3 | +17% | 1484 | 3 | 2448 | 3 | +65% |
| 5 ASEAN countries | 3036 | | 4200 | | +38% | 2738 | | 4252 | | +55% |

**Table IV (e) SINGAPORE**

*[Value in million US dollars]*

| | Import from | | | | | Export to | | | | |
|---|---|---|---|---|---|---|---|---|---|---|
| | *1988* | *Rank* | *1992* | *Rank* | *% + or –* | *1988* | *Rank* | *1992* | *Rank* | *% + or –* |
| World | 43765 | | 72067 | | +65% | 39205 | | 63386 | | +62% |
| Japan | 9554 | 1 | 15122 | 1 | +58% | 3365 | 3 | 4825 | 3 | +43% |
| USA | 6808 | 2 | 11878 | 2 | +75% | 9369 | 1 | 13391 | 8 | +43% |
| Malaysia | 6426 | 3 | 10613 | 3 | +65% | 5292 | 2 | 7901 | 1 | +49% |
| Germany | 1618 | 6 | 2351 | 7 | +45% | 1364 | 6 | 2689 | 5 | +97% |
| China | 1688 | 5 | 2252 | 8 | +34% | 1178 | 8 | 1112 | 9 | +95% |
| Thailand | 1186 | 9 | 2681 | 5 | +126% | 2137 | 5 | 3947 | 4 | +85% |
| South Korea | 1264 | 8 | 2370 | 6 | +88% | 769 | 9 | 426 | 7 | +85% |
| Hong Kong | 1208 | 10 | 2202 | 9 | +82% | 2456 | 4 | 4960 | 2 | +102% |
| United Kingdom | 1273 | 7 | 2015 | 10 | +58% | 1144 | 7 | 1845 | 6 | +62% |
| Saudi Arabia | 1926 | 4 | 3696 | 4 | +92% | 276 | 12 | 412 | 12 | +19% |
| India | 2616 | 12 | 533 | 12 | +101% | 736 | 10 | 932 | 11 | +27% |
| France | 789 | 11 | 180 | 11 | +128% | 653 | 11 | 972 | 10 | +49% |

**Table IV (f) MALAYSIA**

*[Value in million US dollars]*

| | Import from | | | | | Export to | | | | |
|---|---|---|---|---|---|---|---|---|---|---|
| | *1988* | *Rank* | *1992* | *Rank* | *% + or –* | *1988* | *Rank* | *1992* | *Rank* | *% + or –* |
| World | 12589 | | 35183 | | +179% | 17911 | | 34300 | | +92% |
| Japan | 2746 | 1 | 9541 | 1 | +247% | 3504 | 1 | 5388 | 3 | 54% |
| USA | 2363 | 2 | 5596 | 2 | +137% | 2970 | 3 | 5802 | 2 | +96% |
| Singapore | 1824 | 3 | 4072 | 3 | +123% | 3252 | 2 | 7992 | 1 | +146% |
| Germany | 528 | 4 | 1595 | 4 | +196% | 612 | 5 | 1242 | 6 | +103% |
| United Kingdom | 518 | 6 | 1165 | 5 | +124% | 569 | 6 | 1503 | 5 | +164% |
| France | 204 | 11 | 466 | 12 | +128% | 238 | 13 | 476 | 12 | +100% |
| Australia | 526 | 5 | 960 | 7 | +82% | 400 | 10 | 586 | 10 | +47% |
| South Korea | 334 | 9 | 989 | 6 | +196% | 951 | 4 | 1516 | 4 | +59% |
| China | 376 | 8 | 803 | 9 | +114% | 279 | 12 | 639 | 9 | +129% |
| Hong Kong | 276 | 10 | 680 | 10 | +146% | 499 | 9 | 1152 | 7 | +130% |
| Indonesia | 176 | 12 | 494 | 11 | +180% | 146 | 14 | 503 | 11 | +244% |
| Thailand | 448 | 7 | 890 | 8 | +101% | 512 | 8 | 1094 | 8 | -114% |
| Philippines | 148 | 13 | 164 | 14 | +11% | 323 | 11 | 330 | 13 | +2% |
| India | 100 | 14 | 282 | 13 | +182% | 519 | 7 | 318 | 14 | -39% |

**Table IV (g) THAILAND**

*[Value in million US dollars]*

| | Import from | | | | | Export to | | | | |
|---|---|---|---|---|---|---|---|---|---|---|
| | *1988* | *Rank* | *1992* | *Rank* | *% + or –* | *1988* | *Rank* | *1992* | *Rank* | *% + or –* |
| World | 20225 | | 40467 | | +200% | 15952 | | 284156 | | +78% |
| Japan | 5880 | 1 | 11900 | 1 | +102% | 2546 | 2 | 5133 | 2 | +102% |
| USA | 2749 | 2 | 4774 | 2 | +74% | 3200 | 1 | 6062 | 1 | +89% |
| Germany | 1084 | 4 | 2149 | 4 | +98% | 735 | 4 | 1469 | 4 | +100% |
| United Kingdom | 582 | 6 | 911 | 9 | +56% | 588 | 6 | 1028 | 6 | +75% |
| France | 491 | 8 | 944 | 8 | +92% | 379 | 9 | 700 | 7 | +84% |
| Australia | 342 | 10 | 788 | 10 | +130% | 296 | 11 | 463 | 9 | +56% |
| China | 680 | 5 | 1149 | 7 | +69% | 475 | 7 | 335 | 12 | -30% |
| South Korea | 563 | 7 | 1786 | 4 | +217% | 255 | 12 | 459 | 10 | +80% |
| Singapore | 1503 | 3 | 2950 | 3 | +96% | 1225 | 3 | 2336 | 3 | +91% |
| Hong Kong | 250 | 11 | 492 | 12 | +97% | 710 | 5 | 1348 | 5 | +95% |
| Malaysia | 425 | 9 | 1596 | 6 | +276% | 472 | 8 | 684 | 8 | +45% |
| Indonesia | 174 | 14 | 291 | 14 | +67% | 85 | 14 | 213 | 15 | +50% |
| Philippines | 190 | 13 | 121 | 15 | -37% | 59 | 15 | 105 | 13 | +77% |
| India | 171 | 15 | 335 | 13 | +96% | 221 | 13 | 63 | 14 | -12% |
| Saudi Arabia | 203 | 12 | 518 | 11 | +150% | 356 | 10 | 445 | 11 | +25% |

**Table IV (h) PHILIPPINES**

*[Value in million US dollars]*

| | Import from | | | | | Export to | | | | |
|---|---|---|---|---|---|---|---|---|---|---|
| | *1988* | *Rank* | *1992* | *Rank* | *% + or –* | *1988* | *Rank* | *1992* | *Rank* | *% + or –* |
| World | 8729 | | 15465 | | +78% | 708 | | 9790 | | +38% |
| USA | 1850 | 1 | 2821 | 2 | +53% | 2522 | 1 | 3843 | 1 | +52% |
| Japan | 1519 | 2 | 3282 | 1 | +116% | 1424 | 2 | 1745 | 2 | +23% |
| Germany | 342 | 5 | 699 | 4 | +104% | 298 | 5 | 521 | 3 | +75% |
| United Kingdom | 171 | 9 | 314 | 8 | +84% | 328 | 4 | 436 | 5 | +33% |
| Australia | 314 | 6 | 452 | 6 | +46% | 111 | 8 | 113 | 9 | +2% |
| China | 269 | 7 | 202 | 9 | -25% | 67 | 10 | 114 | 8 | +70% |
| Hong Kong | 388 | 3 | 745 | 3 | +92% | 346 | 3 | 463 | 4 | +34% |
| Singapore | 352 | 4 | 573 | 5 | +63% | 224 | 6 | 252 | 6 | +13% |
| Malaysia | 258 | 8 | 401 | 7 | +59% | 117 | 7 | 128 | 7 | +9% |
| Indonesia | 91 | 10 | 196 | 10 | +115% | 27 | 11 | 41 | 10 | +48% |
| India | 29 | 11 | 95 | 11 | +228% | 71 | 9 | 8.6 | 11 | -88% |

*Source :* Same as for Table II.9.

## TABLE V

**Commodity composition of exports and imports in 1992 for China and selected ASEAN countries : Proportions in percentages of total**

(a) Exports for 1992

| *Country* | *Manufactured Exports* | *Texiles* | *Metal Manufactures* | *Chemical* |
|---|---|---|---|---|
| China | 87% | 36% | 23% | 9.5% |
| Thailand | 81% | 21% | 29% | 5.5% |
| Philippines | 88% | 12% | 20% | 4.6% |
| Malaysia | 76% | 6% | 45% | 4.5% |
| Indonesia | 58% | 22% | 7% | 7.5% |
| Average for 5 countries | 78% | | | |

(b) Imports for 1992

| *Country* | *Processed Foods* | *Combustible Fuels* | *Capital Equipment Machinery* | *Parts Accessories* | *Cars* | *Consumer Goods* | *Total* |
|---|---|---|---|---|---|---|---|
| China | 42.9% | 4.4% | 24.4% | 4.7% | 1.7% | 5.1% | 83% |
| Thailand | 33.0% | 8.2% | 21.3% | 9.9% | 2.3% | 4.9% | 80% |
| Philippines | 28.2% | 13.8% | 14.9% | 5.7% | 1.9% | 4.9% | 68% |
| Malaysia | 25.7% | 4.33% | 28.4% | 17.4% | 2.6% | 5.9% | 84% |
| Indonesia | 35.2% | 7.5% | 33.1% | 3.5% | 0.6% | 2.0% | 82% |
| Average for 5 countries | | | | | | | 80%. |

*N.B. Source* : International Trade Statistics Yearbook, UN, 1992, Vol. I, Trade by Country.

## TABLE VI A (i)

### Commodity composition of China's exports to ASEAN countries : 1984

Exports :

| Commodity | Quantity Metric Tons* (a) | Total Value US $ (Mi) To all Countries | Malaysia (a) % of Total | Malaysia (b) % of Total | Indonesia (a) | Indonesia (b) | Singapore (a) | Singapore (b) | Philippines (a) | Philippines (b) | Thailand (a) | Thailand (b) | Brunei (a) | Brunei (b) |
|---|---|---|---|---|---|---|---|---|---|---|---|---|---|---|
| Country Totals (for China) | | 24416 (100%) | — | 0.79% | — | 0.28% | — | 4.89% | — | 0.94% | — | 1.0% | — | 0.12% |
| Cereals | 3439673 | 776 (3.18%) | 3.0% | 2.9% | 2.7% | 3.0% | 5.7% | 3.7% | 3.4% | 2.8% | 0.54% | 0.5% | Nil | Nil |
| Rice | 1189089 | 285 (1.17%) | — | — | 4.8% | 0.28% | — | 4.89% | — | 0.94% | — | 1.0% | — | 0.12% |
| Soyabean | 834445 | 252 (1.03%) | 6.2% | 5.6% | 4.3% | 4.3% | 0.5% | 0.54% | Nil | Nil | Nil | Nil | Nil | Nil |
| Maize | 910731 | 115 (0.45%) | 4.0% | 4.1% | 3.9% | 3.8% | 15% | 14.0% | Nil | Nil | Nil | Nil | Nil | Nil |
| Pulses | 124820 | 49 (0.2%) | 1.9% | 1.54% | Nil | Nil | 5.4% | 5.5% | Nil | Nil | 0.35% | 0.3% | Nil | Nil |
| Vegetable Oil | 134333 | 10 (0.04%) | 0.07% | 0.11% | Nil | Nil | 4.7% | 1.41% | Nil | Nil | Nil | Nil | Nil | Nil |
| Groundnut Kernels | 124535 | 118 (0.48%) | 0.44% | 0.4% | 5.6% | 4.3% | 5% | 4.61% | Nil | Nil | Nil | Nil | Nil | Nil |
| Vegetables | 368524 | 128 (0.52%) | 0.66% | 1.1% | Nil | Nil | 3.8% | 4.3% | Nil | Nil | Nil | Nil | Nil | Nil |
| Canned goods | 402951 | 390 (1.6%) | 1.62% | 2.1% | Nil | Nil | 3.0% | 3.5% | 0.08% | 0.07% | 0.05% | 0.07% | 0.05% | 0.07% |
| Cotton | 202481 | 295 (1.2%) | 0.07% | 0.91% | 0.67% | 0.51% | 0.38% | 4.2% | 0.05% | 0.04% | Nil | Nil | Nil | Nil |
| Cotton Yarn | 681775 | 304 (1.24%) | 0.04% | 0.06% | Nil | Nil | 0.05% | 0.06% | 0.06% | Nil | Nil | Nil | Nil | Nil |
| Cotton Piece | 151197015 | 981.2 (4%) | 0.84% | 0.7% | 0.003% | 0.003% | 2.7% | 2.1% | 0.01% | 0.1% | Nil | Nil | Nil | Nil |

* Unless otherwise stated.

TABLE VI A (ii)

**Commodity composition of China's exports to ASEAN countries : 1984**

Exports :

| *Commodity* | *Quantity Metric Tons* (a)* | *Total Value US $ (Mi)* | *Malaysia (a) % of Total* | *Malaysia (b) % of Total* | *Indonesia (a)* | *Indonesia (b)* | *Singapore (a)* | *Singapore (b)* | *Philippines (a)* | *Philippines (b)* | *Thailand (a)* | *Thailand (b)* | *Brunei (a)* | *Brunei (b)* |
|---|---|---|---|---|---|---|---|---|---|---|---|---|---|---|
| Spun Rayon Rice Goods | 13178752 | 44.5 (0.18%) | 1.21% | 1.32% | Nil | Nil | 2.23% | 2.23% | Nil | Nil | Nil | Nil | Nil | Nil |
| Garments including Silk Readymade | — | 1110 (4.5%) | — | 0.16% | Nil | Nil | — | 0.36% | Nil | Nil | Nil | Nil | Nil | Nil |
| Tea | 140209 | 299.6 (1.22%) | 0.76% | 0.94% | Nil | Nil | 1.66% | Nil | Nil | Nil | Nil | Nil | Nil | Nil |
| Carpets Sq. metre | 319839 | 193.6 (0.8%) | 0.01% | 1.11% | Nil | Nil | 0.18% | 0.16% | Nil | Nil | Nil | Nil | Nil | Nil |
| Cotton Shoes Pair | 11774370 | 106.7 (0.43%) | 2.06% | 2.14% | 1.61% | 1.30% | Nil | 0.27% | Nil | Nil | 0.07% | 0.08% | 0.22% | 0.2% |
| Leather Shoes Pair | 9154234 | 46.8 (0.19%) | 0.57% | Nil | Nil | 1.4% | 0.57% | Nil | Nil | Nil | NIl | Nil | Nil | Nil |
| Electric Sets | 1119478 | 29.1 (0.12%) | 0.1% | 0.1% | — | — | 0.4% | 0.03% | Nil | Nil | Nil | Nil | Nil | Nil |
| Embroidered Articles | — | 347.2 (1.42%) | — | 2.03% | — | — | — | 0.03% | — | 0.1% | — | — | — | — |
| Pottery in 10000 Porcelain Pieces | 48453 | 109.6 (3.1%) | 3.1% | 2.7% | — | — | 2.9% | 7.9% | 0.05% | 0.54% | — | — | 0.001% | 0.08% |
| Jewellery | — | 33.9 (0.14%) | — | 0.02% | — | 0.024% | — | 3.38% | — | 0.1% | — | 0.02% | — | — |
| Steel Products | 268049 | 67.7 (0.28%) | — | — | — | — | — | 6.64% | 0.04% | 0.4% | — | — | — | — |
| Coal | 6955471 | 28.9 (0.12%) | 0.07% | 0.074% | — | — | 0.34% | — | 4.2% | 4.3% | — | — | — | — |
| Petroleum Products | 5817456 | 142.1 (0.58%) | 0.02% | 0.04% | — | — | 12% | 0.56% | — | — | 6.0% | 5.7% | — | — |
| Rubber Tyres Unit | 505512 | 27.7 (0.11%) | 0.08% | 0.02% | — | — | — | 11.2% | — | — | — | — | — | — |

* Unless otherwise stated.

## TABLE VI A (iii)
## Commodity composition of China's exports to ASEAN countries : 1984

Exports :

| *Commodity* | *Quantity Metric Tons (a)* | *Total Value US $ (Mi)* | *Malaysia (a) % of Total* | *Malaysia (b) % of Total* | *Indonesia (a)* | *Indonesia (b)* | *Singapore (a)* | *Singapore (b)* | *Philippines (a)* | *Philippines (b)* | *Thailand (a)* | *Thailand (b)* | *Brunei (a)* | *Brunei (b)* |
|---|---|---|---|---|---|---|---|---|---|---|---|---|---|---|
| Pharmaceuticals | — | 247.3 (1.01%) | — | — | — | — | — | — | — | 0.12% | — | — | — | — |
| Tools | — | 10.5 (0.04%) | — | 4% | — | — | — | 4.7% | — | 0.13% | — | 2.6% | — | — |
| Agricultural Implement | — | 20.3 (0.08%) | — | 6% | — | — | — | 1.83% | — | — | — | 0.8% | — | 0.04% |
| Machine Tools Set | 5787 | 18.2 (0.07%) | 6.66% | 5.2% | — | — | 14.2% | 11.1% | 0.1% | 0.16% | 2.16% | 2.1% | — | — |

*Source :* Almanac of China's Foreign Economic Relations and Trade, Beijing 1985 (pp. 1050-65).

## TABLE VI B
## Commodity composition of China's imports from ASEAN countries : 1984

Exports :

| *Commodity* | *Quantity Metric Tons (a)* | *Total Value US $ (Mi)* | *Malaysia (a) % of Total* | *Malaysia (b) % of Total* | *Indonesia (a)* | *Indonesia (b)* | *Singapore (a)* | *Singapore (b)* | *Philippines (a)* | *Philippines (b)* | *Thailand (a)* | *Thailand (b)* | *Brunei (a)* | *Brunei (b)* |
|---|---|---|---|---|---|---|---|---|---|---|---|---|---|---|
| Machine Sets Tools (Units) | 2668 | 41.9 (0.16%) | — | — | — | — | — | — | — | — | — | — | — | — |
| Ships (Units) | 170 | 311.4 (1.2%) | — | — | — | — | — | — | — | — | — | — | — | — |
| Aircraft (Units) | 30 | 92.8 (0.36%) | — | — | — | — | — | — | — | — | — | — | — | — |
| Automobile Unit | 94291 | 700.2 (2.7%) | — | — | — | — | — | — | — | — | — | — | — | — |
| Steel Products Metric Tons | 13314482 | 408 (0.77%) | 0.004% | 0.008% | — | — | 0.12% | 0.19% | — | — | — | — | — | — |
| Copper Ingots | 310960 | 471 (1.81%) | — | — | — | — | — | — | 0.32% | 0.29% | — | — | — | — |
| Aluminium Ingots | 206314 | 199.4 | 41% | 40% | — | — | — | — | — | — | — | — | — | — |
| Zinc Ingots | 240258 | 226.2 (0.87%) | — | — | — | — | — | — | — | — | — | — | — | — |
| Natural Rubber | 260314 | 199.4 (0.77%) | 41.4% | 39.6% | — | — | 24.5% | 24.7% | — | — | 16.2% | 15.9% | — | — |
| Pharmaceuticals | | 121.5 (0.47%) | — | — | — | — | — | 0.01% | — | — | — | 0.02% | — | — |
| Cereals | 10645387 | 161.8 (6.21%) | — | — | — | — | — | — | — | — | — | 2.6% | 0.4% | — |
| Timber Cubic Metre | 8238388 | 688.4 (2.65%) | 4.3% | 5.2% | 0.64% | 1.12% | — | — | 0.07% | 0.01% | — | — | — | — |
| Rice | 246126 | 51.3 (0.2%) | — | — | — | — | — | — | — | — | — | 73% | 78% | — |
| Sugar | 1228668 | 233 (0.9%) | — | — | — | — | — | — | 2.6% | 1.5% | 3.6% | 2.2% | — | — |

*Reference :* Alamanac of China's Foreign Economic Relations and Trade.

TABLE VII A (i)

**Commodity composition of China's exports to ASEAN countries : 1993**

Exports :

| *Commodity* | *Value US $ in Million to all Countries* | *Malaysia % Share* | *Indonesia % Share* | *Singapore % Share* | *Philippines % Share* | *Thailand % Share* | *Brunei % Share* |
|---|---|---|---|---|---|---|---|
| Animal Products | 2562 (2.8%) | 0.15% | 0.02% | 0.81% | 0.003% | 0.34% | — |
| Vegetable Products | 4371 (4.8%) | 3.94% | 1.8% | 3.55% | 0.15% | 0.33% | — |
| Cereals | 143.2 (0.16%) | 8.65% | 21.9% | 1.5% | — | — | — |
| Prepared Food Stuffs | 3611.7 (4.0%) | 0.98% | 1.02% | 5.7% | 0.72% | 1.14% | 0.01% |
| Sugar and Sugar Confectionery | 654.5 (0.71%) | 0.24% | 0.49% | 3.3% | 0.05% | 0.01% | 0.02% |
| Mineral Products | 4873.9 (5.3%) | 0.38% | 1.44% | 8.32% | 0.74% | 0.91% | — |
| Mineral Fuels | 4108.2 (4.5%) | 0.22% | 1.53% | 9.5% | 0.81% | 0.86% | 0.1% |
| Products of Chemical and Allied Industries | 4398.3 (4.8%) | 1.8% | 1.7% | 2.47% | 0.71% | 2.76% | 0.1% |
| Raw Hides and Skins | 3442.8 (3.75%) | 0.04% | 0.61% | 0.53% | 0.04% | 0.32% | — |
| Paper and Paper Board | 502.1 (0.55%) | 2.6% | 0.7% | 6.41% | 0.39% | 0.71% | — |
| Textiles and Textile Articles | 26063.6 (28.4%) | 0.3% | 0.42% | 1.4% | 0.21% | 0.45% | 0.0006% |
| Cotton Textiles | 2783.6 (3.1%) | 0.7% | 3.1% | 3.5% | 0.71% | 1.25% | — |
| Knitted Clothing | 5032.2 (5.5%) | 0.06% | 0.03% | 1.0% | 0.18% | 0.10% | — |

TABLE VII A (ii)

**Commodity composition of China's exports to ASEAN countries : 1993** *(Continued...)*

| *Commodity* | *Value US $ in 1000 to all countries* | *Malaysia % Share* | *Indonesia % Share* | *Singapore % Share* | *Philippines % Share* | *Thailand % Share* | *Brunei % Share* |
|---|---|---|---|---|---|---|---|
| Non-knitted Clothing | 11541 (12.5%) | 0.17% | 0.01% | 0.49% | 0.04% | 0.10% | — |
| Footwear and Head gear | 6290 (6.9%) | 0.15% | 0.09% | 0.49% | 0.08% | 0.07% | — |
| Base Metals and Articles of Base Metal | 4670 (5%) | 1.48% | 1.17% | 5.5% | 0.6% | 1.81% | 0.02% |
| Vehicles Aircraft Associated Transport Equipment | 1926 (2.1%) | 0.6% | 0.36% | 3.8% | 0.19% | 1.93% | — |
| Machinery and Mechanical Appliances, Television Sound Recording System and Parts thereof | 13906 (15.2%) | 1.08% | 1.4% | 2.2% | 0.38% | 1.01% | — |
| Total of all Commodities | 91744 | 0.77% | 0.75% | 2.4% | 0.31% | 0.81% | 0.01% |

*Source :* China Customs Statistics Yearbook 1993.

TABLE VII B (i)

**Commodity composition of China's imports from ASEAN countries : 1993**

| *Commodity* | *Value US $ in 1000 to all Countries* | *Malaysia % Share* | *Indonesia % Share* | *Singapore % Share* | *Philippines % Share* | *Thailand % Share* | *Brunei % Share* |
|---|---|---|---|---|---|---|---|
| Animal Products | 548.7 (0.53%) | 0.77% | 1.35% | 1.2% | 0.51% | 6% | — |
| Vegetable Products | 1277.1 (1.3%) | 0.56% | 1.79% | 0.23% | 0.46% | 4.3% | — |
| Cereals | 997.3 (0.96%) | — | — | — | — | 3.5% | — |
| Prepared Food Stuffs | 841.1 (0.81%) | 3.6% | 0.43% | — | 1.38% | 2% | — |
| Sugars and Sugar Confectionery | 132.6 (0.13%) | 1.13% | 0.6% | 1.95% | 0.03% | 4.8% | — |
| Mineral Products | 7157.3 (6.9%) | 1.27% | 0.98% | 23.8% | 1.1% | 0.26% | — |
| Mineral Fuels | 5818.9 (5.6%) | 1.51% | 10.6% | 29.2% | 1.26% | 0.33% | — |
| Product of chemical and allied industries | 4398.3 (4.23%) | 0.55% | 0.5% | 2.1% | 0.44% | 0.37% | — |
| Raw hides and Skins | 1842.4 (1.78%) | 0.03% | 0.29% | 0.07% | — | 10.7% | — |

TABLE VII B (ii)

**Commodity composition of China's imports from ASEAN countries : 1993**

| *Commodity* | *Value US $ in million to all Countries* | *Malaysia % Share* | *Indonesia % Share* | *Singapore % Share* | *Philippines % Share* | *Thailand % Share* | *Brunei % Share* |
|---|---|---|---|---|---|---|---|
| Paper and Paper Board | 1620.4 (1.6%) | 0.35% | 1.7% | 0.83% | 0.06% | 4.4% | — |
| Textiles and Textiles Articles | 9668.5 (9.3%) | 0.29% | 0.33% | 0.13% | 0.03% | 0.48% | — |
| Cotton | 1236.8 (1.19%) | 0.09% | 0.63% | 0.11% | — | 0.15% | — |
| Knitted Clothing | 132.4 (0.13%) | 2.2% | 0.53% | — | — | 0.73% | — |
| Non-knitted Clothing | 377.3 (0.36%) | — | 0.09% | — | — | 0.16% | — |
| Footwear and Headgear | 379.7 (0.36%) | 0.07% | 0.21% | — | — | 0.08% | — |
| Base Metals and Articles of Base Metals | 16540 (15.9%) | 0.32% | 0.36% | 0.42% | 0.41% | 0.29% | — |
| Vehicles, Aircraft and Associated Transport Equipment | 8723.2 (8.4%) | — | 0.1% | 1.96% | — | 0.03% | — |
| Machinery and Mechanical Appliances Television Sound Recorders | 35846.9 (34.5%) | 0.03% | 0.03% | 0.95% | 0.02% | 0.18% | — |
| Total of all Commodities | 103959 (100%) | 1.04% | 1.4% | 2.54% | 0.2% | 0.58% | — |

TABLE VIII

**Foreign direct investment in selected Asian countries 1987-93**

*($ Million)*

| *Country* | *1987* | *1988* | *1989* | *1990* | *1991* | *1992* | *1993* | *1987-93* |
|---|---|---|---|---|---|---|---|---|
| People's Republic of China | 2314 | 3194 | 3393 | 3487 | 4366 | 11156 | 26000 | 53910 |
| Singapore | 2836 | 3655 | 2773 | 5263 | 4395 | 5635 | 6829 | 33400 |
| Indonesia | 385 | 576 | 682 | 1093 | 1482 | 1774 | 2004 | 7999 |
| Malaysia | 423 | 719 | 1668 | 2332 | 4073 | 4118 | 4351 | 17960 |
| Philippines | 307 | 936 | 563 | 530 | 544 | 228 | 763 | 3871 |
| Thailand | 352 | 1105 | 1775 | 2444 | 2014 | 2116 | 1621 | 11427 |
| Bangladesh | 3 | 2 | — | 3 | 1 | 4 | 14 | 27 |
| India | 181 | 287 | 350 | 112 | 200 | 390 | 600 | 2120 |
| Pakistan | 129 | 186 | 210 | 244 | 257 | 349 | 346 | 1721 |
| Sri Lanka | 60 | 46 | 20 | 43 | 48 | 123 | 195 | 535 |
| Total for 4 countries of South Asia | | | | | | | | 4403 |
| Total for 5 countries of ASEAN | | | | | | | | 74657 |

*Source :* Asian Development outlook, Reports by the Asian Development Bank Published by OUP, Hong Kong, p. 17 (1994 Report); p. 17 (1995 Report).

# 11

# Regional Trade Arrangements

NITISH SENGUPTA

The SAFTA agreement reached by the South Asian countries in Dhaka in April 1993 was an auspicious silver-lining on otherwise sombre political environment in the subcontinent. Through this treaty, the seven countries decided to forget their political differences, at least temporarily, in the overall interest of their "commitment to promote regional cooperation for the benefit of their people", their awareness "that the expansion of trade could act as a powerful stimulus to the development of their national economies" and the knowledge that there is "need to establish and promote regional preferential trading arrangements for strengthening intra-regional economic cooperation and the development of national economies." These are highly promising signboards. The question is whether these seven nations are equally serious about doing what they say, and whether in taking future steps they would truly accept the precept that economic developments should precede the resolving of political conflicts, and that once regional economic cooperation in trade and investment becomes a reality, the solution of political differences can only be a question of time.

Indeed one important lesson in international development experience in the last four decades has been that countries with outward-looking economies have, by and large, been pushed backwards. Also, the emergence of regional markets has been taken place side by side with the process of globalization, almost hand in hand, starting with the Treaty of Rome (1960) creating the European Common Market, the remarkable progress made by the EEC and its eventual transition to E.C., the concept was taken by several other regions, some successfully, some not successfully. The most successful story was the ASEAN which has completely transformed the South East Asian economic landscape. This has become economically the most successful trading block today. Along with economic progress it has brought about dramatic changes in the living standards and quality of life of the people. In conjunction with Japan, Korea, Taiwan and China, the ASEAN is promising to grow into an even larger Asian-Pacific region which, according to current indications, will be the fastest growing regional market in the near-term future.The latest illustration of a regional market is the North American Free Trade Area (NAFTA) which, despite the initial hurdles, is being viewed as a way out of the currently dismal economic scenario in the USA, Canada and Mexico. Interestingly, it is developing Mexico which is pushing the hardest among the three to achieve this regionalisation of investment and trade.

If the SAARC countries are to draw any lesson from ASEAN, E.C. and NAFTA, it is that the route to future economic prosperity lies through the regionalisation of trade and investment, the removal of the existing barriers that separate these countries and the encouragement given to entrepreneurs to set up projects based on wherever comparative advantages lie. Indeed we all must subordinate every other consideration to this exciting vision of making South Asia a unified and vibrant market. This will mean a market of 1200 million people, the largest trading block in the world. There are vast natural resources, a great reservoir of technological and scientific manpower and strong elements of entrepreneurship and management. All efforts should, therefore be directed towards transforming the South Asian Preferential Trade Area into the South Asian Free Trade Area.

But what seems a very logical development is bugged by serious political differences, strong national prejudices and misgivings and a log of perceived economic and commercial interest clashes. Pakistan and India have serious outstanding political issues. Bangladesh is full of mistrust against India over Farakka barrage and host of other issues. India in turn is seriously worried about illegal immigration. Nepal with whom India has a pattern of border 'trade and cross-border investment which should provide a model for liberalization among other SAARC countries, is worried about Indian hegemonism and economic strength. Nepal and Bhutan are locked up in a dispute over Bhutan's expulsion of Nepali migrants. These are serious obstacles to the realization of a pan-South Asian economic identity. But the vision of all-round economic and commercial prosperity through regionalisation of trade and trade-related investment is exciting, should outweigh political differences and military suspicions.

Some intellectuals in the SAARC countries have for a long time stressed the importance of economic cooperation among SAARC nations and questioned the wisdom of the on-going political cacophony, and the diversion of scarce resources to ruinous military purposes, all the more regrettable in a region where history and culture have been shared for thousands of years and poverty and domestic instability continue to be common and major threats. We should heed these isolated voices and perceive the obvious advantages of close influence on the international stage, greater ability to sell its goods and services to the world market, and more effective control over the marketing and pricing of key commodity exports like tea, jute, rubber, cotton and agricultural products. The ASEAN provides a model.

The SAPTA provides a workable basis to start from. The operational gaps in this treaty should be filled by borrowing from the ASEAN treaty. The biggest road block is India's overwhelming size in relation to the other partners, and the misgiving that it causes in smaller nations. But Indian market is huge enough to boost the industries of all neighbouring countries. India can afford to show the way by taking a unilateral decision to open her market obligation to do the same. India, with her size and growth potential, can take the risk. Indeed it is worth taking. Once this happens there will be exciting possibilities of regional trade, the growth of joint ventures, and further possibilities of closer ASEAN-SAARC-Gulf countries commercial and economic linkages. All countries will stand to gain in the long run. Regionalisation of trade and investment have played a great catalyst role in our times of accelerating economic performance and improving the living standards and quality of life of the people. The realization must dawn on the governments and peoples of South Asia. Once the SAPTA is transformed into SAFTA, this region, with its huge market, substantial economic resources and the natural entrepreneurial instincts of its people will have the potential to catch up with and even go past the ASEAN region by the year 2000 AD. That potential must be translated into a promise, and the promise into an achievement.

There are several other interesting possibilities in India's commercial and economic linkages with the neighbouring countries in several directions. About a year ago, South African Foreign Minister, Mr Botha, suggested during a visit to Delhi on the possibility of forming Indian Ocean Economic Zone. This opens up exciting prospects of a regional arrangement covering countries like India, Sri Lanka, Mauritius, Australia, South Africa, Zanzibar, Tanzania, Kenya, Mozambique, Somalia, Saudi Arabia, Yemen, UAE, Iran and several other countries, including Pakistan after India's relationship with her improves. These countries could easily start on the basis of a customs union and thereafter move cautiously towards a closer economic union. In these days of easy communication and easy information technology, there is no reason why we should not consider this as a possibility that can be seriously looked at.

Secondly, there was a proposal from a Chinese minister suggesting that China and India form an economic zone. We should appreciate the vast geo-political changes which have taken place in the last two decades. India has opened up motorable roads up to Nathu La pass and the Chinese have constructed motorable roads from Nathu La pass to Lhasa and on to China itself. There is no reason why we should not take advantage of this one continuous route and revive the vastly enlarged version of the old mule caravans that existed from time immemorial until 1959. We should also consider opening up newer routes accepting the fact that the Himalayas are no longer an inseperable obstacle. There are many aspects of complementarily between the economies of China and India. Frankly, once India and China can come together on the economic plane and perhaps also involve the former CIS republics in this arrangement, that can provide the basis for great economic prosperity for Asia in the future.

Lastly, there are talks of India becoming associated with ASEAN and for that matter with the Asia Pacific community. If India's foreign economic policy centers on these three tripods plus the fourth prospect of turning South Asia into an economic zone, that will really herald a new dawn for all the countries concerned.

# 12

# APEC and India: Emerging Linkages

V.V. Bhanoji Rao

## THE APEC ECONOMIES

### The Constituents

Asia Pacific Economic Cooperation (APEC) stands for a process of intergovernmental cooperation inaugurated in Canberra in 1989. Presently there are 18 economies represented in APEC. These are the six ASEAN countries; USA, Canada, Mexico, Australia, New Zealand, Papua New Guinea, China, Hong Kong, Taiwan, Korea, Japan and Chile. Since late 1993, there has been a three-year embargo on further expansion of APEC.

### Economic Indicators

The 18 APEC members present an enormous diversity. In terms of population size, while Singapore, Hong Kong, New Zealand and Papua New Guinea had between 3 to 6 million persons each in 1992, Japan, USA and Indonesia had populations in the 125-255 million range and China had 1.2 billion persons. The smallest to largest ratio here is 1 to 400. Per capita GNP differences are also substantial. The lowest (China, US $ 470) and the highest (Japan, US $ 28,190) portray a ratio of 1 to 60. Some economies are still predominantly agricultural, with the sector's share in GDP at about 20 per cent or more (China, Papua New Guinea, Indonesia and Philippines). Some are distinctly industrialised and have agriculture's share in GDP of less than 10 per cent (e.g., Japan, USA, Canada, Australia, New Zealand and Mexico).

Of the 106 economies in World Development Report 1994 with data on the average annual rate of growth of per capita

GNP during 1980-92, 44 economies had negative growth rates. Another 44 economies had growth rates below 3 per cent per annum. The economies with a relatively high growth rate are a mere 18 in number, of which 9 are APEC members. (Note: The remaining 9 include India with an average annual growth rate of GNP per capita of 3.1 per cent during 1980-92.)

### APEC and the World

Most APEC members have high levels of trade orientation. Of the 18 economies, 13 have export to GDP ratios of 20 per cent or more. APEC members as a group accounted for 40 per cent of world exports in 1992. They also account for 38 per cent of the world population, 52 per cent of the world GDP, and 42 per cent of the global international reserves. APEC also has some of the world's major foreign investors (USA and Japan) and major recipients (China and ASEAN countries, in addition to USA). Its dominant role in the world economy, the members' trade and investment linkages, the large economies like fact that USA and Japan and several fast growing ASEAN and East Asian economies are in APEC, and the leaders meeting in Seattle in late 1993 have brought APEC into sharp focus.

## APEC EVOLUTION AND GOALS

### Future of APEC: EPG View

An important way of gauging the future of APEC is to look at the vision articulated by the Eminent Persons Group (EPG), created at APEC's Fourth Ministerial Meeting in Bangkok in September 1992. Members of EPG are reputed intellectuals from the member economies.

The first report of EPG submitted to the APEC Ministers in late 1993 called for the eventual establishment of free trade in the Asia Pacific. The Chairman of EPG (Fred Bergsten of USA) formally presented the second report to President Soeharto, current Chairman of APEC, on the 31st of August, 1994. The title of the report is "Achieving the APEC Vision: Free and Open Trade in the Asia-Pacific". The report has a number of specific recommendations to promote free trade within APEC. The important EPG recommendations are detailed below.

**Trade and Investment Facilitation**

There are a set of five concrete steps recommended for the growth of trade and investment flows within APEC. These are described below:

(1) *Concord on Investment Principles* : EPG recommends that an APEC Concord on Investment Principles be adopted. The Concord would embody several key principles: (a) Investment policies should be fully transparent and firmly adhered to. (b) Foreign investors should be guaranteed national treatment. (c) Compensation should be assured in any cases of nationalisation. (d) New performance requirements or investment incentives should be avoided, and existing practices of both types should be rolled back.

In addition, the Concord would also include an effective dispute settlement mechanism to help resolve any problems of interpretation and application that subsequently arise. The Concord would begin as a voluntary instrument, in the sense that each member can decide whether or when to apply the agreed principles. (The report notes, however, that those who choose to abstain for even a brief period could be placed at a competitive disadvantage with respect to attracting new flows of investment from abroad.)

(2) *Standards* : Differences in national product standards and testing procedures raise the costs of international transactions and can impede cooperation. The EPG recommends that APEC work toward: (a) adoption of an APEC Standards and Conformance Framework to guide progress on this range of issues; (b) identification of sectors where harmonization of standards could eliminate or reduce trade distortions, as a basis for developing proposals for each; (c) development of a model mutual recognition agreement among member governments that could provide the basis for acceptance of each others' standards, and of procedures for implementing that concept; (d) identification of sectors where early progress on mutual recognition would be most valuable and most feasible; and (e) acceptance of the conformity assessment principle "tested once, accepted everywhere", which will require mutual recognition of testing laboratories in APEC economies so that products need not be tested several times to gain acceptance in different markets. In addition, EPG recommends that APEC members who have developed their research

and accreditation procedures should offer technical assistance to members whose processes have not advanced so far. This is to enhance the prospects for APEC-wide progress in this area.

(3) *Monetary and Macroeconomic Policy* : EPG recommends that the APEC Finance Ministers have regular consultations. They should bring central bank officials into their discussions. The achievement of free trade in the region will require a means to address trade and macroeconomic imbalances among the members, which will inevitably develop from time to time. The Finance Ministers can assess the root causes of such problems and take appropriate action.

(4) *The Environment* : Sharing pro-environmental technologies, joint funding of environmentally sound development projects, encouraging the most widespread possible adoption of the "polluter pays principle", advancing proposals for creation of new institutional mechanisms for international environmental management, embodying the "polluter pays principle" as a global norm, and the gradual convergence of environmental standards among APEC members are suggested.

(5) *Antidumping Policy and Restrictive Business Practices* : This is an area that the GATT has decided to place on its post-Uruguay Round agenda. EPG recommends that APEC create a task force on antidumping and restrictive business practices, to address antidumping practices and the impact of national antitrust laws on international trade with eventual expansion into the broader aspects of competition policy. Initially, the task force would review national practices in each of these areas, especially as they may affect trade and investment flows. The task force is urged to assess the prospects for developing an APEC agreement on some or all of them, perhaps beginning with such modest steps as assisting each others' investigations in antidumping and antitrust cases through exchanges of information and other measures of "positive comity". For the longer run, the task force should consider the possible harmonization of competition policies, such as has been worked out by Australia and New Zealand, which enabled them inter alia to eliminate all antidumping measures.

### Dispute Settlement

The EPG Report makes references to the US-Japan and US-China trade frictions, and suggests that these disputes should be channelled into multilateral rather than bilateral channels. "Doing so could, in some cases, improve the prospects for resolving the disputes successfully. Any determination by the two parties directly involved should not hurt other economies in the region". (EPG Report, pp.17-18).

The Report acknowledges the reform of the dispute settlement mechanism in the Uruguay Round. "We strongly support this reform, hope and believe that it will greatly enhance the effectiveness of the new World Trade Organization, and urge all APEC members to make full use of it in resolving trade problems between them". (EPG Report, p. 33). However, issues outside the purview of GATT-WTO need to be addressed. Regional arrangements can fill this gap. For instance, NAFTA has extensive dispute settlement mechanisms. In regard to antidumping and countervailing duties, binational panels can be called upon to review whether the country implementing such duties in a given case has applied its domestic law fairly. A panel finding that a country has failed to do so requires the country to reconsider its decision and the United States has in fact reversed itself in all eight cases vis-a-vis Canada where such a finding has been handed down.

For applying GATT-WTO and NAFTA precedents on an APEC-wide basis, two requirements have to be met. First, there should exist a set of agreed rules against which to judge compliance. Second, there should be a significant degree of comparability of domestic laws among the participating economies. Since these conditions are not yet in place to a large extent in APEC, EPG believes that APEC should develop a dispute settlement mechanism that emphasizes mediation rather than arbitration. Accordingly a Dispute Mediation Service is recommended to provide assistance in resolving (and thus, over time, perhaps avoiding) economic disputes among APEC members. Beyond this mediation service, EPG recommends that any new APEC-wide agreements should include procedures for resolving different interpretations of their own provisions. The process of dispute mediation or interpretation would be voluntary.

**Trade Liberalisation**

*Liberalisation within APEC and Conformity with GATT :* There are three alternative ways to meet the GATT test for regional liberalisation: (a) declare that the regional grouping's objective is to eliminate barriers on "substantially all trade", including both goods and services now that there is a General Agreement on Trade in Services, (b) extend the benefits of regional liberalisation to all economies (including non-members) on an unconditional MFN basis, or (c) seek a GATT-WTO waiver from the prevailing rules. EPG opted for the first provision since the second implies a give away to others and the third does not imply a commitment to global liberalisation.

*Trade Related Domestic Policies :* Competition policy, dispute settlement, environmental issues, financial services, government procurement and intellectual property rights are among the domestic policy issues to be addressed by APEC. EPG believes that APEC may be able to make a major contribution to future global progress on all these issues by developing regional accords that would subsequently be placed before the entire GATT membership for general adoption.

*Open Regionalism :* First, members of APEC are urged to carry out the maximum extent of unilateral liberalisation. Second, members are urged to continue reducing their barriers to non-members while liberalising within APEC on an MFN basis. Third, APEC benefits are available to non-members on a reciprocal basis. (However, non-members who took up the offer would not become members and would have no voice in APEC decision-making). Fourth, any APEC member can extend its APEC liberalisation to non-members of the developing country as a whole. (GATT does not permit extension of preferences selectively to non-members of free trade arrangements, except for the developing countries as a group.) EPG considered and "rejected the concept of unconditional MFN treatment of non-members...." (EPG Report, p. 49).

*Safeguards :* When there are special balance of payments or other economic difficulties, members should be permitted to temporarily halt or even reverse the liberalisation programme they have announced, in respect of a particular product for a temporary period. EPG suggests that the concerned member, whose domestic industry is unduly threatened by an import surge, could increase the tariff on the relevant product, for a short period of, say, 3 years, and would have to phase down the re-instituted protection, based on the principle of degressivity.

Compared to existing safeguards in GATT Article 19, the APEC safeguard system should be more comprehensive.

**Subregional and Bilateral Free Trade and APEC**

The EPG Report considers the risks arising from an expanding NAFTA and increasing bilateral free trade agreements between APEC members and non-members. APEC members, who may not belong to the subregional or bilateral ties might underemphasize APEC-wide cooperation. The Report recommends that the subregional arrangements within APEC publicly indicate their willingness to equalise the margins of preference that their members now enjoy in trade with each other with their other APEC trading partners, and eventually eliminate these margins on an APEC-wide basis.

*Rules of Origin* : Subregional arrangements may come in conflict with regional arrangements especially in regard to rules of origin (ROO). They can also become a guise for protectionism. The EPG recommends that APEC adopt rules of origin that support free trade through simplicity, transparency and application across-the-board (i.e., without sectoral exceptions). The approach suggested is a straightforward "substantial transformation" rule. This would require that a product undergo significant upgrading to count as an "APEC product" for intra-APEC customs purposes. Efforts are also needed to harmonize the ROO at subregional and regional levels. To simplify further , APEC should ignore the ROO issue for products where tariffs are very low (say, below 3 per cent ) or where all APEC members have identical tariffs on a product (as NAFTA members have agreed on computers). EPG urges APEC members to provide strong support for the timetable for ROO reform included in the Uruguay Round Agreement.

*Promoting Global Free Trade* : The EPG took pains to point out that free trade within APEC is not just GATT- consistent, but in fact goes beyond. First, free trade within APEC proposed by EPG covers all trade in the region, not just "substantially all trade" as required by Article 24. Second, APEC members make commitments to further reductions in their trade barriers to non-members, not just to avoid increases in such barriers as required by Article 24. Finally, APEC extends the benefits of its liberalisation to non-members, on a reciprocal basis, which no free trade area constructed under Article 24 has ever done.

## THE BOGOR DECLARATION

### A Significant Achievement

Presidents Clinton and Suharto, and Prime Ministers Keating, Mahathir and Murayama and 13 other leaders met for the second APEC summit at Bogor, Indonesia on the 15th of November. At the end, the Bogor Declaration (see box at the end of this study) adopted a two-tiered time-frame for free trade in the region. Developed APEC members such as United States and Japan will achieve free trade by 2010 while the developing APEC economies will achieve it by 2020.

It is by no means an insignificant achievement for leaders of 18 diverse economies (which include demographic-economic giants like China, Japan, and USA as well as several smaller economies) to commit themselves to achieve free trade, (that is, to get rid of all barriers to trade) and investment within a specified time frame. With few exceptions, several of the APEC members have used and been using fairly high tariff and non-tariff barriers to boost domestic industry. For instance, as the Asian Wall Street Journal (November 18-19) reported, the host country Indonesia's effective protection rate is 52 per cent for 269 categories of manufactured goods. For countries such as Indonesia to agree to dismantle trade barriers, albeit over the long period of 25 years, must be considered a great victory for free trade.

Why did APEC succeed in making the free trade commitment? In an article published in the Washington Post and reproduced in IHT , November 14, C. Fred Bergsten, Chairman of the APEC Eminent Persons Group points out that the APEC initiative has jelled at this time because nations on both sides of the Pacific have concluded that it will advance their interests. On the Asian side, in addition to the obvious advantages of trade expansion with the US, Bergsten notes that virtually all the countries rely on the US "to preserve a security balance in the region, providing assurances against future uncertainties such as those generated by a huge and rapidly growing China". The gain for the United States is the access to the large and dynamic Asian economies. Moreover, for the US, APEC provides a chance to engage Japan and China within a multilateral framework.

**Liberalisation at Different Speeds**

While the intention is to remove tariff and non-tariff barriers within APEC by 2020, the pace at which different countries move towards the goal may differ. This is what is conveyed in the following passage in the declaration: "In order to facilitate and accelerate our cooperation, we agree that APEC economies that are ready to initiate and implement a cooperative arrangement may proceed to do so, while those that are not yet ready to participate may join at a later date".

Malaysia, however, did not think that the timetable for free trade within APEC should be interpreted to mean that all the APEC members should achieve free trade by 2020. The country submitted an annex of reservations to the Bogor Declaration. The Malaysian Prime Minister said: " As far as we are concerned, we interpret the declaration as allowing us to go beyond 2020 if, by then, our country is still not yet at that stage of development where we can open up everything... We will make our best efforts. But if by the year 2020, we still cannot compete, I don't think anyone should force us to open up our economy to competition from companies from developed countries".

The Malaysian annexure to the Declaration also affirmed that the dates 2010 and 2020 are indicative targets and non-binding, and that the APEC free trade area would be GATT-WTO consistent. Of significance is the observation by the Malaysian Prime Minister that although he was the only one to put up an annexure, some others too had reservations.

In spite of Malaysia's reservations, the Bogor Declaration is seen by the leaders as a commitment for APEC free trade by 2020. The commitment, however, has to be translated by APEC members into credible timetables to cut tariffs and lift non-tariff barriers. If no such action takes place within the next year or if most nations prefer to produce timetables that provide maximum concessions only towards the last couple of years (prior to 2010 or 2020 as the case may be), then the so-called APEC free trade process will not have much credibility within APEC itself.

The Japanese Prime Minister Tomiichi Murayama, after the Bogor summit, said that next year's APEC forum meetings would focus on the specifics of free trade in member economies. According to him, Japan, the new chairman of APEC, will take a positive approach in the creation of an action agenda. All eyes now turn to the APEC summit at Osaka in November 1995 and the preceding official and ministerial deliberations.

## INDIAN ECONOMY: TRENDS AND POTENTIALS

### Trends

India's per capita income expanded at an insignificant rate of 0.5 per cent per annum during 1860-1910 and stagnated during 1911-46 (Rao 1993, p. 7). In sharp contrast, the period 1950-90 witnessed an average annual rate of economic growth of 4 per cent. In 1990-91, India's per capita GNP at current market prices was Rs. 6,197 (or US$ 345 at the then prevailing exchange rate). India remains a low income country, even though the rate of economic growth has improved in the 1980s to 5.5 per cent compared to less than 4 per cent during the earlier decades. India today possessed a broad-based industrial sector. The industrial base comprises food, textiles, metallurgical, mechanical engineering, electrical engineering and chemical industries. Industrial production expanded at an average rate of 5.9 per cent over the 1950-90 period.

Commands and controls have evolved over a period of time to regulate industrial progress in the country. The industrial sector in India has been most directly influenced by licensing of capacity, industrial location policy, administered prices, phased manufacturing programme, regulation of foreign investments, small enterprise reservations, controls on large companies, and reservation of certain industries for the public sector.

During the 1950s and 1960s import substitution was the main strategy and import controls were severe. The late 1970s saw the first moves towards import liberalisation primarily to encourage exports that needed capital and intermediate goods imports. Subsequently, in the 1980s import liberalisation was also aimed at allowing the domestic production and assembly of certain consumer durables.

One of the features of the Indian economy in the 1970s and 1980s has been the growing fiscal and budget deficits. In 1990-91, the Central Government's deficit on revenue account was an all-time high of 3.3 per cent of GDP, as against 2.6 per cent in 1989-

90. The gross fiscal deficit of the Government rose from 7.9 per cent of GDP in 1989-90 to 8.4 per cent in 1990-91. The balance of payments deficit also widened in 1990-91 compared to 1989-90. The fallout of the Gulf war entailed an additional cost of US $ 2.9 billion on the current account during 1990-91. The balance of payments was also adversely affected by the loss of confidence in India's short-term viability because of the domestic political uncertainties (two prime ministers ruled the country for a total period of 14 months during December 1989-March 1991 and the popular and charismatic leader, Rajiv Gandhi, then in opposition and expected to come to power again, was assassinated in May 1991). Gross national product at constant prices expanded at only 0.6 per cent during 1991-92. Since June 1991, responding to the economic crisis, the government announced a number of economic reform measures. They included tax reforms, trade policy reforms, convertibility of currency on current account, industrial policy reforms, financial sector reforms etc. (See Rao, 1993 and 1994).

Compared to the crisis year 1991-92, economic growth recovered to 4 per cent in 1992-93 and 3.8 per cent in 1993-94 (Table 1). The liberalisation of the trade and exchange rate regimes, especially the incentives to exporters (the applicability of the free market exchange rate, for instance), has begun to show its impact on export growth. Despite the fact that the rupee remained firm, exports in dollar terms appear to have grown significantly in 1993-94 after relative stagnation in the previous three years. Foreign currency reserves amounted to close to US$ 20 billion by the end of 1994, some twenty times the level of reserves in mid-1991.

**Medium Term Potentials**

*Growth Scenario :* The estimated growth rate for 1994-95 is 5.3 per cent. It is still within the 5.5 limit set by the average growth experience of the 1980s. In the medium term the economy should be able to move to a higher growth path and register a rate in the range of 6.5 to 7 per cent, since the economy in the 1980s did not work under an environment as liberal as the mid-1990s. The time-path of the rate of economic growth is expected to be around 6.3 per cent in 1995-96 and 6.5 per cent from 1996-97 through 2000-01.

**Table 1**
**India : Selected economic indicators, 1990-95**

| | 1990-91 | 1991-92 | 1992-93 | 1993-94 | 1994-95** |
|---|---|---|---|---|---|
| Growth rate of gross domestic product (%) | 4.9 | 1.1 | 4.0 | 3.8 | 4.2 |
| Growth rate of agricultural GDP (%) | 4.2 | -2.1 | 4.9 | 2.3 | n.a |
| Growth rate of industrial GDP (%) | 6.3 | -1.1 | 2.6 | 3.2 | n.a |
| Fiscal deficit as per cent of GDP | 8.4 | 6.0 | 5.8 | 7.4 | 7.6 |
| Central Government budget deficit as per cent of GDP | 2.1 | 1.1 | 1.8 | 1.2 | 0.7 |
| Inflation : annual change in CPI (%)+ | 13.6 | 13.9 | 6.1 | 8.2 | n.a |
| Annual change in GDP deflator | 11.5 | 14.9 | 9.8 | n.a | 67.9 |
| Export earning (US $ billion) | 18.1 | 17.9 | 18.4 | 21.0 | 25.5 |

* Extrapolated on the basis of $15.7 billion for the 9 months (April 1993-December 1993).

** Forecasts by the Centre for Monitoring the Indian Economy.

\+ CMIE (1994) from 1991-92, see source (ii) below.

*Source :*

(i) From *Economic Survey, 1993-94,* Government of India, pp. 2 and 20, RBI estimates of May 1994 and 1994-95 budget documents.

(ii) Centre for Monitoring the Indian Economy, *Monthly Review of the Indian Economy, June 1994,* Bombay: CMIE.

*Investment Requirements and Domestic Saving* : Since a considerable amount of long-gestation infrastructure investment will be needed, the incremental capital output ratio (ICOR) is anticipated to rise from 4 in 1995-96 to 4.5 in 1999-2001. The domestic saving rate in India rose from 10 per cent of GDP in 1950-51 to 24 per cent of GDP in 1989-90. Even at this pace of change, the rate can improve to about 25.5 per cent by 2000-01. Thus, the foreign capital requirements, of which DFI is a major component, will be between 3 to 4 per cent of GDP during the next five years. In US dollars terms the capital requirement will be in the region of 10 to 20 billion.

*Inflation and the Exchange Rate* : India's annual rate of inflation (measured by the GDP deflator) was 8.5 per cent during 1980-92. U.S. inflation average 3.9 per cent. It is assumed that the Indian GDP deflator will settle for slightly lower rates of change in due course and the average rate will be about 7.0 per cent moving from 8 per cent in 1995-96 to 6 per cent in 2000-01. The US inflation rate is expected to average 3.5 per cent. The Indian rupee will thus depreciate at an average rate of 3.5 per cent which is healthy from the point of view of export growth. Under these assumptions, the exchange rate works out to Rs. 32.6 per US dollar in 1995-96 and Rs. 38.6 per dollar in 2000-01 as against Rs. 31.37 during 1994.

*Exports and Imports* : The export and import ratios relative to GDP over the 1980s and early 1990s indicate a shift in export orientation of economy starting from 1988-89. Exports as a percentage of GDP steadily rose from 5.1 in 1988-89 to 9.0 in 1994-95. Even on fairly conservative terms, the ratio should reach a level of 9.5 per cent in 1995-96 and 12 per cent by 2000-01. Imports too must be of slightly higher order by then, assuming an average 2 per cent trade deficit. The orders of magnitude can be US $ 30 billion exports and US $ 37 billion imports in 1995-96 and US $ 60 billion exports and US $ 71 billion imports in 2000-01.

*Business Potentials : A Summary.* Increments to exports and imports during 1995-2000 are projected to be US $ 30 billion and US $ 34 billion respectively. Foreign capital requirement is expected to be in the range of US $ 10-20 billion during 1995-2000. Projects to build infrastructure will be worth billions of dollars and foreign partnership opportunities abound. An extremely large market will also be evolving for a whole variety of consumer goods, especially in electrical and electronic durables, since the per capita GDP will be US $ 500 by the turn of the century.

**Table 2**

**India : Indicative macro-economic projections**

| | *1995-1996* | *1996-1997* | *1997-1998* | *1998-1999* | *1999-2000* | *2000-2001* |
|---|---|---|---|---|---|---|
| GDP growth (%)* | 6.3 | 6.5 | 6.5 | 6.5 | 6.5 | 6.5 |
| GDP deflator growth (%) (drop by 0.4 points annually) | 8.0 | 7.6 | 7.2 | 6.8 | 6.4 | 6.0 |
| GDP at m.p. (Rs. billion)* | 10413 | 11881 | 13509 | 15305 | 17280 | 19440 |
| Exchange Rate (Rs. per US$) (US inflation = 3.5 per cent) | 32.6 | 33.6 | 34.8 | 36.0 | 37.2 | 38.6 |
| GDP at m.p. ($ billion) | 319.4 | 353.6 | 388.2 | 425.1 | 464.5 | 503.6 |
| Population (million)+ | 927 | 943 | 960 | 976 | 992 | 1008 |
| GDP per capita(US $) | 344 | 375 | 404 | 436 | 468 | 500 |
| ICOR (Infrastructure-led) | 4.0 | 4.2 | 4.3 | 4.4 | 4.5 | 4.5 |
| Investment GDP ratio (%) | 25.2 | 27.3 | 28.0 | 28.6 | 29.2 | 29.3 |
| Domestic Saving/GDP Ratio (%) | 22.0 | 24.3 | 24.6 | 24.9 | 25.2 | 25.5 |
| I-S Gap (%) | 3.2 | 3.0 | 3.4 | 3.7 | 4.0 | 3.8 |
| Foreign Capital Required ($ billion) | 10.2 | 10.6 | 13.2 | 15.7 | 18.6 | 19.1 |
| Exports/GDP(%) | 9.5 | 10.6 | 10.5 | 11.0 | 11.5 | 12.0 |
| Imports/GDP(%) (2 per cent trade deficit assumed) | 11.5 | 12.0 | 12.5 | 13.0 | 13.5 | 14.0 |
| Exports (US $ billion) | 30 | 35 | 41 | 47 | 53 | 60 |
| Imports (US $ billion) | 37 | 42 | 49 | 55 | 63 | 71 |

* GDP estimate for 1994-95 (Rs. 9110 billion) is derived from the revised fiscal deficit of the central government and the estimate of the deficit at 6.7 per cent of GDP. Growth rate for 1994-95 was 5.3 per cent. It is expected to pick up by one percentage point by 1995-96 and then stabilize at 6.5 per cent (possibly conservative).

\+ Assumed growth rate : 1.87 per cent in 1992-93 going down annually by 0.03 percentage points. India's population in 1992-93 was 878.6 million (*Economic Survey 1993-94*, p.S-1).

## APEC AND INDIA: TRADE AND INVESTMENTS

### Trade Linkages and Potentials

Data on direction of trade by IMF indicate an increase in Indian exports from US $ 9.1 billion in 1986 to US $ 23.3 billion in 1993. The corresponding figures for imports are US $ 15.1 billion in 1986 and US $ 25.1 billion in 1993. APEC's share in Indian imports declined during the period from 35.5 per cent in 1986 to 27.2 per cent in 1993; however, APEC's share in Indian exports has remained relatively high and stable at about 41-42 per cent (Table 3). The share of exports to Canada, Mexico and USA (with USA dominating) has declined, while the shares of East Asia and ASEAN have moved up— a shift that reflects the initial success in India's "Look East" policy.

**Table 3**
**India : Export and import shares of the major APEC members**

| *APEC Members* | *Imports* 1986 | 1992 | 1993 | *Exports* 1986 | 1992 | 1993* |
|---|---|---|---|---|---|---|
| Canada, Mexico and USA | 11.4 | 10.9 | 9.8 | 20.8 | 19.0 | 16.6 |
| China, Hong Kong, Japan and South Korea | 16.5 | 12.0 | 10.8 | 15.8 | 16.1 | 17.3 |
| ASEAN** | 5.2 | 4.1 | 3.4 | 3.2 | 6.2 | 6.4 |
| Australia and New Zealand | 2.4 | 3.1 | 3.2 | 1.4 | 1.4 | 1.3 |
| APEC Share | 35.5 | 30.1 | 27.2 | 41.2 | 42.7 | 41.6 |
| World total ($ billion) | 15.1 | 23.6 | 25.1 | 9.1 | 20.7 | 23.3 |

*Source of basic data* : IMF, *Direction of Trade Statistics Yearbook, 1993.*
* Annual estimates are based on data for the first three quarters.
** Excluding Brunei.

The principal exports out of India used to be primary commodities. Even in 1980-81, agricultural and allied products accounted for 31 per cent and ores and minerals for 6 per cent of total exports. The export structure changed significantly by the late 1980s and early

1990s. Thus, in 1992-93, agriculture and allied products share in total exports was down to 16.5 per cent and the share of ores and minerals was down to about 3 per cent. Some of the fast growing export commodities have been gems and jewellery, leather and leather products and fabrics and garments.

India's share in total world exports (US $ 3575 billion in 1992), was only 0.6 per cent, for a nation with a labour force which accounts for 14.7 per cent of the world's labour force. If the vast human resource could take a mere 2 per cent share in the global export market, India's 1992 exports would have been some US $ 72 billion as against the actual US $ 20 billion.

A little over half of total imports in 1993-94 was concentrated in three commodity groups: crude petroleum and products (24.8 per cent of total), machinery and transport equipment (18 per cent) and pearls, precious and semi-precious stones (11.4 per cent). The narrow import base is the natural consequence of a policy of importing what is most needed (crude petroleum and machinery, for example). The policy shied away from a deliberate encouragement of import dependent export orientation except for the recent growth of the gems and jewellery exports. Over a period of time, along with the development of human resources, the evolution of comparative advantages in new sectors and the carving out of market niches are possible by developing trade linkages with the fast growing APEC region.

The bottom-line for APEC-India trade expansion is the recognition by all concerned that growth in exports as well as imports (not one or the other only) constitutes the win-win situation. APEC expertise in the field of trade promotion in conjunction with India's human resources can lead to significant expansion in APEC-India trade.

APEC should take note of the untapped potential in the Indian market, especially in the post-liberalisation period. It has been noted that India's imports may be close to US $ 70 billion by the year 2000. It should not be difficult for APEC to take a hefty 35-40 per cent share in the market, especially by raising DFI and setting up import dependent export industries.

**APEC Investments in India**

Since India has not attracted sizeable DFI for several years, the accumulated DFI stock in India by the end of the 1980s was less than a billion dollars, even though the stock for the world as a whole was US $ 1496 billion by 1990 of which US $ 83 billion was in ASEAN as a whole and US $ 10.6 billion in China (UN, 1993).

Until 1991, there was considerable uncertainty as to the sectors into which DFI was permitted in India and whether or not approval could be obtained in the face of relatively stringent regulations. The Government now has a clear list of 35 industries in which foreign investment is permitted upto 51 per cent automatically. Existing companies with less than 51 per cent foreign equity are automatically permitted to raise it. Hundred per cent foreign equity is permitted for setting up and operating power plants, and for wholly export oriented units. In other areas, investment of over 51 per cent equity will be considered on a case by case basis by the Foreign Investment Promotion Board. India signed the Multilateral Investment Guarantee Agency (MIGA) convention, thus signalling its keenness to promote DFI. India also signed its first ever Investment Guarantee Agreement with Britain in March 1994.

The 35 priority sectors identified for promoting DFI include metallurgical industries, electrical and electronic equipment, agricultural, industrial and earth moving machinery, industrial and scientific instruments, chemicals, drugs and pharmaceuticals, plate glass, cement products, printing machinery, food processing, hotels and tourism and software development.

During 1991-94, some 82 per cent of approved investment was into the identified 35 sectors. Within the identified sectors, the distribution of approved DFI was 20.3 per cent in oil refineries, 17.1 per cent in power, 11.9 per cent in food processing, 11.6 per cent in metallurgical industries, 9.6 per cent in electrical equipment and electronics, 7.9 per cent in chemicals, 6.1 per cent in hotels and tourism, and 4.4 per cent in transportation, together making up almost 90 per cent. The wide array of industries selected for DFI thrust and the fact that all of them received DFI within a short span of three years signifies the attractiveness and potential of India.

Approved DFI into India during 1991-94 (May) amounted to US $ 5.5 billion. APEC's commitments in India (within the short span of three years) are almost half of the total DFI approval. The potentials for DFI into India from APEC are enormous, partly because India is a late comer to active soliciting of foreign investment and partly because of the well-known advantages India offers to the investors. Among others, the attractions of India include an educated manpower of about 50 million and a total labour force of 340 million, a large and expanding domestic economy and an estimated 200 to 300 million and growing middle class. India's foreign capital requirements are of the order of US $ 9 billion in 1995-96 rising to over US $ 18 billion in 2000-01. US, Japan, Hong Kong, Korea, Singapore and Taiwan may be expected to take up some 50 to 60 per cent of the projected DFI.

In the final analysis, decision to invest in a country depends on profitability. Indian economic reforms have set the framework for increasing international competitiveness and profitability of a wide range of product lines. For instance, the pre-tax cost of cold rolled steel in 1992-93 from the government owned Bokaro Steel Plant in India was the lowest among similar (blast furnace based) units (*The Hindu*, International Edition, November 6, 1993, p.11). The pre-tax cost in India was $372 per tonne as against $ 513 in US, $ 572 in Japan, $ 468 in Australia , $ 511 in South Korea and Taiwan. The labour cost per tonne was a mere $ 32 in India as against the $ 90-150 range in the others despite the fact that the Indian steel workers have always been well organised and among the better paid.

There is no doubt that eventually DFI will go to India driven by an astute business sense of investors from US, Japan, Australia, Hong Kong, Korea, Singapore and Taiwan. The process can be greatly expedited and facilitated through formal cooperation arrangements and linkages between APEC and India.

## THE CASE FOR A FORMAL APEC-INDIA RELATIONSHIP

There is strong case for building a formal relationship between APEC and India. Such a relationship will also be of benefit to the world economy at large. The bases for the case for a formal relationship are elucidated below.

### Pursuance of APEC Objectives

It is well known that APEC stands for open regionalism and is aimed at strengthening (not weakening) multilateral and global processes and institutions. (EPG 1993 and 1994). Given the strong APEC foundation of open regionalism and the agenda that is pro-multilateral trade and investment, it is only natural and logical that APEC and India develop formal linkages, particularly because of the projected trade and investment potentials of emerging India noted in the earlier section. The Seattle Vision Statement and the Bogor Declaration also alluded to the need for cooperation initiatives in human resource development and promotion of small and medium enterprises. Linkages with India can be of significant use in both the areas, and India will be a compatible and valuable partner within APEC.

**Special Relationships with Key APEC Members**

The Indian economic reforms have been fast and pervasive. This naturally promoted the building of special economic ties between India and some of the key APEC members. These are briefly reviewed below.

*Australia* : Australia, the nation which actively promoted the founding of APEC has been very quick to recognise India's potentials. The Australian Department of Foreign Affairs and Trade (ADFAT) has also recently formulated the "Australia's India Strategy". (ADFAT, 1994). The strategy is based on the following perception: "In the 1990s, India will attract international attention as it grows at a rate comparable to that projected for South-East Asia. At average annual growth rates of some 6 per cent per year, by the year 2000 India will have a GDP of around US $ 430 billion (in 1992 dollar terms). Based on this assessment, India, with a GDP less than that of Australia in 1992, would overtake Australia in economic size by the year 2000. Projected annual imports of US $ 49 billion (in 1992 dollar terms) by the end of 1990s suggest that Australian firms should take India's potential into consideration as they formulate their trade and investment strategies. India's economic growth outlook could mean a doubling of Australian annual exports to the market by the year 2000." (ADFAT,1994).

"Australia's India Strategy" identifies several regions (Tamil Nadu, Karnataka, Gujarat, Maharashtra, Haryana, Punjab and West Bengal) and various specific activities (infrastructure materials including specialised steel and alluminium products; transport, telecommunications and power equipment; processed food; a wide variety of services; wool, vegetables and dairy products, and coal and LNG) (ADFAT, 1994:211). The strategy also calls for securing market access prior to further tariff reductions in India and blending Australian technology with India's natural and human resources (Ibid., p. 212). Australia should like to see not only an expansion of its bilateral economic relations with India but also a role for both in APEC.

*United States* : Jeffery Garten, the US Under Secretary of Commerce for International Trade, and the author of the thesis of big emerging markets (BEMs), thinks that the United States should now look at India "in terms of a great opportunity". (Parthasarathy, 1994:3). According to a study on "U.S-India Commercial Relations 1993-2000", there is now a strong case for a change in US policies towards India, in order not to forego "an unprecedented opportunity to develop a long term commercial relationship in a market that is bound to become increasingly open and competitive." (Parthasarathy, 1994:3). Garten is also reported to have observed that unlike China and other BEMs, India has the advantage of a highly developed commercial infrastructure, an extremely sophisticated business class and potential for partnership. (Ibid).

In trade and investments vis-a-vis India, US ranks number one. US sees vast potential for investments in infrastructure—upto some US $ 100 billion during 1995-2000 (The Economist, March 26,1994:34). Both countries share strong democratic traditions. Some of the top scientists and professionals in US are of Indian origin. Highly qualified Indians enter USA to perform services in a speciality occupation—on a short-term basis. Indian computer programmers are increasingly sourced for short-term engagement. Cooperation between the two countries is natural and inevitable. Beyond the bilateral context, US should be keen to see linkages between APEC and India.

*Singapore* : Among the members of ASEAN, Singapore is India's largest trading partner, largest investor and attracts the largest number of tourists from India. India looks to Singapore as the gate-way to ASEAN and the rest of Southeast Asia. Singapore attracts Indian workers into its construction industry. Indian professionals work in several junior, middle-level and high-level management positions in Singapore companies. In general, Indian human resources complement the highly developed infrastructural and service sectors of Singapore.

Prime Minister Goh Chok Tong of Singapore went to India in January 1994 as the guest of honour at the Republic Day of India. Prior to that he encouraged Singapore investors to look to India. At the time of his visit he laid the foundation to the Bangalore Information Technology Park costing US $ 150 million in which Singapore's share holding is 40 per cent. An India Business Interaction Group has been formed in Singapore. It brings together members of the Singapore Manufacturers Association and the Confederation of Indian Industries. A number of Indian companies have or are about to set up offices in Singapore. The Trade Development Board and the Economic Development Board have offices in India. Singapore's premier government linked Development Bank of Singapore opened its first Indian branch recently.

The growing Singapore-India economic relations received a further boost with the visit of the Indian Prime Minister to Singapore in September 1994. The growth of the economic relationships between the two countries are such as to strengthen the linkages not only between Singapore and India but also with the Southeast and East Asian countries of which several are APEC members. This development should augur well for a formal link between APEC and India.

*Japan* : The Japanese Government's 1994 White Paper on Economic Cooperation places India next only to China and Vietnam in terms of its target nations for increased cooperation. "First comes official aid, followed by Japanese direct investment, and then the arrival of Japanese banks and portfolio capital flows." (Rowley, 1994). With production costs rising in East Asia, an increasing number of Japanese industries will be looking at India as an important location; they may wish to invest in upgrading Indian infrastructure and human resources as necessary; and take advantage of the huge domestic consumer market. Suzuki, Mitsubishi, Toyota, Nissan and Mazda are already in India in the auto sector. Fujitsu is producing telephones and software. Hitachi and Sanyo are producing household appliances while windscreens are manufactured by Asahi Glass. These modest investments are considered miniscule given India's market and export potentials.

*Thailand* : Thailand too is upbeat about the prospects for collaboration with India. The leader of a Thai Government study team is reported to have observed: .." it is believed that India will be the next rapid growth (area) after China and Indonesia". (Boyd, 1994). Thailand has even sounded the possibility of formal cooperation between ASEAN, India and Sri Lanka. Thailand is now India's fourth largest source of direct foreign investment. Animal feed, shrimp farming and fish processing have attracted Thai investments. Jewellery and electronics are also likely to attract Thai interest. With four million engineers and technicians, and a huge labour force trained to assembly level, India is an attractive destination for ASEAN investments.

## INDIA'S POSITION AND POLICY AGENDA

### Development Imperatives

India needs an annual growth rate of 6.5 to 7 per cent to make a dent on poverty and human resource underutilisation. This would call for annual injections of capital inflow of the order of US $ 10 to 20 billion. Much of this has to come from APEC countries. Commensurate with the required economic growth, exports and imports must grow rapidly-reaching levels of at least US $ 65 and US $ 75 billion respectively by the year 2000. APEC shares in these can easily go up to as much as 50 per cent (presently they are around 45 per cent and 30 per cent respectively in exports and imports). Developing such strong investment and trade linkages with APEC countries will be greatly facilitated if India has a formal relationship with APEC, preferably in the form of full membership, with benefits in regard to trade and investment facilitation, and the development of small enterprises and human resources.

### Links with the World via APEC

On the 8th of September, while delivering the 13th Singapore Lecture, the Indian Prime Minister said: "India has already taken steps to liberalise its currency regime, open the economy to more imports and investment, and educate its people on the benefits of exposure to the outside world. The Asia-Pacific could be the springboard for our leap into the global market place..." In bilateral discussions between the India and Singapore delegations on the same day, the Singaporean Prime Minister informed his

Indian counterpart that Singapore would welcome India's eventual membership in APEC (and also the ASEAN Regional Forum).

**Policy Agenda for India**

India should position itself over time to be invited to be a member of APEC. To facilitate that, an Indian policy agenda should be developed along the lines suggested below.

1. *Continued Liberalisation* : India should continue with its own liberalisation. The full convertibility of the rupee (after reserves reach a comfortable level), further simplification of income tax (maximum 30 per cent), abolition of gift and wealth taxes, simplification of indirect taxation (move towards VAT) and a timetable to bring down the peak customs duty to 30 per cent, with most duties at 10 per cent or less by the year 2000, combined with GATT binding, are some of the reforms that will help in making India a major player in the global economy.

2. *Links with AFTA* : AFTA is expected to be a reality by the year 2003. By then, if Indian import duties are reduced to 5 per cent or less on most manufactured goods, it should be possible to establish a special relationship with AFTA. This should be actively pursued.

3. *Keeping in Touch with APEC* : India should be fully abreast of the deliberations, recommendations and agreements of the various APEC Committees, working groups and officials, ministers and leaders meetings. It will be a tribute to Indian diplomatic efforts if India can be invited to be an observer in the key committees. (Committee on Trade and Investment is the most important. There are various working groups on trade promotion, investment, data review, industrial science and technology, human resource development, regional energy cooperation, telecommunications, fisheries, marine resource conservation, transportation and tourism.)

4. *Upgrading Key Bilateral Relations* : Just as India-Singapore relations have been upgraded over the past three years, a major thrust is needed for upgrading relations with Indonesia, Malaysia, Australia and Japan, in addition to a deepening of ties with USA. These are all countries which are emerging as key players in APEC. Indian academics, officials and opinion makers should speak with one voice about the breadth, depth and pace of the economic reforms in India, the characteristic of the emerging

mega economy, unprecedented trade and investment opportunities, etc., and build solid relations with their counterparts in Indonesia, Malaysia, Australia and Japan.

5. *Cultivating Opinion Makers* : Indonesian, Malaysian, Australian and Japanese intellectuals and opinion makers should be routinely invited to India, and due recognition should be given to the role they can play as favourable commentators on India in their home countries. Research institutions in various parts of India should be designated for the cultivation of linkages. External donors (Ford Foundation, IDRC, Asia Foundation etc.) should be encouraged to set up over the period 1995-2000, exchange programmes with the four countries with the express intention of achieving strong economic relationships.

6. *Economic and Commercial Diplomacy* : The Indian Ministry of External Affairs should continue to emphasize economic and commercial diplomacy, with possible investment and trade targets vis-a-vis key APEC members, the achievement of which must be one of the major tasks of the Indian missions abroad.

## ANNEXURE

### Extracts from "APEC Economic Leaders' Declaration of Common Resolve", Bogor, Indonesia, November 15, 1994

- As we approach the 21st century, APEC needs to reinforce economic cooperation in the Asia Pacific region... with the objective of APEC leading the way in:
  - strengthening the open multilateral trading system;
  - enhancing trade and investment liberalisation in Asia Pacific; and
  - intensifying Asia Pacific development cooperation.
- To strengthen the open multilateral trading system, we decide to accelerate the implementation of our Uruguay Round commitments...
- We also agree to commit ourselves to a continuing process of unilateral trade and investment liberalisation.
- As evidence of our commitment to the open multilateral trading system, we further agree to a standstill under which we will endeavour to refrain from using measures which would have the effect of increasing levels of protection.

- ... we agree to adopt the long-term goal of free and open trade and investment in Asia Pacific. This goal will be pursued promptly by further reducing barriers to trade and investment and by promoting the free flow of goods, services and capital among our economies. We will achieve this goal in a GATT-consistent manner...
- We further agree to announce our commitment to complete the achievement of our goal of free and open trade and investment in Asia Pacific no later than the year 2020. ... with the industrialised economies achieving the goal of free and open trade and investment no later than the year 2010 and developing economies no later than the year 2020.
- We are determined to pursue free and open trade and investment in Asia Pacific in a manner that will encourage and strengthen trade and investment liberalisation in the world as a whole. Thus, the outcome of trade and investment liberalisation in Asia Pacific will not only be the actual reduction of barriers among APEC economies but also between APEC economies and non-APEC economies. In this respect we will give particular attention to our trade with non-APEC developing countries to ensure they will also benefit from our trade and investment liberalization, in conformity with GATT/WTO provisions.
- To complement and support this substantial process of liberalization, we decide to expand and accelerate APEC's trade and investment facilitation programs.
- We emphasize the importance of trade facilitation because trade liberalization efforts alone are insufficient to generate trade expansion.. . In particular we ask our ministers and officials to submit proposals on APEC arrangements on customs, standards, investment principles and administrative barriers to market access.
- Our objective to intensify development cooperation among the community of Asia Pacific economies will enable us to develop more effectively the human and natural resources... Cooperative programs in this area cover expanded human resource development (such

as education and training and especially improving management and technical skills), the development of APEC study centres, cooperation in science and technology (including technology transfer), measures aimed at promoting small and medium scale enterprises and steps to improve economic infrastructure, such as energy, transportation, information, telecommunications and tourism. Effective cooperation will also be developed on environmental issues, with the aim of contributing to sustainable development.

- Recognizing the role of the business sector in economic development, we agree to integrate the business sector in our programs and to create an ongoing mechanism for that purpose.
- ... we agree to examine the possibility of a voluntary consultative dispute mediation service, to supplement the WTO dispute settlement mechanism, which should continue to be the primary channel for resolving disputes.
- We will start our concerted liberalization process from the very date of this statement...
- We direct our ministers and officials to immediately begin preparing detailed proposals for implementing our present decisions. The proposals are to be submitted soon to the APEC economic leaders for their consideration and subsequent decisions. Such proposals should also address all impediments to achieving our goal.
- We express our appreciation for the important and thoughtful recommendations contained in the reports of the Eminent Persons Group and the Pacific Business Forum. ... We agree to ask the two groups to continue with their activities to provide the APEC economic leaders with assessments of the progress of APEC and further recommendations for stepping up our cooperation.

## REFERENCES

ADFAT (Australian Department of Foreign Affairs and Trade). 1994. *India's Economy at the Midnight Hour: Australia's India Strategy,* Canberra: Australia Government Publishing Service.

Bergsten, C. Fred 1994. APEC and World Trade : A Force for Worldwide Liberalisation. *Foreign Affairs,* 73(3), May-June, 20-26.

Boyd, Alan. 1994. "A New Regional Grouping in the Works?", *Business Times,* Singapore, August 12.

EPG (Eminent Persons Group of APEC). 1993. *A Vision for APEC : Towards an Asian Pacific Economic Community.* Report of the Eminent Persons Group to the APEC Ministers, October.

EPG (Eminent Persons Group of APEC). 1994. *Achieving the APEC Vision: Free and Open Trade in the Asia Pacific,* Singapore: APEC Secretariat.

Parthasarathy, Malini. 1994. US Sees in India a "Great Opportunity". *The Hindu,* International Edition, 20(32).

Rao, V.V. Bhanoji. 1993. *India's Economic Future: Government, People and Attitudes,* Delhi: Tata McGraw-Hill.

Rao, V.V. Bhanoji. 1994. *Indian Economy: Past Progress, Recent Reforms and Medium-Term Potentials,* MPP Working Paper Series No. 2., Singapore: National University of Singapore, Centre for Advanced Studies, Public Policy Programme.

Rowley, Anthony, 1994. "Japan Seeks to Get Friendlier with its Next, Next-Door Neighbour," *Business Times,* Singapore, July 27.

UNITED NATIONS. 1993. *World Investment Report 1993: Transnational Corporations and Integrated International Production,* New York: United Nations.

# Index